Church and society in
Catholic Europe of the eighteenth century

Church and society in Catholic Europe of the eighteenth century

Edited by
WILLIAM J. CALLAHAN
Professor of History, University of Toronto
and
DAVID HIGGS
Professor of History, University of Toronto

CAMBRIDGE UNIVERSITY PRESS

CAMBRIDGE
LONDON · NEW YORK · MELBOURNE

Published by the Syndics of the Cambridge University Press
The Pitt Building, Trumpington Street, Cambridge CB2 1RP
Bentley House, 200 Euston Road, London NW1 2DB
32 East 57th Street, New York, NY 10022, USA
296 Beaconsfield Parade, Middle Park, Melbourne 3206, Australia

First published 1979

Phototypeset by
Western Printing Services Ltd, Bristol
Printed in Great Britain at the
University Press, Cambridge

Library of Congress Cataloguing in Publication Data
Main entry under title:
Church and society in Catholic Europe of the eighteenth century.

'This collection of essays . . . arose from a conference . . . held at
the University of Toronto in November 1974.'
Bibliography: p.
Includes index.
1. Catholic Church in Europe – History – Congresses.
I. Callahan, William James, 1937– II. Higgs, David, 1939–
BX1490.C49   282'.4   78-12165
ISBN 0 521 22424 1

Contents

Preface

This collection of essays on the Catholic church in eighteenth-century Europe arose from a conference on the topic held at the University of Toronto in November 1974. Although the present volume has been expanded to include countries not covered at that time, we owe a debt to those who participated in the conference and who generously offered suggestions. We are grateful to Harvey Mitchell, Roger Clark, T. J. A. LeGoff, David Smith, William Slottman, Charles Jago, Helen Liebel and Pierre Hurtubise and the other participants for their stimulating contributions to the conference discussions. We express our thanks to Stanley Golowacz for translating chapter 9; the editors are responsible for the English versions of chapters 5, 7 and 10. We also wish to acknowledge the generosity of the Canada Council and Varsity Fund and the History Department of the University of Toronto, which enabled the conference to take place.

William J. Callahan
David Higgs
Toronto, March 1978

Notes on contributors

Gerhard Benecke, University of Kent, is the author of *Society and politics in Germany, 1500—1750*, and other studies of German history.

Jean Bérenger, Université de Haute-Bretagne, is the author of *Finances et absolutisme autrichien dans la seconde moitié du XVIIe siècle; Les 'Gravamina', Remontrances des Diètes de Hongrie de 1655 à 1681; Lexique historique de l'Europe danubienne*, and other books and articles on central European and French history.

William J. Callahan, University of Toronto, is the author of *Honor, commerce and industry in eighteenth-century Spain*, and articles on the social history of Spain and Spanish America in the eighteenth century.

David Higgs, University of Toronto, is the author of *Ultraroyalism in Toulouse*; co-author with Grace M. Anderson of *A future to inherit: the Portuguese communities of Canada*, and has written various articles on French social history.

Olwen Hufton, University of Reading, is the author of *Bayeux in the late eighteenth century; The poor of eighteenth-century France, 1750—1789*, and numerous other studies of French history.

Béla K. Király, Brooklyn College of the City University of New York, is the author of *Hungary in the late eighteenth century*, and other studies and articles on Hungarian history.

Jerzy Kłoczowski, Catholic University of Lublin, is the author of (in Polish) *The Dominicans in Silesia*; general editor of *The History of the Polish Church*, and has written numerous studies and articles on Polish ecclesiastical history.

Mario Rosa, Institute of Medieval and Modern History of the University of Bari, is the author of *Riformatori e ribelli nel '700 religioso italiano* and other books and studies of the religious and political history of Italy.

Marc Venard, Université de Paris I – Panthéon-Sorbonne, is the author of *La Vie religieuse à Avignon au XVIe siècle* and other studies of French religious history.

1 Introduction

WILLIAM J. CALLAHAN
DAVID HIGGS

The eighteenth century witnessed the final flowering of the reforming efforts of the Counter-Reformation, but it also saw deep cracks appear in the facade of the traditional alliance of throne, altar and orthodox belief. These rifts have often been explained by the development of an intellectual movement, the Enlightenment, which displayed hostility both to the institutional church and even to the practices of traditional Christianity. The struggle between reforming states and the church over the use of ecclesiastical wealth, the extreme differences between the high and low clergy, the growing tension between the extravagances of baroque popular piety and simpler forms of religious expression, the inequalities of an archaic organization, the uneven distribution of resources between the urban and rural church, all pointed to the beginnings of a crisis within the church and between it and the larger society.

The historiography of the church is, of course, extensive. The shelves of libraries are heavy with studies of bishops, seminaries, religious orders, relations between church and state and the analysis of theological disputes. Members of the church have studied its history with careful detail and much of their work is of considerable merit. In France, A. Schaer's work on the Alsatian clergy, in Spain, López Ferreiro's well-documented history of the archdiocese of Santiago, are examples of the solidity of clerical scholarship. But many of these works, though valuable for the information they provide on the operation of ecclesiastical institutions, neglect the problem of the relationship of the church to the wider society. New departures in the study of the church emerged before the Second World War and from within the church itself. The obvious decline in religious practice, especially in France, led clerics to ask the question why it was taking place. Many realized that simple moral explanations of religious behaviour were inadequate. There developed a demand for analysis informed by the social sciences, particularly sociology. This new approach owes its greatest debt to Gabriel Le Bras, a French sociologist and historian, who stressed the necessity of studying those who worship and why they did so in contrast to the traditional emphasis on the history of ecclesiastical institutions. Le Bras's work, first published in the 1930s, was to lead to a flourishing discipline of religious sociology in the countries of Catholic Europe. The efforts of Canon Boulard in France, J. M. Vázquez and R. Duocastella in Spain, attest to his widespread influence. The Le Bras approach, though stressing the historical background to religious problems, focuses attention on the crisis of belief and the incidence of observance in the contemporary world. But its emphasis on sociological investigation has stimulated historians to look at the church from a new vantage point. The place of the church within society and religious behaviour in the past are seen as legitimate objects of scholarly enquiry separate from the historian's personal beliefs or the problem of religion in the modern world.

Current research on the religious history of eighteenth-century Europe varies from one country to another. Progress has been greatest in France where an abundant monographic literature has provided the foundation of a recent innovative historiography of religion. Maurice Agulhon has investigated the confraternities of eighteenth-century Provence and their relation to the social life of the times; Michel Vovelle has analysed the content of wills in Provence to trace the rise and decline of religious sentiment during the century. Southern Europe has been less well served, but in Italy the pioneering work of Candeloro Giorgini on Tuscany, Guiseppe Orlandi on Modena and Gabriele de Rosa on the south reflect the new trends. For Spain, the monographic literature has been growing. The work of Saugnieux and Appolis on Jansenism, Olaechea on church–state relations, and Batllori on the Jesuit exiles are signs of serious scholarly interest in the history of the Spanish church, and the recently published *Diccionario de historia eclesiástica* with a broad range of articles on such problems as ecclesiastical demography promises further advances. In central and eastern Europe, Grete Klingenstein and others have done work on the German and Austrian churches, while Jerzy Kłoczowski and his colleagues at the Institute of Ecclesiastical Studies at the Catholic University of Lublin have published important studies on the socio-religious history of Poland.

The essays in this volume, though national in focus, deal with a series of general problems significant to understanding the place of the church within society. The social role of Catholicism, for example, has often been linked to the study of the recruitment of the clergy. Although theology taught that all members of the church from pope to peasant would stand one day on equal footing before the judgement seat, the church of this world possessed an elaborate organization which mirrored the complexities of the Old Regime's social structure. Cardinals, archbishops, bishops and cathedral canons formed an elite whose wealth and prestige rivalled the nobility's in civil society. The study of episcopal recruitment is valuable for analysis of the relationship between the secular and ecclesiastical worlds. The stereotype of the cultivated, aristocratic bishop of the eighteenth century has worked its way into countless textbooks. The reality was more complex. In France, it is true, the aristocracy monopolized high church office just as it dominated social life and the officer corps. Elsewhere, the situation, reflecting the peculiarities of each nation, was mixed. Jean Meyer in a recent study of the eighteenth-century European nobility has stressed the importance of the numerous and relatively poor nobles of northern Spain, Hungary and Poland. This genteel, impoverished nobility found clerical service an acceptable occupation for its sons. In Spain and Portugal, lesser nobles formed the majority of the episcopacy at any given moment. In Italy, aristocrats dominated the hierarchy in Naples, Venice and Piedmont but their numbers declined in the Papal States in favour of ecclesiastical bureaucrats. In central and eastern Europe, the nobility dominated the wealthiest sees such as Salzburg, Estergom and Gniezno.

The faithful found few noble priests at the centre of the church's life, the parish. Its place as a basic unit of society is evident. The parish served as a vehicle for making the desires of government known to local populations; it was often the first link in the chain of authority running from village to royal council. Social life at the parochial level revolved around the festivals of an elaborate liturgical calendar. For the peasantry, parish membership furnished an identity against the outside world.

Despite the importance of the parish priest to the life of the church, the existence of an underpaid, often ill-prepared and unevenly distributed parochial clergy prevented the church from conducting an effective pastoral mission, although this was not always true. The clergy and the parish functioned well in France, in contrast to Spain where thousands of parishes lacked priests; Italy, where an archaic parish structure blocked attempts to serve an expanding population; and Poland, where the relative poverty of the church created large and inefficient parishes. In Hungary, new parishes were created in districts such as that around the River Temes recently freed from Turkish rule, while in Austria the resources of the more than 700 monasteries and convents closed by Emperor Joseph II permitted the establishment of more parishes, as in Lower Austria where 231 were founded. Everywhere parish priests were predominantly commoners, often from towns where grammar schools and local monasteries provided the foundation of clerical education. In France and Poland, parish priests even in the countryside came from modest urban families. There is little evidence for the Iberian peninsula, although there are indications that the better-off peasantry provided some priests in rural Portugal. But nowhere did the very poor enter the clergy.

The education of parish priests left much to be desired. The need for improved professional training of the clergy particularly concerned Benedict XIII (1724–30), who encouraged the foundation of new seminaries. The eighteenth-century episcopacy had the same high expectations of education shared by eighteenth-century bureaucrats everywhere. The location of seminaries at the beginning and the end of the century shows the substantial progress accomplished, although there were setbacks. In the Austria of Joseph

II, for example, small seminaries were closed in favour of a handful of general seminaries. Improvements in clerical instruction and the related campaign promoting spiritual conferences for the clergy revealed the continuing preoccupation of the church's leadership with improving the intellectual quality of the priesthood.

These efforts produced disappointing results in the view of the hierarchy. Confidence in educational improvement was clearly misplaced. The real problem was the unequal distribution of the church's material resources. The archbishops of Braga, Toledo, Rheims, Venice, Salzburg and Gniezno enjoyed handsome revenues; many of their parish priests eked out a bare living. The inadequate income of the parish clergy was a serious problem in many countries.

The poverty of the rural clergy illustrates the most serious weakness of the eighteenth-century church. Its wealth, power and prestige rested not in the countryside where the majority of the population lived and worked but in the cities. In an overwhelmingly rural society, the church was urban. Diocesan seats, cathedral chapters, charitable and educational foundations abounded in the cities. There too the religious orders established their houses. The successful cleric of the eighteenth century was above all an urban man who had studied in a university and obtained livings in important towns. The rural priest, perhaps educated in a seminary, faced a lifetime of hardship and little or no advancement. The immense wealth of the church remained in the ecclesiastical capitals. Although there is abundant evidence of the administrative abilities and good intentions of the majority of the bishops, the concentration of ecclesiastical riches and talent in the cities constituted a glaring weakness never overcome.

This wealth did not lie idle. The supreme achievements of Counter-Reformation architecture distracted notice to some extent from ecclesiastical building in the eighteenth century. As well as the construction of great basilicas and monasteries, especially in central Europe, there was everywhere a wave of church building. The increasing level of luxury with which large segments of the European population were familiar was first displayed in ecclesiastical buildings. The refinement of decoration, the use of elaborate gilding, painting and fine liturgical vessels was characteristic of the century. These efforts in *arts appliqués* were not solely restricted to churches; there was a parallel demand for the application of the same decorative techniques (and often from the same artisans and craftsmen) for *Schloss* and townhouse. However, clerical patronage always provided a powerful stimulus to the luxury crafts. This is most obvious in celebrated commissions given to artists, like those to A. Canova to sculpt the tombs of Clement XIII and Clement XIV. An interest in the fine arts was displayed at the highest levels of the hierarchy: Benedict XIV charged Winckelmann to establish the Vatican Museum of Antiquities. Still more eloquent testimony to the general increase of opulence were the numerous commissions given by the clergy for the embellishment of churches, chapels and local shrines throughout Europe. Whether in Beja, Santiago de Compostela, Florence, Breslau or Estergom, communities of silversmiths, embroiderers, carpenters, roofers, candle-makers and a host of others depended on the expenditure of bishops, monasteries and cathedral chapters.

The funnelling of clerical revenues into the towns served another purpose: it made the church in ecclesiastical centres the single most important consumer and the principal source of charity for the masses of impoverished produced by the fragile agrarian economy of the Old Regime. The church provided the equivalent of the modern state's spending on public works in societies where chronic unemployment was a fact of life. There is no doubt that the charity distributed to the poor by the church did not resolve the problem of massive poverty in eighteenth-century Europe, and that the alms dispensed by the devout often flowed to the indigent in an inefficient and haphazard stream. But the church and its institutions – the parish, monastery, hospital and charitable foundation – were the major sources of social welfare during the Old Regime. How much of the church's wealth went into charity is impossible to say, but the efforts of ecclesiastical institutions contributed to the hold of the church over the mass of the population. Expenditures on charity compensated in part for the immense sums spent on church building and decoration. The declining charitable role of the church in western Europe, and there are indications of this beginning in the second half of the century, signalled a change in the relationship between church and people.

The wealth financing the great facade of the basilica of Santiago de Compostela, the church-monastery of Mafra, the splendid baroque monastery of Melk and a multitude of hospitals, orphanages and asylums came primarily from the land. The urban church of the eighteenth century supported itself on income from ecclesiastical properties in the countryside and the tithe. The church was perhaps more visible in the countryside as a landowner and tithe-gatherer than as a dispenser of spiritual comfort. Clerical land-holdings varied in extent depending on the region and country. By 1714 the church had acquired one-sixteenth of the land area of Bohemia, one-twentieth of the land of the region of Toulouse, and so on. During the second half of the century a decline in ecclesiastical property-holding took place as the result of expulsion of the Jesuits, whose land and endowments were taken over by governments, although often for religious purposes. More serious was the attack carried out in Austria and the Habsburg dominions of Italy during the rule of Maria Theresa and Joseph II. In Austria alone 738 religious houses were closed in the 1780s. Moreover, governments sought through legislation to prevent the accumulation of property in ecclesiastical hands. In spite of these measures, church property remained essentially unchanged in most states of Catholic

Europe until the massive sale of ecclesiastical lands which took place in France during the Revolution.

The relationship of the church to the economics of rural society is vital to an understanding of its social role. The nature of the relationship was determined by regional conditions. In areas where the church possessed substantial property – southern Iberia and Italy, for example – its social ties to the local population differed from those in districts of peasant ownership such as northern Portugal, the Basque Provinces, Brittany, or Poland. In certain areas the ability of the church to maintain its following among the rural masses may well have been due to the lesser presence of the church as landowner.

Imposing in wealth, internal organization and education, the eighteenth-century church laboured to fulfil its primary mission, to save the souls of its members. The problem of assessing the quality and incidence of religious practice during the Old Regime, however, is immense. The historian would like to see maps drawn of the main features of European Catholicism to show the similarities and differences in ritual and belief across Europe. We are still poorly served in this regard, although historical geographers are now turning to the task. Pierre Deffontaines in his highly general but inventive work on the geography of religion took as a departure point the impact of religion on the geography of population distribution. The *Atlas zur Kirchengeschichte* edited by Jochen Martin, the religious maps of the *Atlante storico italiano dell'età moderna* and the articles on the subject published by the *Miscellanea historiae ecclesiasticae* of Louvain show the insights offered to historians by cartography. Comparative maps over time of the incidence of pilgrimages, feasts, festivals, seminaries, new religious building, vocations and so on may point us towards regional explanations of these features. Indeed, the mid-twentieth-century map of 'messalisants adultes par diocèse' of western Europe drawn up by Canon Boulard and his collaborators provides a map of contrasting levels of religious practice. Did this have its origin in the Counter-Reformation? Recent work on the religious sociology of France suggests that the modern pattern of observance running from Brittany, Normandy through eastern France to Alsace and Franche Comté was already forming during the eighteenth century. It may be that the areas which were most recalcitrant to post-Tridentine reform were those which subsequently remained most faithful to the church, just as those parts of France where reforms were more easily accepted by clergy and the laity became the first to show signs of dechristianization. The present day low incidence of practice in the Portuguese Alentejo and in Andalucia, both areas of large estates and impoverished rural populations, can be traced in part to a simpler cause, the pastoral neglect of country districts already evident during the eighteenth century. The parishes of southern Spain, for example, were extremely large and ineffective compared to those in the north. The questions raised by a cartography of ritual, belief and even more by something as diffuse as resistance to reform, are evident enough.

The practices of popular religion contributed to the influence of the church over the urban and rural masses. Clerical laments about ignorance of the basic truths of the faith were commonplace. Indeed, for the vast majority of the population, religion combined colourful ceremony, the appeasement of divine wrath and folkloric custom. However distressed ecclesiastics were by popular religious practice, the novenas, processions, confraternities, pilgrimages and devotions formed the basis of piety which made religion an integral part of daily life. Toward the close of the century there were indications that the traditional instruments of popular religion were beginning to lose favour, particularly in urban centres. The *Bruderschaften* of south German towns often fell under municipal control and thus had an incipient independence of the clergy which may have been heightened in the atmosphere of the *Aufklärung*. The *irmandades* of Portugal, the confraternities of Italy, and parallel forms elsewhere appeared originally to offer an excellent vehicle for clerical guidance and control of popular religious life, but they may well have been a nursery for secular associations. Agulhon's study of Provençal confraternities, those pious associations of laymen found everywhere in Catholic Europe, revealed a marked decline in their religious vitality during the eighteenth century. A similar pattern developed in Seville and Gerona among confraternities of artisans, and in Lombardy and Tuscany the number of confraternities fell over the course of the century. The confraternity, essential to lay participation in the elaborate ritualism of the church as well as to local sociability, may have declined during the urban expansion of the eighteenth century. Economic changes and the flow of rural migrants into the towns made the traditional forms of religious association outmoded and less effective.

The distinction between the Catholicism of the elite and popular religion has a further dimension as a result of the importance of magic. Recent scholarly interest in this topic has been most evident for north-western Europe in the seventeenth century and for non-European peoples in the twentieth. In Catholic Europe of the eighteenth century belief in necromancers and witches was far from vanquished, although the educated of France and Germany showed scepticism and contempt for the reality of magic, that 'deliberate production (or attempted production) of physical effects or the gaining of knowledge by means which were regarded as occult or supernatural' (K. Thomas). Yet if the number of witch trials plummeted, this did not mean the clergy could assume that magical beliefs no longer existed. Indeed, the concern with destroying belief in the powers of sorcerers and witches was widespread among the clergy who were themselves sometimes accused of deforming Catholic rituals for magical purposes. Belief in supernatural powers was still common among the peasantry. If religion in the formal sense was intercessionary and magic was coercive, much popular religion was perilously close to an attempt to coerce intercession. The idea that fervent devotionalism could produce results in non-religious aspects of life was common. There seems to be some linkage between what Michel Vovelle has termed baroque Catholicism, characterized by numerous masses for the dead and elaborate funeral processions, ostentatious expenditures on ritual objects, ex-votos and candles, and the persistence of belief in magical powers.

Increasing emphasis on devotionalism in the eighteenth century showed the desire of the clergy to use affection for specific rituals and intercessional worship as a means of deepening religious sentiment without the dangers inherent in the practices of popular religion or in uncontrolled flights of personal piety. The eighteenth century witnessed the spread of devotions such as the Sacred Heart and the Stations of the Cross which provided the basis for a new popular religion directed by the church itself. In many states the episcopacy, trained to abhor the dark side of popular religion based on shrines and the magical qualities often attached to statues, relics, fountains, rocks and other features of the natural landscape, tried to suppress these practices in favour of the new devotions. The religious orders, particularly those engaged in missionary activity, were the most important instruments for spreading clerically directed piety. The Sacred Heart, first popularized in France by St John Eudes (1601–81), became a favourite devotion of the Jesuits who promoted it throughout Europe in their missions. The Capuchins encouraged the Stations of the Cross in their missions, while the Redemptorists, an order founded by the most effective exponent of the new piety, St Alphonsus Liguori, promoted devotion to Our Lady of Perpetual Help. These practices, however, did not displace the primitive appeal of traditional popular religion, as shrines, pilgrimages, and curious rituals existed alongside the devotions created by the church.

Popular religion suffered also from the attacks of reform-minded clergy intent upon purifying the liturgy and providing the masses with at least a rudimentary knowledge of the basic truths of religion. Though often described as Jansenist, the clerical reformers conformed to the official doctrinal orthodoxy of the church. They insistently called for a purer, interior religion to replace what seemed to them to be the superstitions of popular religion. This 'Enlightened Catholicism' found supporters everywhere: Bishops Climent and Tavira in Spain, Ricci in Italy, Dillon in France, were all examples of the reforming impulse that was felt within the church during the second half of the century. The establishment of new seminaries, the burgeoning number of spiritual conferences for the clergy and, above all, the vigorous evangelizing missions of the religious orders testified to the reality of the reforming movement.

Since the Council of Trent the church had relied upon groups of priests, drawn generally from the regular clergy, to revive religious fervour and spread knowledge of sound doctrines through popular missions. The evangelizing campaigns of the eighteenth century produced a number of extraordinary figures whose instinctive grasp of mass psychology produced highly effective preachers. St Alphonsus Liguori (1696–1787) founded the Redemptorists in 1732, and the order soon proved its worth in southern Italy as did the Passionists established by St Paul Francis Danei in 1720. Elsewhere missionary activity was carried on by the Jesuits and Vincentians (France and Poland) and by the Capuchins and Jesuits (Spain) with the Redemptorists active in several lands. The religious orders involved in missionary work improved preaching and evangelizing techniques in contrast to the more traditional reliance on extravagant and sometimes incomprehensible sermons. The missions themselves were exercises as carefully prepared as those of any modern evangelist. How effectively they achieved their goal of deepening religious sensibilities among the illiterate is difficult to say, but there is some evidence that the missions served as a mechanism for halting the slippage of faith among the rural population.

Internal reform preached by the episcopacy and the evangelization of the masses carried out by the religious orders revealed the vitality of the eighteenth-century church. But the reforming effort failed to penetrate deeply enough to produce a general movement of transformation similar to the Counter-Reformation of the sixteenth century. Improved clerical education and the zeal of domestic missionaries, though partially successful, did not halt the decline of religious practice in areas where it had already begun nor did it replace religion based on the devotions of popular piety with the pastoral and spiritual faith demanded by the reformers. And except in a few cases – the reform of the Austrian church by Joseph II and the Tuscan by Scipione de' Ricci, for example – no serious attempt was made to alter the church's archaic and imbalanced administrative and financial structure. And there were other danger signs. A decline in religious vocations took place in every country after a period of expansion during the first half of the century. In Italy, the number of priests fell due to the pressure of government reformers on the religious orders in Lombardy–Tuscany, but even in Naples the secular clergy declined by twenty-one per cent between 1773 and 1801. In Spain, the decline was less noticeable for the secular clergy and the mendicant orders but was marked among the great monastic foundations: the Benedictines, Carthusians, Cistercians, etc. The near collapse of the monastic orders occurred elsewhere as well.

The life of the church was everywhere affected by the changing character of relations between the state and Rome. The struggle, almost as old as Christianity itself, took on new dimensions during the eighteenth century as the balance between states and the papacy shifted in the former's favour. There were still areas, to be sure, where the temporal power of the church was evident, starting with the Papal States. In the Germanies there had been a decline in the number of *Geistlichen Staaten* from the Reformation until the collapse of the Holy Roman Empire at the dawn of the nineteenth century, although the great north German bastions of Catholicism, Münster, Trier and Würzburg, continued to enjoy a certain importance.

The eighteenth-century papacy proved unable to resist the pressure brought to bear by governments staffed by bureaucrats intent on extending secular control over the internal affairs of the church even at the level of religious practice and discipline. States first sought to expand the traditional right of patronage over ecclesiastical appointments. Between 1740 and 1760 the governments of Portugal, Sardinia, Naples and Spain acquired for all practical purposes the right of appointment to the most important and lucrative benefices. In many lands, governments succeeded in tapping church revenues for secular purposes. Although doctrinal ties between local churches and Rome continued, monarchs everywhere worked toward the creation of what were in effect 'royal' churches subordinate to the state in almost every aspect of their temporal administration, even Frederick the Great, who insisted on exercising the right of patronage over the church in Catholic Silesia. Nor were the prince-bishops of Germany averse to extending their authority at the expense of Rome. Moreover, in the age of Enlightenment the rulers of Catholic Europe used the church to promote schemes for social and economic improvements. Whether in the Portugal of Pombal or the Austria of Joseph II, priests, especially the secular clergy, were seen as agents of the state advancing material progress, improving education, building public works and in general promoting in their dioceses and parishes the utilitarian policies enunciated by the absolutist states. The degree to which churches became 'royal' varied from state to state. It was most feeble in Poland because of the weakness of the national state. It was strongest in the Austria of Joseph II and in the duchy of Tuscany under the Emperor's brother, Leopold, where the state came closest to realizing the idea of a royal church serving temporal as well as spiritual interests. Joseph's closing of more than 700 monasteries and the subsequent use of their property to finance new parishes and central seminaries constituted an attack so direct on the traditional ecclesiastical structure of the Austrian church that Pope Pius VI took the unheard of step of journeying to Vienna in 1782 in the hope of restraining the Emperor from further measures. But in 1786 Joseph's younger brother, Grand Duke Leopold of Tuscany, encouraged the convocation by the reforming bishop of Pistoia, Scipione de' Ricci, of a diocesan synod which sought to strengthen episcopal authority vis-à-vis the papacy, purify the liturgy and limit the growth of the religious orders.

Between 1750 and 1790 the states of Catholic Europe achieved a degree of control over their respective churches never attained before. Rulers appointed bishops, founded seminaries and regulated church discipline. But the triumph of 'royal' churches did not rest on solid foundations. A weak papacy could not halt the progressive extension of state control over the church, but doctrinal ties and an undercurrent of sympathy for Rome among some clerics maintained a measure of papal influence which appeared to offer a counter-weight to the seemingly insatiable demands of secular governments. In Spain during the 1760s, the bishop of Cuenca, Carvajal y Lancaster, suffered for his out-spoken opposition to the ecclesiastical policies of the state, while in the 1780s, the prince-archbishop of Vienna, Cardinal Migazzi, and the primate of the Hungarian church, Count József Batthyány, resisted the policies of Joseph II. At the end of the century, the outbreak of revolutionary upheaval and the financial exactions of Catholic rulers on the church led to the beginnings of a modest revival of papal influence, a process, indeed, which would continue unabated throughout the nineteenth century.

The most celebrated victims of the widespread efforts to create 'royal' churches were the Jesuits. Once the glory of the Counter-Reformation church, the Society of Jesus, though it had lost the militant élan of its earlier history, continued to enjoy prestige and influence. Its missions in the New World, China, India and Persia, its more than 600 colleges providing education to national elites, and the social background of its members as well as the order's evident prosperity, made the Jesuits, though by no means the largest order within the church, one of the most successful and certainly the most envied. Inside the church their prominence and prosperity aroused the jealousy of the Augustinians, Franciscans, Dominicans and others. Governments gradually came to regard the order with its special vow of obedience to the popes with deep suspicion. As monarchs began to exert more authority over their respec-tive churches, hostility against the Jesuits increased. It was Catholic Portugal under the direction of its chief minister, Pombal, that first devastated the order in 1759 when the Society was expelled from the Portuguese empire, some Jesuits executed and hundreds more imprisoned. Against his personal inclina-tion Louis XV dissolved the order in France in 1764 after charges of dubious financial dealings in Martinique. Spain followed in 1767 in spite of the personal piety of Charles III, who obtained from a reluctant papacy the extinction of the order which was decreed by Clement XIV in 1773. The Jesuits fell not simply because irreverent and sceptical opinion was hostile to them but because Catholic princes – the 'Most Faithful King' of Portugal, the 'Catholic King' of Spain and the 'Most Christian King' of France, all by papal title – moved to destroy an order which did not fit into the pattern of the eighteenth-century 'royal' church.

The history of eighteenth-century toleration, once it is divorced from its literary manifestations, still remains to be written. While Protestants, Jews, and members of other religious and Christian sects saw their situation improve compared to the first half of the century, it everywhere fell short of the loftier flights of the Parisian and Milanese intelligentsia. Yet as governments sys-tematized attitudes towards minorities they diminished, at least implicitly, the primacy of Catholics. The toleration of Jews and Protestants in France in the 1780s was actually part of an oblique governmental compression of the church's authority.

The decline in vocations, tension between popular piety and the religion taught by the ecclesiastical elite, the dominance of a wealthy urban church over an impoverished rural one, the difficult relationship between papal and national authority, made apparent by the end of the century that the church had failed to resolve fundamental problems. On the eve of the French Revolution, the church's place in society was less secure than it had been a century earlier, and its institutional power had been diminished by Catholic but reformist absolute monarchs. The expulsion of the Jesuits and the suppression of the order by a weak papacy revealed how far the alliance between throne and altar had shifted in the former's favour. The church saw its internal unity disturbed by a series of strident theological disputes over Jansenism, Molinism, etc. It also had to face the intense criticism of intellectuals, especially in France. By the late eighteenth century the church was caught in a crisis leaving it ill prepared to face a period of revolutionary change.

We have touched here on a few of the subjects which need fuller examination for an understanding of the eighteenth-century church. These and other themes deserve investigation if we are to see the place of the church in traditional society and how it responded to new political, social and economic conditions which would alter its place within European society.

2 The French church

OLWEN HUFTON

The historian who would seek to summarize the history of the French church in the eighteenth century must be conscious of an unwieldy legacy. There can be few who have sat in departmental archives who have not encountered the individual in clerical collar or monk's habit, hard at work in the series G, carefully amassing material on his parish, diocese or order at any century since the middle ages, ready to embody the fruits of his labours in the *Semaine religieuse de . . .* , the *bulletin* of his local *Société Savante*, or in mammoth tome probably entitled *Histoire du diocèse de . . . depuis l'époque gallo-romaine jusqu'à 1789*, an individual endowed with those most luxurious of research prerequisites – time and freedom from economic worry. Since the second half of the nineteenth century, the church has provided its own historians, and in our own day – to cite merely three – the Abbé Plongeron, the P. Bertholet du Chesnaye at Rennes and the Abbé Baccrabère at Toulouse must be conscious that they belong to a time-honoured yet living tradition. Admittedly until the 1950s much of the work was stereotyped. Diocesan history pivoted (as far as the eighteenth century was concerned) upon certain *illustres prélats*, Jansenism (the universal garnish and a term used with the same discrimination as communism during the McCarthy era), or the debate between Catholicism and Enlightenment in the shape of the local renegade canon or *abbé un tel* who dabbled with freemasonry and hence in his own small way was responsible for the revolutionary debacle; and the work inevitably comprehended those whose generosity made possible the construction of pious edifices, the foundation of seminaries, hospices and *petites écoles*; and concluded with the evident divorce between high and low clergy (Richerist inspired) as manifest in the elections to the Estates General. Conspicuous by their absence from the study were the laity, whose presence was also difficult to define in the coexistent but rarely contiguous intellectual history, the *laïque* approach to the eighteenth century of, say, a Daniel Mornet, which probably reached its full flowering in the United States where a particular fondness for intellectual history has always been demonstrated. The Catholics and unbelievers of R. R. Palmer's study were not ordinary Catholics, who could barely grapple with their tax assessment and a chapbook, let alone the further flung passages of a Helvétius (the illiteracy rate was around sixty-five per cent), and the unbelievers were indeed a distinguished bunch – no chance here of running across the loud-mouthed innkeeper of Lodève or Béziers who consciously defied the parish priest every Sunday by opening his bar during mass and so turned the male faithful from their worship, but rather a collection of genteel intellectuals reinforcing each other as they gleefully demolished the intellectual underpinning of the established church. One is obviously not intent upon denigrating productive historical traditions but upon explaining the impact of the approach of Gabriel Le Bras, canon lawyer, sociologist and historian, when, just before the war and subsequently reiterated in 1955 in his celebrated *Etudes de sociologie religieuse*, he asked a series of questions designed to give an entirely new direction to ecclesiastical studies. Broadly speaking, he urged a historical approach to the present day map of religious worship in France, as drawn up by Canon Fernand Boulard, in order to locate and explain past discrepancies in religious worship – in short, a historical approach to modern religious sociology and a sociological approach to religious history. Dissatisfied with the concept of a France dechristianized since 1789, he sought to discern irregularities long before the Revolution. He emphasized the need to use episcopal and archdeacons' visitation registers to determine the strength of religious worship, the quality of the clergy and the state of the church. He asked, to cite a few examples, whether the existence of Protestantism in an area strengthened Catholics in their faith or whether proximity to a grasping religious house intensified anticlericalism and so caused a turning from the church. What did folklore and popular cults tell about the religion of the people? He did not leave the clergy untouched: turning to the *insinuations ecclésiastiques* (notarial contracts registering the resources behind an aspirant to the priesthood who had to show he had 100 livres of independent income and which also state the origin and parental profession of the aspirant cleric), he urged an examination of who became priests, their socio-economic standing and whether they were of local or distant recruitment. Yet more ambitiously, he asked what at any time was quintessential religion and posited that more than anything else it was an approach towards death. What could one find out about this in a historical context?

It is perhaps not surprising, given the range and chronological span of Le Bras's suggestions, that he was not the founder of any single school. Yet since his imaginative elaboration for future research into religious history, there has been a steady trickle of work along the lines he suggested and the eighteenth century has been by no means neglected. Moreover, a generation of obsessive quantifiers has established a grid for conveniently analysing visitation registers and *insinuations ecclésiastiques*. The recent emphasis on the history of *mentalités* has taken Le Bras's approaches to religious history still further and has asked questions that he did not broach. Maurice Agulhon has considered the degree to which Provençal religion was an expression of parochial sociability and solidarity; Gérard Cholvy's brilliant study of the religious behaviour of the department of the Hérault has investigated amongst many other questions the relationship between religion and radical politics, the degree to which the zone of recruitment of a town population could effect its religiosity, etc. Most recently, Michel Vovelle has succeeded in applying quantitative methods to the most qualitative subject – approaches to death – in his analysis of shifts in the religious content of Provençal testaments, a method so admired that Pierre Chaunu and a substantial *équipe* have usefully applied the same principles to several thousand Parisian wills. Hence anyone who in the 1970s seeks to weld together these differing traditions of approaches to religious history has an immense and very uneven task. He disposes of a 'patchwork' of information in which the religion of the Midi is better explored than that of the north: that of the west better than that of the east and so on, and he must already be conscious of striking differences in behavioural patterns. He has as well to contend with something of a stock image of the eighteenth-century church as a decadent church, stinking of worldliness, cracking from within, rent by quarrels between high and low and characterized by fat prelates, atheistic, masonic canons, skeletal and dissident priests, the whole tending towards imminent collapse in 1789 and only shored up by an ignorant, superstitious, semi-pagan laity. Was this the true legacy of the Counter-Reformation? Before considering whether this image belongs with myth or reality and the nuances of regional worship, let us embark with a few foundation facts.

Numerically, the ecclesiastical population totalled some 130 000 persons (or two per cent of the French population). Of these fifty per cent were regulars, between sixty and seventy per cent being women. Some 8000 might be styled 'upper clergy', i.e. they were bishops, abbots, cathedral canons, disposing of an income of 10 000 livres or more. Ecclesiastical wealth was based on a number of sources: in terms of landed wealth the church disposed of six to ten per cent of the national territory and probably a higher percentage of national income from land since what the church possessed was indubitably worth having. Its estates were unevenly scattered: at their thinnest in Brittany and at their thickest in Burgundy and with, generally, a heavier proportion in the south than in the north and centre. Seigneurial privilege was often attached to land. Over all land was the right to tithe, and tithing rights could account for anything up to one-seventh of the harvest (with a norm of one-eleventh to one-twelfth). Rights to tithe had often been alienated or had passed into the hands of the upper clergy against a nominal payment to the parish priest. The latter had the right to demand from his congregation for his services the surplice fees, set payment for offices performed. The church enjoyed fiscal exemptions but voted every five years a 'free gift' to the crown which could amount to up to twelve per cent of clerical revenues (no mean proportion), and to meet this the cleric paid a contribution – the *décimes*. Spiritual director of the lives of all but a tiny minority of Frenchmen (the Protestants of the Cévennes,

La Rochelle, Normandy and the Jews of Alsace), the church had a virtual monopoly of education: religious feasts dictated the pattern of one's life and the triumph of Counter-Reformation principles ensured that welfare institutions were religious-run and that charity remained the concern of the faithful – the means whereby the rich might be given the means to achieve eternal life. In short, for economic and social influence the church as an institution had no equal.

In terms of both wealth and power an episcopacy of some 139 (large by European standards) disposed of an important share. Though dioceses varied in size from a handful of parishes in the miniscule Avignonnais creations of the Midi to 600 or 800 parishes in the north and east, and annual revenues stretched from 10 000 to 200 000 livres, no bishop was poor: some were merely less rich than others. Moreover, if in Languedoc, Provence and Brittany the actual wealth at the disposal of the bishop was at its least, political experience as garnered in the Provincial Estates could be effective compensation for a bishop. There was a careerist aspect to the episcopacy – especially in the second half of the Old Regime. One can make a number of simple generalizations: all bishops were of aristocratic birth – they owed their position to the nomination of an influential person at court and it helped if one already had a kinsman in the episcopacy. The aspirant bishop had never been either a parish priest or a member of the regular clergy: he usually leapt from university and ordination into the *grand vicariat* of a cathedral chapter and was often a bishop by the age of twenty-seven, certainly thirty-five. Nor did he necessarily begin with a modest diocese: a de Luynes (ducal family) embarked with Bayeux (number ten) and moved to Sens (number two) after twelve years: a Rohan could expect to begin with the archidiocese of Bordeaux and move to Rheims or even Strasbourg (number one): a de Cheylus of more modest origin could however anticipate a humbler beginning, at Tréguier (20 000 livres) to Cahors (60 000 livres) to Bayeux (90 000 livres). In the diocese of Gap, no one after 1738 held the office for more than twelve years, and these Provençal bishoprics, many of them creations of the Avignon papacy, were, along with Breton dioceses, classic *sièges de passage*. But to set against these was, for example, the forty-five year tenure of office of Monseigneur de Partz de Pressy, bishop of Boulogne until the Revolution. Few careers embraced more than three moves and few positions were held for less than twelve years, which at least ensured continuity of direction. Moreover, although a situation in which patronage determined high office might appear to lay the way open to corruption and incompetence, this was emphatically not so. If sanctity was not the hallmark of the eighteenth-century French bishop (and it might be questioned whether it ever was so), administrative efficiency most certainly was. One aspect of this was the enormous expansion in bureaucratic business a bishop was prepared to undertake. Visitation registers begin after about 1740 to be concerned increasingly with the *spirituel*, as well as the *temporel*. They deal with the

condition of the clergy, the le
observance of Easter duties, S
a dozen dioceses from the 17
the bishop and addressed to
clerical income, responsibil
and *bureaux de charité*, the phy
of these were demanded by a
clergy sought detailed know
easy by the gradual extens
seminary which assured a
dioceses where seminaries
bishop had his doubts retu
this could make a real diffe
example – in raising the le
seminary, as in Coutance
assemblies, synods and ec
over which the bishop pre
of, say, a Maximilien Mer
with politics (a Loménie c
trator, leaving the grand
ordinances and returnin
conferences. An eighteen
he had only viewed hir
descended on a periodic
contact – probably more
the lower clergy toward
that these gentlemanly urbane bureaucrats, with ... ,
preferment albeit at the national or provincial level, knew about the economic
problems of the *curé* and did little to help him.

The system did of course still throw up the bishop who was really concerned
with the physical as well as the spiritual well-being of his diocese. Pestilence at
Marseilles in 1720 produced its local Carlo Borromeo in the shape of Belsunce:
the Breton dioceses, impecunious as they were, somehow contrived to produce
a remarkable series of saintly men – Girac at Rennes, de la Marche at Saint-
Pol-de-Léon, Urbain de Hercé at Dol-de-Bretagne, all of them deeply concerned with charitable foundations, *bureaux de charité, petites écoles*, some of them
forced to grapple with the social dislocation produced by typhus and typhoid
epidemics and all of them approaching their episcopal functions in much the
manner of the late-seventeenth-century bishops who in the full flowering of
Counter-Reformation sentiment laboured to endow their dioceses with
hôpitaux (part workhouse, part hospital) and *bureaux de charité* (pools of voluntary alms for the sustenance of the poor). Generally speaking, the concern of
the episcopacy with these institutions diminished very considerably after the

1720s when it became apparent that they could not cope with the demands made upon them. Nevertheless, bishops continued to put in a nominal appearance as directors of the *hôpital* of the diocesan centre, were usually prepared to put up some funds in face of impending bankruptcy and above all remembered the institutions in their testaments. Indeed there are impressive instances at Tulle, Condom, Mende (and probably elsewhere if an exhaustive study were made) of *hôpitaux* as the sole beneficiaries of bishops' wills. A Monseigneur de Piéncourt at Mende (worth 40 000 livres a year) left over 600 000 livres to the *hôpital général*, never failed to perform the foot-washing ceremony on Maundy Thursday and irritated urban officials throughout his diocese by his sudden decisions to present himself at recurrent distributions to the poor from ancient foundations. In short, charity did not desert this elite but it generally ceased to be a preponderant consideration for the majority.

If charity and pastoral care were part of the routine of an efficient bureaucrat's existence, he did not heavily involve himself in moral theology, indeed he sought in every respect to stand aside from the more burning theological issues of the day. What this demands of course is a careful definition of episcopal attitudes towards Jansenism and the role of Rome within their scheme. Any quick way of dealing with Jansenism must be inadequate but, briefly, the movement had three stages. It began in the seventeenth century as a sophisticated moral and theological reform embracing, in Pierre Chaunu's words, 'l'augustianisme latent de la réforme bérullienne, fondamentalisme chrétien des Dominicains, franc prédestinationisme gomarien, libéralisme arminien etc.'. From this it rapidly became a religion of practical and rigorous austerity, making high demands of personal conduct and with specific attitudes towards confession and religious duties – the form in which it percolated into the seminaries and hence influenced the parish clergy – and challenging by its very presence the authority of both papacy and state to determine the direction of religious worship, a struggle of course summarized in the *Unigenitus* (1713). Then in the eighteenth century it assumed political overtones, was taken up by the *parlements* in their struggle with monarchy, assumed nationalistic overtones as it occasioned attitudes towards the papacy and its Jesuit protagonists, and popular overtones as miracles were reported – the reputed *convulsionnaires* of Saint-Médard. No bishop could be deaf to what was going on. The papal nuncio in 1766 sought thus to define the position of the episcopacy:

> All accept the Constitution [*Unigenitus*], at least no one is known as refractory although, if it were possible, more than one would leave it aside as useless or the cause of disputes and disorders. The current controversies on the limitations of the two powers and the usurpations of the *parlements* have, in my view, reinforced the ties of affection and of interest between the French bishops and the head of the church. On the other hand the nuncio must always keep in mind and never lose sight of the fact that these bishops are just as French as the rest of the nation,

and are in consequence so fiercely attached to their maxims, usages and discipline, so jealous to maintain their so-called privileges and liberties of the Gallican church, that they consider themselves to be so many popes in their dioceses. The result is that if the Holy See undertook anything prejudicial to their supposed authority many of them, I am convinced, would oppose, would resist and would even appeal to the Court and the *parlements*, if it were necessary, to render useless the efforts of Rome, as it already happened on other occasions. It would be good to take a warning from this note, in order to meet and to treat the bishops with a total courtesy, but without opening one's mind to them or confiding in them, or if so only to a very small number, and only counting on them up to a certain point, for what shines in them is certainly not all of gold.

This was, of course, an obviously papal viewpoint. Emile Appolis sought more closely to pick out in the Midi what he called the *Tiers Parti Catholique*, a term used to designate those who found a Jansenist approach to the conduct of life and worship totally desirable but who refused to embroil themselves in the theological pros and cons of the *Unigenitus* and hence to erect the issue into a political conflict. Amongst these were numbered an important group of bishops who will be further relevant to our theme (and who are sometimes referred to as 'Jansenist' bishops though they would scarcely have welcomed the epithet). Those in Languedoc and Provence, often in areas rent by Protestant conflict, were to make efforts to strengthen and reform Catholic practice very much along the puritanical lines of the Jansenists, in order to prevent further slippages, perhaps to win converts, at all events to place Catholicism beyond reproach. These efforts would appear to have been significant in determining curious variations in the attitudes towards religion in contiguous localities. On the whole, however, what is most remarkable is the general refusal (with occasional exceptions, as the case of Christophe de Beaumont, archbishop of Paris and fervent protagonist of the *Unigenitus*, demonstrates) to become involved in the political ramifications of Jansenism.

Let us pass from the episcopacy to the rest of the higher clergy. In each diocesan centre there existed a cathedral chapter of, let us say, on average fifty dignitaries whose purpose was to ensure continuity in the running of the diocese, to assist the bishop, to carry out subsidiary visitations (the function of the archdeacon) and to see that cathedral worship was regularly performed in a suitably opulent manner. The cathedral chapters enjoyed a massive collective income whilst each canonry was attached to a prebend which usually afforded the incumbent several hundred if not thousand livres of revenue. Some cathedral canons were in fact wealthier than many bishops from their offices – the cathedral chapter of Chartres disposed of landed income of 3 500 000 livres for ninety *bénéficiers* – but the canons disposed of only limited power. They could make life difficult for the incumbent bishop in his individual diocese, but they did not influence decision-making within the church as a whole. Often exclusively aristocratic in character (and where they were not they were in process of becoming an aristocratic monopoly) the cathedral canonries drew on a national rather than a purely local recruitment, and jobs frequently passed from one member of a family to another. Bishops complained of the extreme youth of some canons (and there are instances of boys of sixteen) though many more were crumbling into ineffectual senility. They also pointed to frequent non-residence, though rarely to immorality or lax conduct. Above all, they referred to the sheer bloody-mindedness of individuals who were Gallican, Jansenist or Ultramontane in inverse proportions to the leanings of the bishop. Each capitular history – be it Chartres, Tours, Autun, Bayeux, Lisieux, Coutances, Angers (and they are legion) – tells essentially the same story. A heterogeneous grouping which defies simple definition but comprehended antiquaries, botanists, philanthropists, dabblers in industrial projects to assist the poor, occasional theologians, still more occasional freemasons, grand-chanters who were tone deaf and those who too readily did nothing except visit their relatives, the canons only seemed to present a united front when they demanded of an incoming bishop the guarantee of their capitular privileges. They perhaps had one common trait: their irrelevance to the functioning of the eighteenth-century church. No one in 1790 envisaged a church without bishops, but everyone could countenance the removal of the capitular clergy. Along with the contemplative religious orders, they were the main target of anticlerical sentiment both at an intellectual and at a popular level.

The decline of the regular religious life was not of course something which started in the eighteenth century but was a continual process from the late middle ages, a process which the Counter-Reformation did not truly reverse though it temporarily arrested it in a very particular way. That is to say, it did not really arrest the decline in the traditional religious orders, the Benedictines, Cluniacs, Carthusians, Cistercians etc., but stemmed the overall downward decline by the creation of a spate of new religious orders – a few of them contemplative but most of them of a rigorously practical nature: one thinks instinctively of the educational orders, the Eudists, the Frères Chrétiens des Ecoles Chrétiennes, the Ursulines, pioneers of female education, or of the new charitable orders, the Soeurs de la Charité, de Providence, de Sagesse, de Saint-Joseph du Puy etc., orders which knew their full flowering in France and which within highly limited terms served her well. Whatever growth in literacy was achieved in the eighteenth century (speculatively of the order of seventeen per cent) is attributed to the extension of *petites écoles*, and whatever the overall inefficacy of Catholic voluntary charity to cope with mounting numbers of paupers, the Sisters of Charity and allied orders remained the most impressive nursing force in European history until the late nineteenth century.

The decline in the numbers of regular clergy was then at its most marked amongst ancient and heavily endowed male orders. The numbers of Benedictines fell from 6434 members in 1770 to 4300 in 1790, of Augustinians from

2599 to 1765, of Franciscans from 9820 to 6064 – figures which point to an almost total lack of new entrants. Some decline is visible in parallel female orders – though the church as an outlet for the unmarried girl of good family ensured some flow of entrants. The teaching and charitable orders, however, continued to draw women though numbers were not increased and the steady proliferation of new charitable orders so characteristic of the seventeenth century was emphatically at an end. The reasons for this chequered pattern are easy enough to discern. The intellectual scorn expressed by Enlightenment thinkers on the monastic ideal evidently served to deter any aspirant monk. Falling numbers led to internal crises of confidence which had several manifestations: a *Commission des Réguliers* in 1766 voted the amalgamation of houses with under nine inmates; other houses asked collectively to be released from their vows. The wealth of the large empty houses served progressively to draw upon them popular wrath and – though it may not be merely an eighteenth-century phenomenon – proximity to such a house would appear to have hastened a process of dechristianization. The same forces, however, did not militate against the charitable orders. Though the Enlightenment sought to denounce the entire concept of Catholic voluntary charity by declaring it indiscriminate and responsible for the *existence* – and not contributing towards the elimination – of pauperdom, and for the same reason was forcibly against *hôpitaux* as reducing needful thrift in the poor, the opinions of the populace at large ran directly counter to this trend. The only popular complaint about these institutions and the women who ran them was that there were not enough of them to assuage the problems of needy old age or suffering pauper children. In short, the practical religious life continued to serve a social purpose and as long as it did so it commanded a favourable public opinion. The Jesuits, on the other hand, discredited by the *parlements* from their association with *Unigenitus*, could be driven into exile without real popular demur. Practical and pragmatic, popular attitudes in the eighteenth century towards the religious life were shaped by the aid it afforded in the here and now. This was an important aspect of the laicization of social attitudes.

One individual in the church hierarchy, arguably the most significant, remains to be considered, i.e. the parish priest. The traditional image of the eighteenth-century parish priest as a semi-starved, ignorant, well-meaning individual sharing the daily privations of his flock has been much eroded by recent work. As far as training was concerned there can be little doubt that the eighteenth-century priest was a far more 'trained' individual than his seventeenth-century predecessor. As Arlette Playoust-Chaussis observed in her recent study of the diocese of Boulogne, 'the priests who were to confront the revolutionary upheaval had received a better training than their predecessors of the 1720s'. The efforts of the Counter-Reformation to improve the quality of clerical education had real effect and bishops conscious of the obligations attached to their office were quick to establish seminaries which appeared in all substantial diocesan centres. Those desirous of a good living were also often graduates. The seminaries did much to lift the general level of the priesthood and clearly they exercised upon the priest the most pervasive intellectual influence of his life. It was in the seminaries that the priest picked up the seeds of Jansenism and Richerism which coloured his approach to his job. (Indeed the intellectual pressure the seminary exerted upon him is best tested by the number of retractions to the Civil Oath (1790) once the seminary had showed its hand.)

What kinds of people became priests? As far as professional origins were concerned the priest was usually the son of a merchant, notary, lawyer, manufacturer or more affluent artisan. In short, to an overwhelming degree he came from the towns, though against towns and bourgs producing a steady flow of vocations must be set others with an inexplicably low record. In other words, there were towns and towns. What is clear is that though a minority of priests (some six per cent) were sons of *laboureurs* (prosperous peasants), the church was not an outlet that the mass of the peasantry sought for its children. Clearly the children of the poor could not enter the priesthood because every ordinand had to show that he had *c.* 100 livres of independent income. After training, he looked for a benefice with cure of souls or, most often, he became a *vicaire* with a view to inheriting a benefice. Presentation to benefices was nominally either in the hands of the upper clergy, religious houses or the nobility, but in fact the incumbent usually decided upon his successor. Since the geographical incidence of religious vocations was far from even, patrons were pleased enough to be relieved of the burden of finding a candidate. From this followed, of course, nepotism and the traditional infiltration of a region from specific localities outside – of Norman priests, for example, into the Ile de France and the Orléanais, of Auvergnats into the Bordelais, of Rouergats into Aquitaine and Languedoc – whilst certain areas of Normandy (dioceses of Lisieux and parts of Bayeux) actually experienced priest shortage and could not look to local recruitment to fill their needs. Over France as a whole the number of vocations was falling, though not critically. It goes without saying that the most substantial benefices were more attractive than the poorest: an Auvergnat could only better himself by quitting the Auvergne. Even in areas which did not know a long-distance immigration, as in the case of Breton, Picard or Dauphinois parishes where the priests were emphatically of the region, they were not strictly speaking locals, but on the other hand they had usually served a long period as *vicaire* before becoming *curé* and had had ample opportunity to acquaint themselves with their parishioners before they became responsible for their well-being.

The average priest's income was of the order of 800 livres, which theoretically placed him in the ranks of the comfortably off, but consideration needs to be made of the heavy demands upon his income: a five per cent levy for *décimes*; seventy-five livres for the wages and maintenance of a servant (no priest could respectably be seen doing his own washing); these were unavoidable charges. There were often others. A retiring priest handing on his benefice expected a pension (at least 200 livres); this was a sum so small or so irregularly delivered that aged priests well into their seventies in the diocese of Gap reluctantly held on to their jobs. The wages of the *vicaire* and, though very rarely, even the schoolmaster could be further tolls. In some dioceses (Toulouse, Périgueux, Comminges etc.) the parish refused maintenance of the rectory. Then there was aid to the poor. The rectory was the first port of call for every *pauvre passant* and the local indigents were insistent in their demands. In short, the priest had a great deal to do with his income.

The bulk of clerical income was composed of tithe and small ancillary sums from property and the *casuel* (surplice fees attached to church services). In those instances where the priest did not hold parochial tithing rights which had been subsumed by bishop, chapter or religious house, the priest instead received from the tithe-holder the *portion congrue* – statutorily raised by the end of the Old Regime to 750 livres though this regulation may have been ineffectual. Where he was a *prêtre congruiste* he may have been forced to lean more heavily on the *casuel*. Generally speaking these surplice fees were not regarded as a productive or a proper source of income – certainly they were actively resented by a tithe-paying peasantry who considered it implied paying twice for the same thing. Many priests could not exact them and found themselves supplying candles and services free of charge. One priest in Franche Comté ran a dossier on each of his parishioners in which such small sums were recorded, but most priests accepted that they could not withhold burial, marriage and baptismal services simply because payment was not forthcoming. Nor was the tithe invariably paid without demur. The higher clergy usually leased out tithing rights to a substantial member of the community but the parish priest often directly collected his dues. Frequently he was caught up in the pattern of debt which literally enveloped every community. Tithes fell into arrears; the priest became creditor for the parish or embarked upon a running battle with his parishioners over unpaid or contested rights. Throughout France the tithe on new crops was generally resisted but worst of all for the priest was recalcitrance over paying tithe on hay (found at least in Normandy, Franche Comté and the Comminges) which could have serious repercussions, since the priest often needed a horse to reach the further flung reaches of his parish and without free hay this became impossible. Briefly, an average income of 800 livres did not place the priest beyond economic worries and if the studies made of Autun and the Ile de France are typical, the economic standards of the priesthood were falling. There was, of course, considerable regional variation. Fifty per cent of the priests of the diocese of Gap, for example, were men whose assets at death totalled over 1000 livres, and a percentage of these were able to make considerable loans to their parishioners, sometimes against the establishment of a life-annuity aimed presumably at increasing the priest's immediately disposable revenue with guarantees to cover old age. Some farmed seigneurial rights or collected taxes for absentee lords. One in this area was even joint partner in the exploitation of a lead mine.

The parish priest was arguably the most overworked individual in Old Regime France. He was responsible for the spiritual well-being of his flock and the catechetical instruction of the young, he was the spiritual director of the parish, the administrator of sacraments and so on; and he was also used by the government as an unpaid civil servant. He had, by law, to register every birth, marriage and death; he was to be called upon to give information if the intendant required it upon any subject from the economic status of his parishioners to the state of the roads. For the villages he *was* contact with the outside world. In times of dearth or local disaster it was his job to plead the community's case to the intendant or to elicit the bishop's special support. His influence intruded into almost every aspect of parish life. Most parishes did not have a trained midwife but a *matrone*, a local woman with the reputation for being good at delivering children. But whether *sage-femme* or *matrone* her conduct was normally under the priest's supervision. He also kept an eye on the efficacy of the school-teacher. His word was that accepted by the courts as a character reference for the accused. He carefully watched the tavern-keeper's business to see that licensing laws were observed and that the prohibitions on gambling were not ignored. In a society where policing scarcely existed outside the large towns, he epitomized in those remote villages where unpunished murder was not unknown and violence surfaced regularly certain standards which ensured that anarchy did not erupt beyond the ken of authority. Every parish priest considered himself overworked and underpaid – hence his intense resentment of the regular and capitular clergy who did nothing to justify their incomes, of a princely episcopacy intent on promotion and deaf to his cries for financial assistance. The relationship between upper and lower clergy was increasing in acrimony as inflation and social problems multiplied the parish priest's difficulties and one need not be surprised at the *curé*'s repudiation of the upper clergy in 1789.

But how efficient was he in carrying out his job? The overall view, an impressive one, is that whether one starts with the papal nuncio's view that the French parish priest and the Spanish bishop were the most praiseworthy elements of the Catholic clergy; or surveys the evident bulk of the parish priest's work enshrined in the *fonds de l'intendance*; or embarks upon innumerable case histories – such as the efforts of the Breton parochial clergy during the massive typhus and typhoid epidemics which made each priest a Belsunce in his parish, and some martyrs, for they contracted the disease; or takes Saint-Jacob's measured view on the Burgundian clergy subsequently echoed in local social studies; they generally served their parishes well.

One can, of course, introduce a number of qualifying factors: the priest's efficiency obviously depended upon the degree of physical energy of the individual. Local studies, however, indicate that the average priest was a man in his forties and though there were aged priests patently unable to cope with their pastoral duties, they were very much the exception to the rule. Where such an individual was revealed as incompetent by visiting priest or archdeacon, it was insisted that he take a *vicaire*. Secondly, the size and accessibility of the parish and the preparedness of the flock to accept the dictates of the priest were important considerations. And this brings us to the largest theme of this short study, the laity.

On a present day map of France demonstrating patterns of religious worship and using a threefold categorization (*fidèles*, the regular Sunday worshippers fulfilling all spiritual obligations; *pratiquants saisonniers*, i.e. loyal to the Easter observance and marrying, having one's children baptized, and dying according to the rites of the church; and those *indifférents aux traditions chrétiennes*), one is confronted with a pious Brittany, a partially pious Normandy, a belt of fidelity running through Flanders to the east of France where Alsace and Franche Comté equalled Brittany in fervour, and a partially pious Massif with the Lozère and the Velay probably scoring the highest percentage of regular worshippers in France. The rest of France shows seasonal conformity with enclaves of total indifference – notably Paris and the Ile de France, Troyes and its immediate area, Limoges and parts of Languedoc. It is too early to state categorically that such characteristics were already the hallmark of eighteenth-century society, but there is sufficient to indicate that this might well be the case. Local studies, for example, underscore an Ile de France in which certain sectors of the population – fifty per cent in some instances of adult males – had abandoned religious duties. Such studies point to a Norman dualism in which the record of the dioceses of Coutances and Rouen contrasts favourably with the less pious Bayeux, Lisieux and Evreux; to a Languedoc in which (the dioceses of Mende and Le Puy apart) laxity and hostility to the ecclesiastical hierarchy were deeply entrenched; or to an intensely Catholic Mauges, a frontier of Catholicism against the Protestant tradition of parts of the west, or a Franche Comté similarly defining itself in sharp distinction to Protestant Switzerland (the terms were interchangeable). The visitation register tells us little about the intensity of religious faith but something about obedience to an institution which was theoretically backed by state legislation insisting (without the mechanism to check implementation) upon baptism, catechetical instruction, church marriage, Sunday and feast day observance, Lenten fasting and the denial of medical services to those who refused the last rites. The eighteenth-century norm was to Sunday observance and to the performing of Easter duties; abstainers from Paschal obligations were usually no more than a handful yet they could in certain Languedocian parishes rise to seventeen per cent of the total population, in parts of the Ile de France to twenty-five per cent, and this in stark contrast with, say, the Breton diocese of

Tréguier where to find a single individual in any one parish who had not performed his Easter duties was the exception to the rule. Professionally, the traditional disrespecters of religious practice are easy to classify: *vignerons, brassiers, cabaretiers* (anyone involved in the drink trade), *bargerons, bateliers* (and others working on river boats), the entire rank and file of the French army; here and there in new industrial developments, weavers or the flotsam of the towns engaged in fringe trades; or in the villages an occasional rebellious, usually wealthy farmer might stand out, or former Protestants might lapse without regrets. Invariably the wayward were male and above the age of fifteen. In short, already to a limited degree and taking care not to overstress the situation, some dichotomy existed between male and female attitudes towards religious practice. Before one concentrates, however, on the non-conforming few discernible to the quantifier let us look – as far as we are able – at the quality of parochial worship.

The religion of the rural masses conformed in no small degree to the model laid down by R. P. Pin in a recent essay as the commonest discernible form, i.e. one of a provident deity, ever present and ready to interpose himself, capable of beneficent or malevolent intervention and hence whose favour must be won. It was a contractual concept of the supernatural (dear God, I am, as required, doing this on the understanding that you will abide by the rules and respond thus). The key to divine favour is the intermediary, the priest, capable of knowing what the community must do to avoid epidemic or harvest failure, cattle pestilence or like disaster, to ward off evil. One recognizes in such a model the religion of eighteenth-century France in which the priest was often called upon to excommunicate insects, in which the ringing of the parish bell was regarded as the only way to ward off hailstorms at harvest-time, in which penitence alone would keep disease at bay and in which the unbaptized child must speedily perish. *A peste, fame et bello libera nos domine*. Such a religion had rituals which in some respects were not a stone's throw from pagan traditions. Every *manuel de folklore historique* is a monument to a Christianity which had taken paganism as a bedfellow, had adapted its holy days and attendant rituals to fit in with popular tradition, had crowned menhirs with crosses, had reconciled itself to saints who appear in no Gregorian calendar. Vivid and immediate, attuned to popular fears and closely linked to the movements of the agricultural year, such a concept of religion was capable of sustaining regular prayer and practice, but to elevate it to a higher spiritual plane, as a better tutored clergy was concerned to do, must be an uphill struggle. It implied, for example, a collision over the pagan aspects of certain cults and particularly over the popular manifestations of the fête. The supernatural religious residue we have described was intermeshed both with the sense and practical manifestations of family and parochial solidarity and sociability. Mass was meeting time: baptism, marriages and deaths were occasions for family reunions. The feast day was holiday, the processions and imagery an important constituent of popular leisure. The youth groups – village associations of the young who on fête days elected a head, formed processions – even if they had long since degenerated into carousing and violence were, nevertheless, associated with the sociability of the religious feast. In short, there was a *social* as well as a *supernatural* element in religious practice. Moreover, one must recognize that part of society's contract with this particular provident deity was adherence to an exigent moral code, the Christian ethic.

How far was this moral code that of French society as a whole in this period or to what extent did it have its own opposing standards and values? Obviously there is no simple answer to such a question. But if we take certain broad themes – one's conduct towards God, i.e. questions of religious observance and reverence already considered, then conduct towards sex and the family and conduct towards society as a whole – a number of useful generalizations can be made. Just as regular religious observance was the norm so obedience to church teaching on sexual conduct was on the whole impressively high. The illegitimacy rate for France as a whole was of the order of one per cent of all births (though it rose in towns from four to seventeen per cent towards the end of the century). Irregular unions (concubinage) in a village context were almost unknown and though birth control seems to emerge as a clearly discernible phenomenon in the closing decade of the eighteenth century (at least in parts of Languedoc) up to that point demographers do not urge it as a feature of demographic development. True, the spectacle of a chaste France is a deteriorating one: illegitimacy rates were rising: there was an apparent growth in urban prostitution, marital separations with church sanctions were increasing, if not spectacularly, and areas of slippage were most marked in towns and cities amongst immigrant servant girls and textile workers and the mobile work force subject, particularly in the last quarter of the eighteenth century, to deteriorating economic conditions. A growth in rural poverty – a feature of the economic scene after (very broadly) 1750 – may also be the root cause of the erosion of another aspect of family obligation: the care of the old (honour thy father etc.). Neglect of the aged amongst indigent sectors of the population was an increasing worry for the parish priest. The heavy growth in child abandonment and infanticide also points to severe economic pressures upon the family. In short, economic change (population growth without the overall economic growth to support it) obviously took its toll upon the standards of this society.

Economic change also has relevance to community obligations – the succouring of the poor which remained in eighteenth-century France a voluntary affair. By contemporary or, indeed, by any standards, the French were a generous people. Theirs was a generosity which manifested itself in the true St Vincent de Paul approach, i.e. it was charity given by a broad social spectrum and not so much in money as in kind, the bit of bread or shelter given to the down and out, the bowl of milk or scrapings from the soup pot reserved for the children of the local poor etc. It is argued, using the decline in donations to hospitals in testaments, that France after *c*. 1740 was becoming less charitable (another aspect of the laicization of society), but this seems a dubious assumption for it does not comment upon the voluntary charity distributed in the donor's lifetime. Parish priests were insistent that charitable resources were stretched to their utmost. Obviously they were insufficient, but given that about a third of France lived on the fringes of destitution whilst something between an eighth and a fifth had crossed into the twilight world of the destitute, no system of relief, voluntary or compulsory, national or parochial, could have stretched to support everyone effectively. Begging and vagrancy in the last thirty years of the Old Regime were on the increase (and the rootless were poor Catholics), crime rates were soaring with the proliferation of thefts and attacks on property. Inadequately policed, a violent society accustomed to settle its own quarrels by private vendetta lived easily with isolated murders. Indeed, murder, if one examines the numerous attacks on tax officers, employees of the *ferme* and seigneurial agents, was a means of squaring community grievances. Priests were accustomed to wrestling with the total amorality of their flocks on such issues with as little effect as they struggled to suppress charivari (community disapprobation against unsuitable marriages) or the tolls exacted when a local boy sought to marry outside the parish. On these and many other issues the community made its decisions independent of church teaching.

Economic change could certainly be blamed for the erosion of certain standards and for slippage in some aspects of religious practice amongst the affected masses. Economic growth in the period was very positive: the burgeoning of certain industries such as the woollen industry of Languedoc before 1750, the silk industry of Lyons throughout the period, the cotton industry of Troyes and Rouen and the east in the closing decades of the Old Regime, precipitated significant changes often involving movements of men and women from their native parishes. Deteriorating circumstances in the country promoted its own migratory movements whether in search of seasonal or permanent jobs. This brings us firstly to the complicated issue of the effects of urbanization and industrialization upon religious behaviour and secondly to the religious habits of the man on the move for long periods of the year. Canon Boulard has led an energetic attack upon the concept of the city as necessarily a dechristianizing agent and, drawing upon instances in modern France, has shown the zone of recruitment of an urban population to be what matters in determining the continuing degree of practice, i.e. pious peasants in a city with pious traditions will remain pious (the peasant of La Chaise-Dieu or Le Monastier or Céaux d'Allègre in the Velay will not lose his habits by going to nearby Le Puy etc.). One can add to this a phenomenon of which we are all cognizant, that is religious practice as an identifying factor amongst some immigrant ethnic groups, whether the Irish in London, the Italians in

Boston or the Portuguese in Toronto, and we can extend this in some way to apply to French provincials in the eighteenth century: to, for example, the Rouergats in eighteenth-century Lodève or the Gévaudois in Montpellier. As such religion was an expression of sociability. Nevertheless, popular religion was in the long run weakened by the transference from country to town and even in some areas (though we must await a study on the villages surrounding Troyes by Stephen Johnson of Glasgow) by the extension of rural industry, and though this trend becomes more easily discernible in the nineteenth century, already there are indications of it in the eighteenth. Certainly the supernatural aspect of religion could be hard to transplant into an urban environment for it was linked to the agricultural year, to climate and natural phenomena; and the rhythm of urban life, the routine of industrial or commercial activity, the complexity of economic movements (imminent unemployment did not have the immediacy of a crop flattened by hail), involved a psychological process 'which seemed everywhere to produce a retreat of the sense of the sacred and the attachment to religious rites'.

The church was not quick to recognize the threats of slippage by increasing its personnel or building new churches where they were needed. On aggregate France had far too many churches in the period for its needs but in particular instances they were so ill-distributed as to leave burgeoning faubourgs and new complexes chronically under-served. Let us take two instances, the faubourg Boutonnet at the gates of Montpellier studied by Xavier Azéma, and Clermont de Lodève. Boutonnet lost its church during the wars of religion and during the next century the few hundred inhabitants complained of children dying unbaptized and adults sent to meet their maker without the solace of absolution when they petitioned the bishop of Montpellier for a church. In the course of the eighteenth century Boutonnet grew from about 500 to 1500 inhabitants: a *bonneterie* production was introduced which drew Rouergat and Cévennol immigrants (both with a high reputation for piety) but who, churchless and priestless, were unable to practise and progressively lost the habit. At Clermont and nearby Villeneuvette from the late seventeenth century, the development of Levant cloth production caused the tripling of the population in under sixty years. Over 5000 people, an unruly, ill-paid, drink-sodden, crime-prone work force, forming easy, irregular unions, giving in to frequent violence, were the spiritual concern of one priest and a *vicaire*. The former, who worked remorselessly to keep the vices of his flock within bounds, admitted he could not keep track of their activities and that there were streets in which he had never set foot. Interestingly enough, the female work force was largely Rouergat in origin which meant women with a tradition of piety: the male work force, on the other hand, was more widely drawn from the dioceses of Carcassone and Béziers (with a more dismal record) as well as from the Rouergue. Historically there has always been a very marked dichotomy of religious attitudes of men and women in this town, suggesting that the women cling to their practice whilst the men adopted the mores of the majority, like their Parisian counterpart fifty years on. The seasonal migrant was invariably male and equally did not practise during his odysseys, but he spent Easter (he was usually a small-holder with sowing to do) at home and fulfilled his spiritual duties at that time. Mass going was an affair for home: absence was the time to work. No legislation was more flagrantly breached than that requiring a workless Sabbath.

Slippage was not of course synonymous with absence from home or with industrialization or rural poverty. The young man who remained in his native village (and here one is harking back to the phenomenon of lapsing as a discernible trait amongst males over the age of fifteen) stood a chance of making a breach with the church. If one might pick out a collective reason for this, it might be the 'alternative sociability' thesis which emerges from the material offered by Maurice Agulhon in his study of Provence, though Agulhon himself does not use his evidence as a religious historian might. He examines religious processions, *confréries*, the café-bar and the *chambrette* or *buvette* as means of expressing sociability in the eighteenth-century Midi. The first grouping, processions and *confréries*, were ostensibly religious; indeed, the *confréries* had been an important Counter-Reformation weapon, and were usually founded in the wake of missions to establish particular devotions. Such expressions of baroque piety extended far outside the Midi though it was there that they burgeoned most extensively. Nominally they had different functions: that of the Blessed Sacrament, for example, accompanied the distribution of the host to the sick and had particular masses in which the brothers formed processions: that of the Rosary had a female following and was particularly espoused by Dominican missions. This *confrérie* was predominantly a cult of the Virgin. There were myriad others. Popular attention could still be attracted by vivid imagery, as the extension of the cult of the Sacred Heart throughout the eighteenth century demonstrates, and the *confréries* with banners and candles, chapels in churches, sometimes bizarre garb and ritual meetings appealed to the immediate aspect of popular religion.

But Agulhon insists upon their progressive laicization, upon their growing social, not religious, aspect. He also underscores the growth in the Midi – and here the phenomenon has universal application – of tavern sociability. The *cabaret* and the drink shop offer a great deal of potential to a social historian. Agulhon touches upon the extension of the business of the *cabaret* in the eighteenth century, an extension linked to the immense growth in the drink trade common to the whole of Europe (whether it was in the form of gin, *marc* or *eau de vie*) in the eighteenth century. The *cabaret* became increasingly the nodal point of male sociability, an easily understandable attraction to people who lived and, more and more, worked, given the extension of rural industry, within the confines of a single room. But the worker disposed of *limited* leisure, and priest and *cabaretier* were in constant conflict for this time. It is no accident that cleric and the drink trade were in constant friction as the former struggled in vain to restrict licensing laws. This alternative sociability was, of course, a male option: it is a social truism that the worker prefers to drink without his wife, whether to release himself from family worries or because he does not like to think his wife a loose woman, and hence for women mass followed by gossip continued to be the main manifestation of female sociability. There is a plethora of evidence to back up the 'alternative sociability' thesis, not least if one looks at the issue without the context of Revolution. The removal of the parish priest meant an unbridled increase in the numbers of these establishments which became the cradle of revolutionary and counter-revolutionary sentiment, the rendezvous of popular committees and so on. Female sociability, however, suffered an incredible blow during the Revolution and it was, interestingly enough, the women of France who recreated their own church long before the Napoleonic Concordat, and that a church of a very particular kind, i.e. one unconcerned with doctrine, instruction, confession, but immensely concerned with regular Sunday observance, the parish bell, the honouring of local saints and a liturgy performed by an individual (not necessarily a priest) uncompromised by having taken the oath. Certainly the Revolution accelerated a male exodus from the church, and if the extension of the café-bar played its part in absorbing the leisure of the Sabbath, another factor, obligatory military service, broke entirely the Christian traditions of the young man. The eighteenth-century army represented a rejection of Christian morality; rape, bloodshed, blasphemous utterances, a masculinity defined by holding one's drink and laying the girls needed only revolutionary propaganda to push it from covert to overt irreligion.

Such tendencies then as one can discern in popular religious practice are in the direction of suggesting gradual slippage rather than any abrupt mass exodus, a tendency accelerated by the Revolution and gaining momentum throughout the nineteenth century. Before 1790, i.e. for ninety per cent of our period, one cannot delineate any traumatic incident or series of incidents which dramatically and suddenly disturbed the regular pattern of religious belief and practice. Where localities were heavily dechristianized one may well have a look back to Albigensian or Protestant conflict, the existence of a Cluny or a Vézelay, or to particular incidents embodied in local history. What one does see in the period is economic change, accelerated mobility and the rupturing of parochial life which engendered a tendency to slippage. The disappearance of widespread famine and plague may also have removed an influence which periodically had served to tighten society's religious bonds (and indeed it may be no accident that the popular religious revival of 1796 and again that of 1816 have a background of dearth). But the case could reasonably be argued that such economic change does not make the eighteenth century in any way special. Surely the same was true of the sixteenth century? And what about the Enlightenment: certainly an intellectual movement counter to the very concept of religion must have traumatic and deleterious effects? The two questions are in fact probably intrinsically interknit and indeed crucial to an understanding of the eighteenth century. Such a tendency towards slippage amongst the masses was not new. But whereas in the past there had existed or had come to exist some intellectual movement to bring the aberrant to their senses, perhaps involving an alternative religious philosophy but emphatically of a religious nature, this was lacking in an eighteenth-century context and the intellectual movement which did exist was for the first time in history atheistical. The philosophy of the Enlightenment did not need to reach the masses: they could slip gradually by default.

One does not know how many of the thirty-five per cent of Frenchmen who could write their own names could actually read as well. Moreover the minority who did read Voltaire or Helvétius might well have been ambivalent in how they received the ideas of the Enlightenment. How many of those who approved of *Emile* did so in the way the English intellectual does the comprehensive school, i.e. as something to be applied to other people's children whilst their own are brought up according to strict parental discipline and regular religious worship? What one does know, thanks to the Chaunu death school and the works of Michel Vovelle on Provence, is that bequests for masses for the repose of the soul and requests for intercession on the part of Christ and the Virgin underwent a marked decline in Paris after 1750 and in Provence after 1760 (Christ from thirty to ten per cent and the Virgin from eighty-five to thirty per cent) in the wills of *notables* and hence that attitudes towards death were undergoing a very marked laicization long before the Revolution. One knows in addition that the intellectual efforts of the Catholic church were turned towards the recalcitrant intellectual minority and that authority hardly backed the church in its struggle. The Calas affair stands out by its very abnormality. Perhaps the church, as Marie-Louise Fracard (S. Marie-Pierre), who was one of the first to take up the Le Bras approach in her study of Niort in 1954, said, misjudged the real enemy, needing to concentrate its efforts instead on the masses to make good areas of slippage in the style later adopted with some success by the priests of the Mission of France. Certainly such an appeal to the people, of which the Jesuits knew only too well the value, were conspicuously absent in the period, though there are indications, like the spread of the cult of the Sacred Heart in Languedoc, that such appeals might have borne fruit amongst communities who sought immediacy and colour in their faith. Perhaps this is to ignore the efforts of a strong Jansenist movement amongst the lower clergy of the Midi which might be responsible, as Cholvy suggests, for the continuing phenomenon of enclaves of fervour, say, in the generally dechristianized district of Agde, but Jansenism was also a repellent factor serving to drive a wedge between priest and people, as I hope will be demonstrated in a short study of mine upon the diocese of Lodève before the Revolution. Much of what one says in any case about slippage in religious fervour and worship must be hedged about with qualifications. It may well be that the downward trend long pre-dates the eighteenth century and that the Counter-Reformation failed fully to win back the recalcitrant, or that such efforts were too short lived to have a lasting impact upon social mores – which seems to me might well apply to the Languedocian scene and to Rouen and Châlons. In short, though much is emerging from obscurity, much remains to be discovered. We await the studies of Dominique Julia upon Rheims, of Phillipe Loupès upon Bordeaux, of Frank Tallet upon Bescançon, and there will assuredly be others. There will doubtless be many surprises: Professor Emmanuel Le Roy Ladurie has brought to us a Pyrenean village which by the fifteenth century had not been 'christianized' in any meaningful sense, and above all one awaits some study of the origins of impiety in the aberrant Ile de France. Like a fresco hidden beneath successive coats of paint, layers can only be removed one at a time, but there can be little doubt of the infinite variety of what one will find below.

3 The Spanish church

WILLIAM J. CALLAHAN

The Spanish church of the Counter-Reformation, with its array of saints, theologians, canonists and missionaries, or the church caught in the bitter political struggles of the twentieth century, has offered more attractive fields of study to the historian than an eighteenth-century church that produced no St Theresa of Avila, no St John of the Cross, no Luis de León, no spectacular missionary achievements in distant and exotic lands. Even the Inquisition went about its work with a desultory spirit that would have shocked the harsh inquisitors of an earlier age. But the church of the eighteenth century, if it lacked the vitality of its predecessors, continued to be an immensely rich and powerful institution in a land where religious practice was deeply rooted and luxuriant in its variety. Moreover, an understanding of the problem of the church in modern Spain requires some knowledge of the long process of disintegration of the Old Regime church that began in the late eighteenth century and continued through the far-reaching liberal reforms carried out between 1835 and 1860. It has been fashionable to consider the history of the Spanish church as a long continuum from the time of Ferdinand and Isabella to the militant and intolerant church of the years prior to and during the civil war of the twentieth century. But the structure, economic base and mentality of the church in modern Spain are very different from those of the church in the Old Regime. It was, indeed, the collapse of the eighteenth-century church which produced the problem of the church in modern Spanish history.

The historiography of the eighteenth-century church is sparse, but recently scholars have begun to produce studies of significance. Olaechea's work on the relations between the state and the papacy, Batllori on the Jesuit exiles in Italy, Martín Hernández on seminaries, López Arévalo and Ajo on the church in Avila, Appolis and Saugnieux on Jansenism are signs of a new and objective interest in an institution that lends itself too easily to polemic. In spite of recent progress, however, the study of the Spanish church lags behind that of its French counterpart. There are few local studies, little on religious attitudes and less on the extent of religious practice. This essay will focus upon another largely neglected aspect of the church, its place within the highly structured society of the Old Regime.

The organization of the Spanish church remained substantially unchanged during the eighteenth century. The addition of four new dioceses, Santander, Ibiza, Tudela and Menorca, to the fifty-six existing represented a modest effort to rationalize archaic and unequal diocesan boundaries. Although the number of dioceses was not excessive by European standards, differences in size, wealth and territorial extent made the ecclesiastical map a patchwork of irrational divisions. Madrid, capital of a world empire, failed to attain diocesan status and continued subordinate to the archbishop of Toledo; an expanding Barcelona remained a diocese subject to the provincial metropolitan located in the stagnating town of Tarragona. The archbishop of Toledo presided over an ecclesiastical province of eight dioceses ranging from Valladolid in Old Castile to Córdoba in Andalucia, but the archbishop of Granada served as metropolitan of two small and poor dioceses, Guadix and Almería, in addition to his own. The bishop of Cádiz ruled a tiny diocese of twenty-eight parishes; the archbishop of Tarragona administered nearly 800. The distribution of the financial resources of the church was as imbalanced as its territorial structure. The historic archbishoprics of Toledo, Santiago de Compostela, Valencia and Seville enjoyed immense revenues, but the bishops of Valladolid, Tudela, Tuy and Urgel ran their dioceses on less than a tenth of the income of their wealthier counterparts. The archbishop of Santiago possessed impressive resources; his neighbour in Tuy just a few miles away was impoverished. Small and insignificant dioceses, Osma and Sigüenza, disposed of wealth far in excess of that available to bishops of more important sees, Barcelona, León and Zamora. The poor dioceses were generally concentrated in the north – Galicia, León, the Basque Provinces, Navarra, parts of Castile and Aragón – the richer in the south.

Some churchmen and the reforming ministers of the Bourbon monarchy recognized the need for changes in the administrative and financial structure of the church. Although the state interfered more and more in ecclesiastical affairs during the eighteenth century, it drew back from the task of imposing order on an institution with formidable powers of discreet resistance. The long saga leading to the creation of the diocese of Santander, finally established in 1754, urged a policy of caution. Santander on the Cantabrian coast originally formed part of the diocese of Burgos, located over the mountains on the Castilian *meseta*. Isolated and remote from Burgos, the region of Santander had to fend for itself before the indifference of the diocesan authorities. Philip II had seen the necessity of creating a new diocese in the north, but the king's plans foundered on the tenacious opposition of the Burgos cathedral chapter. For nearly two centuries the chapter successfully resisted similar proposals. The state finally broke its refusal to comply but only after a legal and diplomatic struggle that left little enthusiasm for further battles. Major changes of the ecclesiastical map would await the nineteenth century.

To foreigners visiting Spain for the first time the number of priests, monks, friars and nuns seemed, in the words of one traveller, 'prodigious'. A massive clerical presence was obvious in all the major towns. Barcelona alone had a cathedral, a collegiate church, eighty-two parish churches, twenty-six convents of men, eighteen of women, two oratories, a seminary, a tribunal of the Inquisition and several smaller religious houses. In Valencia, there were 2610 priests and religious in a population of approximately 80 000, while in Seville, the religious orders were so numerous that they could marshal 1600 of their members to participate in the great processions of Holy Week and Corpus Christi. But the impression of a nation overrun by priests, friars and nuns is to some extent misleading. The accurate census of 1797 showed an ecclesiastical population of 182 778 in a population of ten and a half million, but recent studies of ecclesiastical demography have noted that this figure includes a certain number of lay employees of the church, sacristans, administrators, etc., and that the adjusted total, 148 409, or approximately 1.5 per cent of the general population, was not excessive compared with some Catholic countries where the proportion was higher. Although there is little reliable evidence for estimating the size of the religious population early in the century, it appears to have remained stable between 1700 and 1800, with perhaps a slight decline at the century's close. Within the ecclesiastical establishment, the secular clergy numbered 70 840, the regular, 53 098 and the orders of women, 24 471.

The geographical distribution of the religious population shows significant regional differences. The northern coast, Galicia, Asturias and Guipúzcoa, had the lowest proportion of clergy relative to population; clerics formed one per cent or less of the population. The proportion was slightly higher, up to one and a half per cent, in several of the provinces of Castile, Avila, Cuenca, León, Segovia, Guadalajara as well in the south-east, La Mancha, Valencia and Murcia. Other regions, Catalonia, Extremadura, Seville, Salamanca and Toledo approximated the national norm; others, Madrid (city), Aragón, Córdoba, Palencia and Valladolid exceeded it. Local conditions, the presence of a university or long-established religious houses partially account for regional differences. In general, the religious population tended to be less in areas where the regular clergy formed a smaller proportion of the clerical establishment. In Galicia, Asturias, Guipúzcoa and La Mancha, seculars outnumbered regulars by three to one; in Palencia, Madrid (city), Córdoba, Valladolid, Aragón and Salamanca, the regular clergy slightly exceeded the secular, and there the general proportion of priests to the total population was significantly higher.

The distribution of clergy also affected the urban character of the Spanish church. Regions with large rural populations scattered among impoverished country villages and with few sizable towns were badly served. Nearly 3000 of the kingdom's 19 000 parishes at the end of the century lacked incumbents. The problem was greatest in Galicia, where nearly a thousand parishes were vacant in 1797, and in Soria, a mountainous and inhospitable region in the north-east, where a quarter of the parishes had no *cura*. These figures are even more interesting considering the large number of priests without benefices, over 18 000 at the end of the century. Priests without livings formed a floating clerical population concentrated in the cities and towns. The unbeneficed clergy eked out a bare living as salaried employees of cathedrals, charitable and pious foundations. The existence of these institutions in the cities drew them into the towns and away from the hard life of rural parishes.

The tendency of the religious orders to establish their houses in the cities accentuated the urban character of the eighteenth-century church. In large centres the orders could appeal more effectively for the donations of alms and property that financed their work. In Seville, the most popular city in Spain for the orders, the regular clergy formed nearly sixty per cent of the clerical population as religious and social life revolved to a considerable extent around the city's eighty-four monasteries and convents.

Functional and geographical imbalances in the distribution of the clergy created another obstacle to the efficiency of the church in its religious mission. Late-eighteenth-century censuses show clearly that only a minority of the secular clergy, approximately 22 000 of a total of 60 000 ordained priests, were active in parish work as either parish priests or assistants. The majority of the secular clergy surviving on benefices, the endowments established by pious benefactors for a variety of purposes, chaplaincies in noble households, cathedrals, hospitals, etc., contributed little to the pastoral life of the church. Moreover, the very existence of benefices in the towns attracted priests into an unseemly careerism which often conflicted with their priestly character and gave rise to constant criticism and satire on the part of secular and ecclesiastical writers. There was then no shortage of secular clergy in eighteenth-century Spain, but their distribution created a situation in which poor country parishes often had no priests and the cities too many. The Council of Castile frequently received desperate requests from rural villages without clergy. In 1800, for example, several small towns, Cubillos, Posadina and Cubillinos, told the Council that for twenty years they had lacked 'spiritual nourishment . . . because there was no income to support a priest in the sacred ministry'.

The geographical distribution of the secular clergy with 'cure of souls' was also uneven and reflected already in the eighteenth century the classic north–south division between areas where religious practice was more deeply rooted and those where it was not. On a national scale, the average number of parishioners per priest with 'cure of souls' was 497. The regions below or around this average were concentrated in the north and along the Mediterranean littoral. Some areas, Alava, León, Toro, and Valladolid fell well below the average; others, Aragón, Catalonia, and Valencia approximated it. But in the south, the centre of 'dechristianized Spain' in the nineteenth and twentieth centuries, the average was significantly larger, 1115 in Córdoba, 1721 in Murcia, and 1332 in Seville. The disparity between the southern and northern dioceses arose in part from the historic development of parish structures. Parishes in the south were extremely large. In the administrative area called the kingdom of Seville, 303 parishes served a population of over 750 000, while in Catalonia with a population of just over 800 000 there were 2738 parishes. In some southern dioceses, parishes could reach gigantic size, as in Cádiz where a single parish located in the cathedral served a population of 57 000. Numerous convents and chapels in the city provided services, it is true, but the weakness of the parish in the south deprived the church of the influence which local and neighbourhood parishes provided.

The most important group within the religious population, the secular clergy, fell into two unequal groups, a privileged elite in control of lucrative benefices and the government of the church and the mass of the clergy, parish priests, curates and unbeneficed clerics. The elite included the bishops of the sixty dioceses, 2300 canons of cathedral and collegiate chapters and a minority of the priests with benefices, a group of perhaps 5000. Recruitment into the world of ecclesiastical privilege depended on several considerations; a respectable family background and education were especially necessary for advancement. Priests who had studied theology, philosophy and canon law in universities dominated the episcopal hierarchy and cathedral chapters. The clerical minority was as highly educated as any group within eighteenth-century society. Bishops and canons frequently held doctorates in ecclesiastical subjects. The priest without academic training stood little chance of progressing through the ranks of the secular clergy. The critical point for the ambitious ecclesiastic was to gain admission to either a university faculty or a cathedral chapter; eleven canons of Santiago, for example, became bishops between 1716 and 1770.

The dominance of the nobility in the clerical elite complicated the division of the secular clergy caused by academic streaming. Although no legal obstacles excluded commoners from the episcopacy and cathedral chapters, and there were examples of clerics of modest birth attaining high church office, noble status proved a distinct advantage for the ambitious priest. Few bishops, however, came from the ranks of the aristocracy. Francisco de Solís, archbishop of Seville between 1755 and 1775, was the son of a grandee of Spain; his successor, Luis María de Borbón, was the son of a royal infante. But both cases were unusual. The Spanish episcopacy lacked the aristocratic cast of the French hierarchy during the eighteenth century. Bishops and canons came most often from noble families of modest economic circumstances for whom a church career offered the prospect of respectable status and a comfortable existence. Lesser nobles traditionally entered universities and therefore possessed the academic qualifications necessary for a successful ecclesiastical career. The priest of noble birth and with a university degree enjoyed an advantage competing for vacancies in cathedral chapters, the crucial stepping stone for the rising churchman.

The recruitment practices of the clerical elite produced bishops of superior quality. A foreign visitor's remark that 'the higher orders of the Spanish clergy ... are for the most part exempt from those irregularities which are charged on the clergy of other countries' was a judgement repeated by contemporaries and later historians of the eighteenth-century church. Abuses occurred occasionally, of course. In 1735, Philip V assigned the temporal administration of the archdiocese of Toledo to his eight-year-old son, but this was an exceptional case. More common during the first half of the century were bishops who enjoyed the game of court politics. Cardinal Portocarrero of Toledo intrigued with some effect for the accession of the Bourbon dynasty. During the seventeenth century the crown often appointed bishops to high state office. The practice continued under the Bourbons although on a reduced scale especially after 1766. The typical bishop was a secular priest, a university graduate, perhaps with a doctorate, who had begun his career in a cathedral chapter. Few bishops had experience as parish priests. Progress in the church depended on several circumstances. A priest of distinguished family and with good connections at court moved more quickly than his less fortunate colleagues. There was considerable mobility among the upper clergy since priests could apply for vacant canonries throughout the kingdom. Clerics hoped to advance their careers by moving from a less significant diocese or chapter to one of greater importance. Francisco Lorenzana, archbishop of Toledo during the reign of Charles III, began his career with a canonry in the wealthy though minor diocese of Sigüenza. The support of the royal confessor, Ravago, secured him a post in the prestigious chapter of Toledo of which he subsequently became dean. In 1765, he entered the hierarchy with his appointment to the diocese of Plasencia as his career began to move rapidly. In 1766, he received the archbishopric of Mexico City and in 1772, the great prize of the Spanish church, the archbishopric of Toledo. The mobility of the clerical elite was not excessive; from one to three moves from the first episcopal assignment was the rule. The movement of bishop and canons reflected personal career ambitions, but it also provided the leadership of the church with varied administrative and pastoral experience.

The activities of the eighteenth-century bishop ranged from the spiritual to the creation of public libraries, poorhouses and even manufactures. During the first half of the century, charitable and pastoral concerns predominated. Luis de Salcedo of Seville (1722–41) earned a reputation as 'a true father of the poor' for the massive relief efforts he directed in 1723, 1734 and 1737, when thousands of impoverished peasants sought assistance in the city. Amador Merino Malaguilla of Badajoz was widely esteemed for the pastoral visits regarded as an essential obligation of the good bishop. The Badajoz prelate visited every town and village of his diocese at least five times during his tenure of office. Although charity and pastoral work continued among bishops of the second half of the century, interest broadened to include education, economic development, culture and public works. Lorenzana of Toledo tried to revive the decaying silk industry of his diocesan seat; Fabián y Fuero of Valencia and Llanes y Argüelles of Seville opened public libraries in their palaces; Bertran of Salamanca founded a vocational school for the training of goldsmiths. Although bishops generally fulfilled the responsibilities of office, it should be remembered that they formed part of a privileged social elite by virtue of their positions and often by birth. Some bishops lived austerely such as Salcedo of Seville who slept on the floor as a sign of penance. Other prelates lived in comfort suitable to their station and noble origins. Lorenzana delighted in his personal library of rare books. The archbishop of Granada in the 1780s, according to the English traveller Townsend, was 'well lodged' and kept 'a respectable table' and was 'quite the man of fashion'. Yet the archbishop had also acquired a reputation for his generosity towards the poor. Conscientious bishops, of course, saw no contradiction between an aristocratic style of life and their pastoral function. The balance between the bishop as seigneur and priest was not easy to maintain, but the Spanish episcopacy kept it as well as possible within the existing social structure.

The great recruiting ground for the episcopacy, with the exception of the minority of bishops chosen from the regular clergy, was the cathedral chapter. Over 2000 canons lived in a clerical world as diverse and colourful as any within the church. Chapters were large or small depending on the size and wealth of the diocese. Canons in wealthy chapters enjoyed incomes that sometimes exceeded those of bishops of poor dioceses. Eleven canons of Seville received over 60 000 reales a year, approximately the salary of a government minister. Elaborate styles of dress distinguished the canons of one chapter from another. The canons of Zaragoza wore a black cassock covered by a mantle of violet silk; the canons of Barcelona used a scarlet cassock and a surplice trimmed in ermine. Members of cathedral chapters fulfilled a variety of responsibilities. They chanted the divine office daily in the cathedral, supervised the ceremonies of the liturgical year and managed the often extensive properties and investments of the chapter. Of all the groups within the church, the chapters were the most sensitive about their corporate dignity. Disputes with bishops and the civil authorities constantly disturbed the tranquillity of cathedral towns. Although the canons were a factious lot, they also contributed to the relief of the poor. The chapter of Santiago de Compostela gave generously to a campaign to raise funds for the needy during the terrible winter of 1768–9. The life of a canon was not demanding, and left abundant time for the pursuit of personal interests. Many canons undoubtedly chose to languish comfortably performing their not very taxing duties. But the canons were the source of bishops of superior quality, and they produced some of the most progressive clerics of the eighteenth-century church. Jeronimo del Róo, canon and later dean of the chapter in Las Palmas during the 1770s and 1780s, was typical of the ecclesiastic with a broad range of interests. Róo founded a school of design and promoted the establishment of an architectural academy, and was also an early and active member of the Economic Society created in 1777 to encourage economic development in the Canaries.

Contemporary observers of the eighteenth-century church praised the dedication and devotion of the bishops but denounced the ignorance and lax morality of the lower clergy. Townsend said of the parochial clergy: 'One thing is certain, that many of them have families', and he recalled that the bishop of Oviedo insisted that his priests should not keep their children with them, 'this sacrifice at least he insisted they should make to decency. Beyond this he did not think it right to be too rigid in his inquiries.' Jean Sarrailh in his study of eighteenth-century Spain has stressed the ignorance of the lower clergy. Although this picture is probably accurate, in fact little is known of the condition of parish priests and curates. Clearly the majority of secular priests received a catch-as-catch-can education from a variety of sources. Many clerics picked up a smattering of Latin, perhaps from the arts courses offered by local monasteries and grammar schools. The more fortunate received a seminary education. But until Charles III (1759–88) began to promote the creation of new seminaries and the improvement of those already established, the quality of seminary education was abysmal. Until reforms ordered by the crown in 1766, cathedral chapters generally administered seminaries and showed more concern with using the students as altar servers and janitors in cathedrals than with education. One critic complained that the seminaries taught theology badly, 'since nearly all Spaniards, seeing that the peninsula was free of heretics, believed that it was not necessary to study theology, and some have been bold enough to suggest that its study is more damaging than useful'. Although the number of seminaries increased after 1766, there were still only forty-five by the end of the century, and many of these were small and poorly staffed. Throughout the eighteenth century bishops tried to better the lamentable education of their priests through periodic spiritual conferences which were compulsory in many dioceses.

The quality of the lower clergy depended also on the economic condition of individual parishes. On this level as on the diocesan, some parishes were better off than others. Parish priests in urban centres with well-endowed churches belonged or stood close to the clerical elite. Joseph Climent, bishop of Barcelona (1766–75), had once served as *cura* of a wealthy parish before his elevation to the episcopacy. And some of the parish clergy of Cuenca were university graduates who accepted the charge of modestly endowed churches in rural towns. In areas where churches struggled to survive on poor or non-existent endowments, the situation was different, hence the large number of vacant parishes in Galicia and Soria. And complaints about the superstition and ignorance of the lower clergy were most numerous in regions where parish resources were limited. The church leadership believed the problem was one of education and as a result emphasized seminary education and spiritual conferences for parish priests. Such measures, however, could not remove the basic cause of the difficulty, the imbalanced distribution of resources between the urban and rural church.

The situation of the regular clergy during the eighteenth century is difficult to establish. Government officials and some progressive secular priests of the time painted a bleak picture of an ill-educated monkish rabble, 'armies of idlers' and 'the Pharisees of our time'. The reality was more complex although the orders clearly suffered a decline of religious and intellectual vitality. The strictly monastic orders, the Benedictines, Cistercians, Carthusians, etc., suffered most and increasingly found it difficult to recruit new members. In 1797, the sixty-three Benedictine monasteries had only fifty-one novices among them with an average population per monastery of just twenty monks. Government hostility towards the monastic orders partially accounts for their declining role within the church. Equally damaging was the internal strife that frequently disrupted the tranquillity of monasteries. The clerical historian of the celebrated Catalan Cistercian monastery of Poblet admitted that from 1760 onward, life there had become impossible because of bitter factionalism. The troubles of Poblet were extreme, but similar tensions upset other monastic houses. In these circumstances, the intellectual vigour of the monasteries left much to be desired, although there were a few houses of distinction. The monastery of Santa María de Bellpuig in Catalonia emphasized the study of medieval religious history, built a fine library and produced a group of capable historians and archivists of whom the most notable was Jaime Caresmar. The Benedictines produced one of the great figures in the intellectual history of eighteenth-century Spain, Benito Feijóo, and their abbey of Silos in Old Castile imitated in a modest way the work of St Maur. But in general the scholarship of the monasteries was narrowly theological and philosophical in focus. Most of the books that emerged from them have long since been forgotten.

The situation of the mendicant orders, Franciscans, Dominicans, Carmelites, etc., was stronger. The Franciscans, the largest single order with 15 000 of the kingdom's regular clergy, never experienced difficulty finding recruits. In 1768, the order was so inundated with applicants that it tried to control admission. Critics of the mendicants explained their popularity by alleging that the prospect of having a roof over one's head, supper every evening, a free education and freedom of movement attracted many lacking true vocations. But the *frailes* were not the clerical rabble their enemies thought them to be. The mendicants esteemed education as much as the elite of the secular clergy. In university towns such as Salamanca and Santiago de Compostela, religious houses were miniature universities, and many friars held chairs in ecclesiastical subjects. Education provided the key to advancement in the orders. The heads of the Franciscan province of Santiago invariably held doctorates, and this was a pattern among the other mendicant orders as well. A roguish element was certainly present among the friars, but the traditional picture of the orders being made up of rough and tumble Rabelaisian types is plainly inaccurate.

The friars recruited more broadly than the elite secular clergy, and this was one of the reasons for their traditional popularity among the lower classes. Moreover, the two principal functions of the orders, preaching and education, brought them into close contact with the general population. The mendicants often opened their courses in arts and philosophy to local students. The Augustinians of Agreda, for example, maintained a small college for the education of young friars, which also served as the town's only secondary school. And the mendicant orders along with the Jesuits furnished the personnel for the most vigorous spiritual effort of the eighteenth-century church, the missionary movement which sent preachers across the length and breadth of the kingdom. The Capuchins produced a series of great preachers, the friars Villalpando, Zamora and Cádiz, who attained immense popularity. The general quality of the mendicants was not as high as that of the missionary friars. Occasional examples of gentle abuse occurred as in Cádiz where the Capuchins had matins rung every morning but stayed comfortably in their beds, but there were few examples of scandalous departure from the norms of a collective religious life. The intellectual life of the mendicants focused on the teaching and writing of theology, philosophy and canon law; little of it was significant, although occasionally the mendicants produced figures of importance such as the Augustinian Flórez, who authored a multi-volume history of the Spanish church based on documentary sources.

The mendicant orders suffered too from severe internal factionalism. Regional differences among friars of the Franciscan province of Santiago became so extreme that quotas for election to provincial offices had to be established. Similar differences among friars of the province of Extremadura, between those living north and south of the River Tagus, reached such proportions that the province had to be divided in 1769. A similar pattern of dissension existed among other mendicant orders.

The regular clergy cannot be discussed without some reference to the Jesuits. The Society of Jesus was not among the largest Spanish orders. On the eve of the expulsion (1767), it numbered less than 3000, well below the membership of the Franciscans, Dominicans, Carmelites and Capuchins. The Jesuits compensated for their modest numbers in quality of membership and prestige. The order recruited among the nobility and devoted special attention to the education of noblemen. The business of the Jesuits was education, although not university instruction where they were less well represented than other orders, but secondary schooling for the kingdom's noble elite. In 1749, the Jesuits administered 117 colleges including such prestigious institutions as the Colegio Imperial and the Seminario de Nobles in Madrid. In spite of the order's recruitment practices and its emphasis on education, the intellectual level of the order was no more impressive than that of the mendicants. A modern historian of the order remarked of its eighteenth-century theologians: 'they are all obscure enough and scarcely can be distinguished today but for their names'. There were some exceptions to the lack of intellectual vitality among the Jesuits, notably José Francisco de Isla, author of a controversial satirical novel, *Fray Gerundio*, the great Basque linguist, Manuel de Larramendi, and the archivist, Andrés Burriel.

With the exception of the strictly monastic orders, then, the regulars continued to recruit successfully and to enjoy popular esteem. Their work fell heavily into the areas of teaching and preaching; scandalous lapses from the rules of religious life were rare, but the intellectual vitality of an earlier age had disappeared in favour of a comfortable but not particularly stimulating religious and intellectual routine. The kingdom's 30 000 nuns fulfilled a different role from their male counterparts. The vast majority of nuns lived in contemplative communities. Although there are examples of educational and charitable work among the orders of women, in general active work was not common. The Sisters of Charity whose hospital and nursing activities had won the order a reputation elsewhere in Europe experienced the greatest difficulty establishing themselves in Spain. The first community did not appear until the 1780s, and even then the order spread slowly. The long monastic tradition of the women's orders in Spain partially explains the lack of active communities during the Old Regime. Another reason may have been the social function played by convents in a highly structured society. Not every convent was a refuge for genteel women who could not be supported economically in the outside world, but the life of the contemplative orders, however harsh and austere it might be on occasion, fitted into a widespread mentality that such activities were proper for women and that employment in hospitals and other charitable institutions, which was work among the lowest classes of society, was not.

The place of the church within eighteenth-century society rested in large measure on its material resources. The church received an abundant income from tithes, urban and rural property, mass stipends and other investments. The church in Castile possessed one-seventh of the region's agricultural and pastoral lands, and these produced one-quarter of the area's income from agrarian sources. It is not yet possible to establish the total wealth of the church with accuracy. Such information would be useful, although it would be only the first stage in the study of ecclesiastical finances. The wealth of the church was fragmented among countless institutions, dioceses, cathedral chapters, religious houses and charitable foundations; we will need more studies of local ecclesiastical institutions before a general picture emerges. Moreover, references to the wealth of the church or its ownership of land throw a cover over the extreme complexities of land tenure during the Old Regime. Recent studies of the disentailing of church property after 1835 show that in at least some regions, Seville and Navarra for example, church institutions rarely exploited their land directly but rented it through a variety of lease arrangements. Ecclesiastical properties produced a modest return compared to the income they would render when in private hands. In Seville, the church received approximately one-half the income private owners would derive from the same parcels. In Navarra, church lands were leased for relatively long periods of time, often eight to ten years, for rents that sometimes went unchanged for generations. Eighteenth-century critics of ecclesiastical property, the ownership of land by the so-called *manos muertas*, believed that the church was an obstacle to the spread of private ownership and hence an obstacle to agricultural progress. This line of argument was taken up with enthusiasm by the liberal reformers of the nineteenth century. But the opposite may have been true at least in terms of the livelihood of the peasantry. In Seville and Navarra, the church provided the use of land at moderate cost to a far larger agricultural population than would work the same property after disentailment. The 6000 persons employed on church lands in Seville fell to 450 once the disentailing process was complete.

Another aspect of church wealth often overlooked is that fragmented ownership among a large number of institutions provided for the regional and local retention of some of the church's riches. This is not to deny that some of these resources were siphoned off by the state or that they were inequitably divided among poor and wealthy ecclesiastical centres. But in a society in which trade and industry were poorly developed, the church was one of the few sources of heavy expenditure on local economies. The liturgical staff of the Seville cathedral numbered 235, and diocesan administration required the employment of more personnel. The archbishop of Santiago during the 1770s paid out nearly a million reales a year, a substantial amount, to members of his household and the diocesan administration. In large church centres, communities of silver- and goldsmiths, embroiderers, masons, carpenters, waxmakers and other artisans survived on the work provided by the church. An ironic consequence of the disentailing of church lands in the nineteenth century would be the collapse of artisan life in towns dependent on the church. Toledo had declined economically by the eighteenth century, but local life retained a certain vigour because of the presence of an immensely wealthy bishopric and cathedral chapter. Disentailment plunged the town into a depression from which it never fully recovered.

The church's income allowed it to fulfil one of its most important functions within Old Regime society, the provision of charitable assistance to a large population living in marginal economic circumstances. The state assumed some responsibility for the indigent, but it was the church that erected the only effective if fragile barrier against the spread of starvation and death among the lower classes of town and country. The charity of the church was uneven and could be undependable, but the record of the eighteenth-century church in poor relief was impressive. Bishops and cathedral chapters regularly set aside part of their incomes for charitable purposes. The indigent welcomed assistance in good times, but required it desperately in periods of severe economic crisis. When floods and locusts ruined crops in the vicinity of Seville in 1709, the archbishop and chapter provided alms to nearly 20 000 impoverished peasants who had come to the city in search of food. In Galicia, during the destructive winter of 1768–9 after torrential rains had destroyed the harvest, thousands of peasants on the verge of starvation filled Santiago de Compostela. The relief effort was largely the work of the church. The archbishop, Rajoy, provided food for 1300 persons daily; a local monastery cared for 3000 more. The archbishop and chapter donated funds to purchase grain supplies in southern France to relieve famine conditions. The effort of the ecclesiastical establishment in the crisis of 1768–9 is one of the best examples of the importance of church charity in mitigating the disasters characteristic of the fragile agrarian economy of Spain during the Old Regime. It is perhaps too much to say that charity made the church a popular institution, but there clearly existed an unwritten and vague social understanding consecrated by custom that the wealth of the church had to be used in part to relieve the necessities of the poor. Ecclesiastics and paupers understood the terms of the contract; the poor turned to the church as a matter of course when they needed help, and assistance was generally forthcoming. It is significant that the first massive anticlerical riots of modern Spanish history took place in 1834–5 in the midst of a serious food crisis but at a time when the badly eroded finances of the church made the kind of extensive programme of assistance employed in Galicia impossible.

The church was a popular institution in another respect. The life of every member of society, from a Charles III alighting from his carriage as a priest carrying the Eucharist passed, to the peasant invoking the mysterious and magical powers of the saints to ward off natural disasters, was affected by the church. The fundamental stages of human existence, birth, marriage and death, revolved around the ceremonies of the church. Social life in town and country centred on the festivals of the liturgical calendar. Religious ceremonies took extravagant forms whether in the great processions of Holy Week or the sombre flagellation rites of Lent. In every town pious associations, the *cofradías*, provided the vehicle for popular expression of religious sentiments: Seville alone had more than a thousand. The *cofradías* appeared with appropriate splendour on the important feast days of the liturgical year. But if religious life expressed itself more colourfully than in a later age, we know little of the extent or intensity of religious feeling among the population at large. The techniques of Le Bras have only recently been applied to the study of the Spanish church and almost entirely to the modern period. Moreover, to apply to the Old Regime the test of attendance at Sunday mass, fulfilment of the Easter duty, etc., raises serious questions, for religious practice in the eighteenth century more than today reflected community concerns rather than the devotional commitment of individuals. Goñi Gaztambide's study of the certificates of confession required of the faithful before they could receive communion in the diocese of Pamplona towards the close of the Old Regime revealed that nearly the entire population met its obligations. But this says little of the true state of religious sentiment. In this largely rural diocese, clerical and community pressure must have been substantial. In the cities, the possession of certificates meant nothing. Prostitutes did a brisk trade selling them in Madrid to anyone with a few reales in his pocket.

Historians of the eighteenth-century church agree that it did not distinguish itself within the history of Catholic spirituality. Specific cults such as that of the *Virgen de la Pastora* propagated by the Capuchins multiplied to the detriment of solid knowledge of religious doctrine. The church leadership laboured under few illusions when it contemplated the spiritual poverty of the mass of the population. A 1747 survey of religious education on Mallorca showed that the population was fortunate to receive any instruction and what little there was consisted of knowledge of the Our Father, the Hail Mary, the Ten Commandments and the sacraments. Whatever religious knowledge was communicated to the masses came through preaching. Through much of the century, preachers indulged in extravagant language and theatrical gestures (clanging the chains of the damned on the pulpit) which left congregations more confused than terrorized. The state of popular religious education led many bishops from the 1720s onward to engage in pastoral visits to the towns and villages of their dioceses and to encourage the missions of spiritual revival conducted by the religious orders. The missionary movement represented the most far-reaching effort of the Spanish church to bring a rudimentary knowledge of religion to the urban and rural populace. The Jesuit missionary, Pedro de Calatayud, spent his clerical life between 1720 and 1767 preaching in the small towns and remote villages of central and northern Spain. Urban missionaries such as the celebrated Capuchin, Fray Diego de Cádiz, often preached to thousands in spectacular ceremonies. In the end, the hold of the church over the masses depended on the ceremonial and placatory aspects of religion. But even here there were signs of diminished enthusiasm for the extravagances of baroque piety. Many of the celebrated confraternities of Seville failed to participate in religious processions after 1778, and in Catalonia the authorities found the artisan guilds unwilling to take their accustomed place in liturgical ceremonies.

Concern with the quality of religious faith lay behind the development of a reforming spirit within the church after 1760. The reforming movement was complex in its origins; it owed something to the influence of the Spanish variant of Jansenism although its support went beyond the small circle of Jansenist bishops, Climent of Barcelona and later Tavira of Salamanca, to include prelates such as Lorenzana of Toledo whose orthodoxy was above reproach. The reformers opposed certain manifestations of popular religion, novenas, rosaries, the multiplication of cults of the Virgin; they favoured the communication of religious knowledge through editions of the scriptures in the vernacular. Felipe Bertran, bishop of Salamanca during the 1770s and Inquisitor General, summed up a reforming programme that many bishops would have accepted when he told his clergy to proceed against 'all abuses opposed to the true cult of God . . . and all vain and superstitious rites as well as false beliefs'. His successor, Tavira, tried to purify the liturgy and curb the spreading cult of the Sacred Heart. Lorenzana urged his priests to preach simply to their congregations instead of relying on obscure and bombastic rhetoric. The emphasis of the reforming movement varied from bishop to bishop, but in every case the demand for a pure and internal Christianity arose from the clear realization that the faith of the vast majority of the population rested on weak foundations.

In addition to the crisis of faith, there is evidence that the church's place within a traditional society was slowly changing during the second half of the eighteenth century. The centuries old alliance between throne and altar shifted in favour of the state after the concordat of 1753. The church continued to exist as a highly privileged corporation with financial resources of its own, but it fell increasingly under government control. The crown nominated bishops through a chamber of the Council of Castile. Bishops who did not give royal policy their full support faced harassment and even dismissal. The civil authorities humiliated the aged bishop of Cuenca, Carvajal y Lancaster, who dared to express opposition towards the state's policy with respect to the church during the 1760s, and they hounded from office in the 1790s one of the most distinguished prelates of the hierarchy, Fabián y Fuero of Valencia, who had offended the royal governor of the city. The state gradually established more control over the internal affairs of the religious orders. It suppressed two orders outright, the Jesuits and the hospital order of San Anton, and it used pressure and diplomacy to have separate Spanish congregations established for several orders to reduce their dependence on Rome. In 1783, for example, a Spanish congregation of Carthusians was created even though the monks of the order opposed the change. The mendicant orders resisted longer, but they too fell victim to this policy. In 1805, the Dominicans experienced the same fate. The creation of Spanish congregations allowed the crown to interfere much more directly in the affairs of the orders. José Diaz, the first vicar general of the Dominicans after the 1805 change, owed his position to the efforts of friends at court with influence over the royal favourite, Godoy. It is clear that well before the end of the Old Regime the Spanish church had lost much of its institutional autonomy. It had not yet become a department of government, but its ability to act independently had been seriously weakened.

During the last decade of the eighteenth century, the state undermined the institutional strength of the church further by using ecclesiastical revenues to meet the chronic deficits of the royal treasury. The crown had often used the church as a source of funds in difficult financial situations, but after 1793 the demands of the state reached extraordinary proportions. Between 1793 and 1808 Spain was either at war or engaged in preparations for war; the resulting financial drain was more than the government's archaic tax system could stand, hence the desperate search for new sources of revenue. Royal authorities encouraged donations from bishops, cathedral chapters and religious houses and eventually forced ecclesiastical groups to subscribe to massive state loans. The impact of royal fiscal policy on church wealth has not been studied, but the available evidence suggests that it was serious. In 1793, for example, the chapter of Santiago de Compostela offered the king a handsome gift of two million reales; five years later the archbishop and canons sent half a million to Madrid at royal order and another half million to the military commander of Galicia for the costs of defence against a possible English attack. Within a few years, the ecclesiastical elite of Santiago was forced to subscribe to a state loan to the amount of a million reales. And in 1808, the chapter voted a gift of 300 000 in support of the rising against the French who took their revenge in the following year by imposing a forced loan of ten million reales on the secular and regular clergy of Galicia. The decimation of church revenues after 1793 clearly weakened its ability to play its traditional role within Spanish society. The church's capacity to provide employment in ecclesiastical centres and to distribute charity on a massive scale was seriously compromised. Moreover, in 1798 the state ordered the sale of the property of charitable institutions, hospitals, orphanages, poorhouses, etc., many of which had functioned under clerical direction. Richard Herr has shown in a recent study that the sale of the property of charitable institutions began the undermining of one of the church's most important Old Regime functions.

The church of the late eighteenth century slowly became aware of its eroding position within the traditional structure of Spanish society. Reforming churchmen realized the dangerous implications of a church that depended on ceremonial and popular superstition for its hold over the masses. Although the clerical elite dared not challenge the expanding role of the state in church administration and finance, it grew quietly resentful over secular interference. The mood grew ever more pessimistic and foreboding, as Martínez Albiach has brilliantly shown in his study of the ecclesiastical mentality after 1750. Sermons increasingly dwelled on Spain as a Christian nation that had forgotten the basic obligations of religion, thereby inviting the vengeance of the Almighty. The clergy contemplated the society about them with deep unease; everywhere they saw 'a spirit of libertinism and dissolution . . . corrupting the morality and the customs of the nation'. Surrounded by superstition and moral laxity, harassed by the state, the church slowly developed a theocratic and defensive view of itself as the only hope for the protection of Christian Spain. These sentiments, circulating in general and unformed fashion after 1750, crystallized with the outbreak of the French Revolution in 1789. The impact of the Revolution, regarded by the clergy as the most terrible of horrors, government by an immoral favourite (Godoy), military disasters and a series of agrarian crises and epidemics between 1790 and 1808, convinced the clergy that the punishment they had feared and predicted had at last been visited on Spain in just castigation of its sins. The Napoleonic intervention of 1808 seemed the final blow. The sermons of this period turned again and again to a comparison between the Jews of the Old Testament and the Spaniards of their time. A priest could tell his congregation:

> The Lord has punished you for your sins. Oh Spain, do you not think that you are as deserving as Judea of punishment? Have you not provoked the just wrath of the Lord with your sins and crimes? This is the true cause of your calamaties and misfortunes. This is why God has allowed the enemy to sack our provinces and take possession of the riches that have served only to corrupt us.

The clergy emphasized that only through moral reform led by the church could Spain be saved and restored to its former grandeur. For the church, the new Spain that must come forth from twenty years of war and tribulations was to be, according to one preacher, 'a kingdom of priests and holy people'. The Spanish church emerged from its years of crisis with a harsh and theocratic view of its role within society. This would make the task of adapting the church to the new social and political forces already forming in Spain impossible over the short term and painful over the long.

4 The Portuguese church

DAVID HIGGS

The study of church–state relations and theological controversies has held pride of place in the scant modern investigation of eighteenth-century Catholicism in Portugal. This is true of Fortunato de Almeida's standard work on the history of the Portuguese church since the middle ages, *História da Igreja em Portugal*, unkindly but accurately described by one eminent critic as 'dry, external and political'. Alone among historians of this century in the range of his writings on the nature of Portuguese baroque Catholicism, Almeida's work was partisan and attempted no systematic examination of the socio-economic role of the church. During the half-century following the publication of his books little has appeared on the place of the church in the life of the mass of the population, with the notable exception of Jacques Marcadé's study of the poor and sparsely populated Ourique district in the southern Alentejo. In consequence, any discussion of the link between the church and the Portuguese is as much a statement about what remains to be investigated as it is an appraisal of information already amassed by historians.

In the eighteenth century all levels of the Portuguese economy were touched by ecclesiastical wealth deriving from the spending of churches, convents and the revenue raised from land, housing and other investments. A significant amount of this revenue was transferred from clerical ownership into the hands of the laity. Chapel-shrines (*capelas*) endowed for particular devotions were often supported by buildings or lands held in mortmain by families who enjoyed any excess profits generated by the property after having fulfilled ritual obligations laid on them by the founders. Laymen also levied tithes in some situations. These shared revenues raise one obstacle to estimating church wealth, and the lack of assessments of the value of sacramental objects, buildings and land are another. In the early decades of the eighteenth century the profits from foreign trade, royal largesse and private piety channelled extensive sums of money into the hands of the clergy, and while that revenue may have diminished in the later period the church was probably always the major gatherer of capital in the country.

The clergy themselves were, understandably, the keenest students of their financial position, watching vigilantly over everything from the surplice fees for marriages, funerals, and so forth, to the legacies of the wealthy. Conflicts arose among them, like that between dean and parish in Braga over who controlled the lucrative revenues of the Bom Jesus sanctuary; in that case the archbishop was unable to end the unseemly squabble in 1722 and only a decision from Rome in November 1736 ended the dispute. More commonly there were wrangles between clergy and peasantry over the tithes, and at the time of the early-nineteenth-century French invasion some refused to pay them at all. The military orders of Aviz, Christ, Malta and St James were known to enjoy massive endowments which excited the envy of more recent and hence poorer congregations, like that of the *clérigos agonizantes* or of *Senhor Jesus da Boa Morte*. Accurate accounting seems to have been rare in clerical settings, perhaps for fear that what was precisely known would be more easily taxed. Most contented themselves with the satisfaction shown by the industrious Abade Castro who compiled a famous atlas of Portugal first published in 1747 and reedited several times subsequently: 'In truth, in no part of the world is there such greed to gather money as there is in Portugal the ambition to spend it with God.' One modern historian, Magalhães Godinho, has roundly estimated that the church held one-third of disposable public revenue in the eighteenth century with the other two-thirds belonging to the king and nobility respectively.

The economic activity of the Portuguese church was particularly visible during the golden years under King John V (1706–50), the 1720s to 1740s, when many new churches, chapels, hermitages and convents were constructed. The most often quoted example of the redirection of Brazilian bullion for ecclesiastical purposes was the church-monastery of Mafra, situated forty-two kilometres from Lisbon; built between 1717 and 1730, its construction required 50 000 workers. Equally important was the money spent on the import of foreign-made religious objects, like the Italian gold- and silverware so favoured by John V and his successors. These precious things from abroad had a domestic complement of elaborately inlaid altars, gilded woodwork (*talha*), and painted tiles (*azulejos*), produced by Portuguese artisans specializing in church decoration.

The second period of extensive ecclesiastical expenditure came in the wake of the famous 1755 earthquake. Expenditure on religious edifices slowed in the 1770s after this wave of repairs and reconstruction and never regained earlier levels, despite the commissions given by Maria I, most notably for the beautiful Estrela basilica of Lisbon built in the 1790s.

The church's prominence in economic life was so evident that, together with the control exercised by the English over commerce and industry, it was a traditional scapegoat for Portuguese historians who wished to explain the slow development of the national economy during the eighteenth century. Be that as it may, ecclesiastical wealth supported not only religious but a range of ancillary employees, from domestics to artisans. It would be difficult to try to count all those with clerical employers. The church ran a welfare system of sorts and particularly hospitals, like those established in the seventeenth century by St John Britto. The Jesuits held the main responsibility for secondary schools before the expulsion of the order, when the Oratorians replaced them to some extent, while the Ursulines started in the 1750s at Pereira the first girls' secondary school in the country, followed by another at Viana do Castelo (1778) and Braga (1785). Even more important than the variety of urban jobs which the church provided, however, was its place as a landowner and employer of agricultural labourers.

The prominence of the church in the national economy caused many contemporaries in the eighteenth century to assume it supported a greater ecclesiastical population than was the case. A firmly established stereotype of *Portugal setecentista* saw the country as 'priest-ridden'. Fashionably anticlerical Frenchmen (Dumouriez, Carrière, de Chatelet, Laborde) made estimates of the population of religious ranging from 200 000 to 280 000 during the second half of the century. The *Encyclopédie méthodique* topped the poll with a figure of 300 000 at a time when the total population was no more than two and a half million. Contemporary English language accounts were less precise but evinced the same disapproval of an excessive clerical population, like Costigan in the 1780s, Murphy in the 1790s or Rev. Kinsey in the 1820s.

The Italian geographer Adriano Balbi (1782–1848), whose *Essai statistique sur le royaume de Portugal* (Paris, 1822) is the most valuable single printed source on Portuguese conditions at the end of the Old Regime, puts the question in another perspective. Leaving aside the assumptions made by earlier writers, he turned to numerical estimates based on the evidence presented to the commission of the liberal Cortès of 1821 which investigated the number of religious houses. While it is proper to doubt an extrapolation from an enquiry which led to the 1834 suppression of the male regular orders to the situation of the mid eighteenth century, there is a very striking contrast between the earlier figures and those of the 1820s. Balbi found that the total of religious of both sexes did not exceed 29 000.

These figures may be discussed more fully. The effect of Pombal's restrictions on ordinations, reinforced in the 1780s, and the general disfavour with which the regulars were viewed in the later eighteenth century, had an impact on the decline in vocations which touched Portugal as it did so many other countries at the time. However, it seems hardly credible that in sixty years, at a time of rising population, the religious community shrank to one tenth of the size put forward by the *Encyclopédie*.

The apparent deception suffered by foreign visitors in the eighteenth century derived from generalizations drawn from the larger cities. Arriving at Oporto from Dublin in January 1789, the architect James Murphy, a perceptive observer, noted:

> The first thing that strikes the mind of a stranger, on his arrival here, is the

devout appearance of the inhabitants. Religion seems to be their only pursuit. The clattering of bells, the bustling of processions, and the ejaculations of friars, engage the attention by day, whilst every part resounds by night with the chaunting of hymns.

There is no doubt that Lisbon and Oporto exercised a very strong attraction over an under-employed or unemployed clergy, especially the regulars. This had long been the case. At the beginning of the seventeenth century it was observed 'there are so many priests and priors that they devour one another'. A ten-year moratorium on ordinations was seriously proposed during the seventeenth century, and calls were heard that at least 500 'outsider' priests (*clérigos de fora*) present in Lisbon without sufficient cause and who were 'undignified' should be expelled from the city. In Oporto the city administration protested on various occasions during the seventeenth century against the plethora of religious. The eighteenth-century campaign against an excessively numerous clergy in the cities was not without antecedents; its novelty was that it proved more effective.

Lisbon, with its thirty-seven parishes, thirty-two monasteries and eighteen nunneries in a mid-eighteenth-century population of perhaps 270 000, or Oporto, with its ten parishes and numerous religious houses both in the city and surrounding countryside and a total population of 60 000, sometimes appeared to contemporaries to be almost theocracies. The religious presence was almost equally visible in places like Coimbra with two monasteries and seventeen colleges, or Evora with twelve monasteries, Santarém with eleven or Guimarães with four. This highly visible presence was equally obvious in smaller towns like Beja and Braga, respectively in the under-populated Baixo Alentejo and the densely populated northern province of Minho, and both diocesan seats. They show the importance of religious institutions in stagnant administrative and market towns with episcopal bureaucracies. In Beja 5.3 per cent of the probable mid-century population, and in Braga 6.2 per cent, were ecclesiastical. It should be noted that both towns had very large nunneries. Probably one in ten of the adult population was under vows. Much the same could be said of centres like Miranda, Viseu, Castelo Branco, Leiria. In more variegated economies like the coastal towns of Faro, Setúbal, Aveiro and Viana do Castelo the preponderance of ecclesiastical institutions was less evident. The big cities, then, contained an excess of unemployed and often resented clergy. In the smaller centres, episcopal and administrative towns, they were better integrated into a local economy to which their spending was indispensable.

In parts of Portugal there was, paradoxically, a rural shortage of priests, particularly in the south. There assiduity in religion was more urban than rural. In the southern Serra between the Alentejo and Algarve, a barren land of scattered hamlets, numerous children died without baptism, couples lived together for varying periods of time without marriage, and burials without priests were not uncommon. While there are other explanations possible, one reason for the fall in the level of observance, which was to give the Alentejo the twentieth-century reputation of being virtually dechristianized, was the shortage of priests. This had the effect of weakening religious traditions. As a result the migration into urban centres that was a consequence of the eighteenth-century demographic surge in Portugal as elsewhere, especially to Lisbon from adjacent Estremadura and the Alentejo, brought non-practising country people into pious towns. In the north a more extensive network of religious houses and smaller parishes in the densely populated small-holding areas meant that a constant ecclesiastical presence and example stimulated piety.

Regional differences in the distribution of Portugal's population, and changes in the urban and rural presence of Catholicism during the eighteenth century, qualify whatever comparisons can be made at a national level. A rough estimate from the available figures at the end of the eighteenth century, expressed as a percentage of the population, shows Portugal had half the number of ecclesiastics as Spain, and half as many again as France. Yet as has been already observed these figures take their full meaning only when regional and urban comparisons are made.

Population estimates of the Portuguese laity and clergy cannot easily be made because figures for both which exist for the eighteenth century are notoriously unreliable. Nevertheless they are suggestive. The Manuel José Perinlongue census, or rather population estimate, of 1765, gave 4099 parishes, and 493 convents with a clerical population of 42 200 regulars (30 772 males and 11 428 females). Balbi in 1822 showed an increase in the number of parishes, 4232, but a decline to 6292 male regulars and 3093 females. He also gave a round figure of 18 000 seculars. Another rough guide to the incidence of religious in Portugal is provided by looking at the ratio of religious houses to population. The Pina Manique census, taken in 1789 to ascertain the population balance among the provinces of the kingdom to allow a more equitable recruitment of troops, showed a population of some three million unevenly divided between a more densely populated north, with an agrarian system of peasant small-holdings, and the dispersed habitat of the latifundia areas of the southern Alentejo. The number of religious houses in the mid eighteenth century (477 in 1739) was not distributed in the same ratio. Minho in the north with 20.8 per cent of the population had 16.8 per cent of the religious houses, neighbouring Trás-os-Montes had 9.9 per cent of the population but 2.9 per cent of the religious houses. Estremadura, in the centre of the country including the great concentration of Lisbon, held 18.6 per cent of the population but 38.2 per cent of the religious houses. Beira almost reversed these proportions, with 34.9 per cent of the population but 16.6 per cent of the religious houses. Most surprisingly in the south the Alentejo, with only 11.8 per cent of the population (although comprising a third of the national surface area), boasted 22.4 per cent of the religious institutions. The Algarve province on the southern coast exhibited the closest congruence: 3.9 per cent of the population and 3.1 per cent of the religious houses. The Franciscans were the largest order followed by the Dominicans.

Such a scheme takes its full meaning only if we know the number of monks and nuns in these establishments. In his stimulating essay on Portugal's Old Regime structures (1971), Magalhães Godinho emitted the hypothesis, based on the 'extraordinary' increase in the numbers of churches and religious houses between 1500 and 1800, that the rising per capita ratio of seculars to laity was a particularity of Iberian society. However, it appears that there was a change in emphasis between the post-Tridentine fervour of the seventeenth century and the gluttonous monasteries of which the Austrian botanist Link complained at the end of the eighteenth century. Abade Castro wrote admiringly of poverty, asperity and 'such exquisite penitential mortifications' of hermits, imitated by the reformers Balthazar da Encarnação and Francisco da Cruz who established two new houses in 1725 and in 1743. The eighteenth-century foundations exhibited more social concern than had been evident in the past, like those dealing with missions, prisons, welfare and female teaching orders for girls. The seminary of Varatojo (Torres Vedras), chosen by António das Chagas in 1682 to train domestic missionaries in the flamboyant and theatrical style of popular preaching based on Italian and Spanish models for which he was renowned, flourished in the eighteenth century as did other missionary/seminaries at Vinhais, Mesão Frio and Brancanes.

A royal order of 1782, promulgated significantly enough under so pious a ruler as Maria I, forbade the institution of new orders, a measure which was the culmination of a campaign of increasing hostility to the plethora of religious houses. An edict of 1788 required royal permission for youths to enter religion, and there seems to have been a fall-off in the numbers of vocations, especially among the nobility and the more prosperous urban classes. Clearly many religious houses were quite shrunken in population by the end of the century. Visiting the Sintra monastery of St Jerome, Murphy noted in 1789: 'The number of friars who formerly inhabited the monastery amounted to thirty: at present they are reduced to four.' Balbi in the 1820s advanced fifteen as an average for the number of inmates of religious houses, although he did not enquire whether the number of men was lower than that of the nuns.

The decline of vocations at the end of the eighteenth century can be attributed to various causes, although excessive blame was attached to Pombal by an earlier generation of historians in an effort to explain the generalized rise in hostility to regular orders. Other explanations look back to the early seventeenth century and ascribe the decline of the mendicants to overly close collaboration with the Spanish occupation. The expulsion of the Jesuits and the increasing influence of French liberalism as the Portuguese intelligentsia turned away from Spanish models have also been invoked.

The causes are doubtless more various and social. They included perhaps a change in male attitudes towards celibacy at a time of shifting moral values and rising illegitimacy rates. The increasing incidence of migration and emigration disrupted religious traditions. Generalizations here are dubious without more investigation into regional economies, but it seems that the attraction of the religious life was diminishing. The conventual houses of late-eighteenth-century Portugal were increasingly inhabited by dwindling and elderly communities.

As in Spain, the Portuguese higher clergy of the eighteenth century was more cultivated than at any time in the national history. Among the regulars there were those interested in foreign languages, like the Jesuit João de Loureiro who studied Cochin-Chinese, or the celebrated botanist, João de Brotero, and others who delved deeply into subjects related to the overseas possessions. On the other hand, the secular clergy was often quite ignorant, particularly so in the dioceses without seminaries. Certainly the clergy could write, as is shown in the very informative *Memorías Paroquiaes* (1758), a multi-volume manuscript guide to Portugal compiled from the responses of each *pároco* (parish priest) about conditions in his parish. Yet while some of the responses are models of clarity and precision many others were rambling and badly composed. Contemporaries like Carrière often held a poor opinion of the secular's merits: 'this class of clergy is so much in discredit that few persons of an origin above the mediocre wish to enter there: it is given over to the lowest classes of society.' He claimed they were badly trained, that orders were bestowed with no investigation into the morality of the postulants, nor extensive study, nor seminary training. The poverty of the seculars kept them subservient to the regulars, and since they were more numerous than the number of benefices three-quarters of them were without work. They went from church to church asking the sacristans if any special masses needed to be said. Yet, paradoxically, in parts of the country benefices were vacant during the eighteenth century.

The higher clergy and the regulars seem to have been wealthy by contemporary standards, but what was the situation of the seculars? Those without a benefice were financially embarrassed, but it seems that those with a country living were substantially better off than their parishioners. Marcadé, surveying the information about cash revenues and other payments made to the parish priests in the Ourique district, found them to enjoy on average at least four to five times the income of a peasant family and often more. To the peasantry at least, as in France, it seems that the economic situation of the priest was an enviable one.

Theoretically, high religious posts were within their reach, but in fact ascent in the ecclesiastical hierarchy came primarily to aristocrats or members of the religious orders. A child of prosperous peasant stock became a famous agriculturalist and reforming bishop of Faro in the later eighteenth century, but this was thanks to family connections and membership in a religious order. A more typical member of the hierarchy was the archbishop of Braga from 1758–89, a bastard of King John V, noted for both his grand manners and his charity. Of 156 Portuguese bishops in office between 1668 and 1820 more than four-fifths belonged to the aristocracy (Oliveira Marques). The episcopacy received the deference accorded to nobles and titles of marquis and count were attached to certain sees.

In fact the nobility controlled the highest and most lucrative positions in the Portuguese church, and seemed in this regard closer to French practice than that of neighbouring Spain. The office of patriarch, established at the start of the century by John V, was too close to the court to escape the aristocratic monopoly. The court nobility as well as the less prosperous lower nobility (*fidalgos*) found in religion a career for younger sons. Although the overseas empire and its service fulfilled a similar demographic function (and indeed the military orders fulfilled both religious and expansionist roles), the clergy offered a career for those either indisposed or inapt for service in the *Ultramar*. The most socially prestigious lay orders, those of Aviz, St James and of Christ, included poorer members but mainly attracted an important upper-class component. The wealthiest monastic establishments like São Vicente de Fora in Lisbon, built between 1582 and 1704 and housing the *Cónegos regrantes de Santo Agostinho*, the canonries, almoners for distinguished lay organizations, nunneries like Odivelas for sisters and daughters of the nobility, provided a way for ecclesiastical nobles to spend their mortal span.

This comfortable and accommodating structure, involving especially the episcopacy and the regulars, seems fairly distant from the 'public' system of parish priests, together with, particularly later in the century, the handful of working bishops who actually ran their dioceses with close personal attention. Of course, the contrast cannot be drawn too clearly, since there were exceptions. However from a social perspective it might be said Pombal's assault against the regulars of his time was another side of his attack on the privileged place of the nobility in Portuguese life.

Turning to lay organizations we should consider above all the confraternities (*irmandades*) which proliferated in Portugal. They played an important role in male sociability and protected group interests, sometimes in association with Third Orders. These Third Orders, composed of lay people with a deeper commitment to a religious life than the average member of a confraternity, differed from the *irmandades* which were in fact primarily social and only secondarily religious institutions.

Confraternities took three principal forms. First of these was the sacramental, like confraternities dedicated to the Blessed Sacrament (*Santíssimos*), and which were involved with processions and conveyancing the host. The second variety of confraternity found its point of departure in a profession more than in ritual. The corps of beggars, under the invocation of St Alexis in the Lisbon

Misericórdia church, or the blind, under the invocation of the Infant Jesus in St George's and St Martin parishes, are perhaps too often cited. They were hired to take part in processions. The blind carried distinctive green staffs. These confraternities also had privileges in peddling pious tracts, prints and religious bric-à-brac in the streets. A good example of the less picturesque, but economically important, confraternity was the brotherhood of carpenters from the Lisbon naval arsenal, dedicated to St Roch. Its statutes laid down that members should contribute to various funds for providing alms for poor brothers (that is the unemployed and the old), burials, not only of members but 'of their wives and children and even domestics', as well as paying the ransom of members captured by Moorish corsairs. This particular confraternity had its privileges reconfirmed by Queen Maria in 1781; it was specified that the same rights extended to Oporto, Vila do Condé, Viana, Fão, Setúbal. In Lisbon there were confraternities of tailors, masons and others. A number of the confraternities kept 'hospitals', for tailors, armourers shepherds, carpenters, masons. There were occupations with a certain breadth of membership, and with a sufficient economic level to permit them to finance their activities. In this respect they overlap the third , and most Iberian form of confraternity: the *Misericórdia*.

The Portuguese *Misericórdias* took their model from the confraternity established in Lisbon by Queen Leonora in the late fifteenth century, whose regulations remained the model for the internal organization of many *Misericórdias* until the present century. They were under royal protection, and claimed that this exempted them from ecclesiastical control. This did not, of course, mean that there were no clerical members. The *provedores* (the heads, 'providers') of the Braga *Misericórdia* to mid-century were thirty-three religious, twelve nobles and five uncertain, but from 1751 to 1800 the proportions were reversed with thirty-nine nobles and eleven clerics.

The place of confraternities as a basic form of social organization in Catholic countries has not yet been extensively explored. In a brilliantly innovative study of an area of Provence in France, Maurice Agulhon showed the relationship between popular politics, male social activities and class differences. In Portugal some *irmandades*, like the *Santíssimo* of the parish lying between the Carmo and Chiado in Lisbon, had powerful patrons: in that case the Condes de Valladares were hereditary officials. Others were primarily for artisans. As yet no systematic enquiry has been made into activities of members of confraternities in municipal life, if any, or of the emergence of an opposition to clerical attempts to control popular associations. Certainly the number of confraternities greatly increased from the early sixteenth century; that is, at the same time as the large rise in the number of religious orders. Eighteenth-century dictionaries of parishes carefully detailed the altars and patron saints of the confraternities. At São Martinho de Arrifana de Sousa (Penafiel) in the 1760s and 1770s over a third of all funerals were escorted by confraternities, and in the case of the rich there was music, processional crosses and the poor to carry candles. In the countryside and small villages where work was a continuum, part of a station in life, with little sense of productivity and the absence of a clear dichotomy between work and play, confraternity ceremonials like burials, processions, elections and so forth interrupted the working day and were part of leisure. The carpenters of St Roch blurred the distinction still more for they stipulated that they were to be paid while attending to confraternity duties during working hours.

The social composition of the confraternities is something of a mystery, since most membership lists are summary, giving only names and places of residence without details of profession or wealth. On the other hand the regulations of the *Misericórdia* (and these were clearly the most socially prestigious of such associations) required the *provedor* to be a *fidalgo* and his secretary 'a dignified and respectable man'. In the largest *Misericórdia*, that of Lisbon with 600 members, half were to be nobles and half commoners. In the smaller *Misericórdias* of Bragança, Funchal, Coimbra and others the same proportion was required. After 1773 the old 'purity of blood' regulations designed to exclude those with Moorish or Jewish origins from membership was ended, but was immediately replaced by the obscure requirement of 'clean hands' which in fact, like 'purity of blood' rules, meant continuing discrimination against men in commerce and manufacturing. As a result there was probably a fairly clear social divide between the nobles and those of the 'second condition' in the *Misericórdias*. In the northern town of Bragança we know that among the commoners' professions were those of weaver, farrier, soldier, ovenman, tailor, miller, gunner, shoe-maker, horseguard, bailiff, barber, bugler, doctor, carpenter, cavalry officer, prison warden and dyer. In the same town in 1754 it proved impossible to find a suitable *fidalgo* candidate to take the 'provider' position, and the crown named a *comendador* of the Order of Christ, who owned revenues from parishes of Bragança, Baçal, Deilão and Rabal, and who was a lieutenant-colonel of the Trás-os-Montes infantry and father of the bishop of Bragança and Miranda. Clearly it was out of the question to allow a commoner to take this post.

Another important form of lay religious activity was the sinister organization of the familiars of the Inquisition often recruited from the nobility. These were carefully chosen after a scrutiny of their orthodoxy and moral conduct as a watch-dog over the forms of popular religion, sexual morality and heresy. Their power to induce the arrest of anybody suspected of evil doing must have been particularly notable in small towns. The bishops indeed often opposed the Inquisition, both at a doctrinal level, as in the case of the *sigillist* controversy over breaking the secret of the confessional, or at an organizational level of resisting the inroads on episcopal authority made by the para-religious organization of familiars. Indeed tensions between a popular and folkloric religion, the confraternities, the secular clergy, the regulars, and the familiars of the Holy Office provided in a certain sense the 'political universe' of the lower classes of eighteenth-century Portugal.

All these watch-dogs of orthodoxy inevitably raise the problem of religious practice. The Portuguese episcopacy of the eighteenth century seemed little concerned with collecting precise statistical detail on such matters. The *visita pastoral* records may yield information, although in parts of the country these visitations were extremely infrequent. Some registers dealing with Easter observance may still exist in diocesan and parish archives. At all events these were least reliable in the larger cities: Carrière noted of Lisbon that the *párocos* took the names of tenants in the houses in order to see who attended the paschal celebrations, but that it was commonplace to bribe the sacristan to enter the note that the obligation had been observed. Both canonical and civil punishments would befall those who evaded Easter communion and, particularly among the poor residents, there were probably few who made a systematic practice of it. For the poor, communion was cheaper than bribery. At the same time, in the larger cities the floating population of the poorest districts, like São Ildefonso in Oporto or Cais do Sodré in Lisbon, would not be sufficiently stable to figure on such registers. In smaller centres the clergy could take more accurate surveys. The questionnaire circulated throughout the country following the 1755 earthquake probably provides the best guide to levels of religious practice, although many priests did not address themselves to the subject and others may have given replies which would reflect credit on them rather than the light of truth. To take an example of one of the more complete answers to the question 'how many hearths in the parish?', the priest of Benavente (Santarém) replied 650 with 1156 men of whom 1047 commune and 109 confess, and 1052 women of whom 969 commune and 83 confess.

With the exception of the study by Jacques Marcadé of the Ourique district, historians have not investigated in depth the problem of differing regional levels of practice in eighteenth-century Portugal. However, the 'retrospective' approach, which derives from the writings of Gabriel Le Bras, suggests that this would be a rewarding if difficult subject for further study. Augusto Querido's map of different levels of Catholic marriages in Portugal from 1949 to 1953 certainly supports the conventional wisdom on the subject of twentieth-century levels of religious faith. The north of the country appears as an area of popular piety, with an increase in indifference in the centre, especially around Lisbon, reaching levels which have been described as dechristianization in parts of the diocese of Beja. The Algarve in the far south presents a more pious prospect. For Querido this strong north–south contrast coincided with that between a popular, rural Catholicism of small-holders with its own dogma and rites, coexisting uneasily with official orthodoxy, while in the south an urban Catholicism essentially controlled by the clergy contrasts with a dechristianized rural proletariat in the arid lands of the underpopulated latifundia. The historical origins of these differences and their evolution constitute a theme of great significance in Portuguese history, and they appear to have emerged in part by the end of the eighteenth century.

Popular devotions flourished during the century with a particular emphasis on those which might be expected in a period of rapid demographic growth. The Infant Jesus was much revered: there is a splendid baroque example, dressed in red velvet upper-class robes with silver embroidery, in the sacristy of São Vicente de Fora. Infant Jesus was a frequent eighteenth-century vision, as in the case of Sister Ignacia Maria and Mother Custodia do Sacramento who saw him in ecstasy at their Beja convent of Santa Clara. Increasing favour was given to images of Our Lady of Milk, or of the Conception. The devotion to the *anjinhos* ('little angels'), interceding for souls in purgatory, was extremely popular in the eighteenth century. The redemptive devotion to the Sacred Heart, introduced to Portugal in 1731, became widespread as a result of the patronage of Queen Maria I. St Francis Borgia, named protector of the kingdom against earthquakes following the disaster of 1755, was accorded veneration on his feast day, 24 March. These devotions did not, of course, supplant such traditional attachments as that of Lisbon to St Anthony, particularly implored during the plague of 1723 which decimated the capital. The iconography of fertility and deliverance seemed to predominate after the more austere themes of the Counter-Reformation.

The church was uneasy with religious festivals and processions that were insufficiently controlled by the clergy. An excellent example is provided in the islands of the Azores, especially São Miguel and Terceira, where the Holy Spirit festivals (which had originated in thirteenth-century Germany) became by the eighteenth century annual celebrations with many overtones of popular life. The Counter-Reformation clergy (and bishops usually came from the mainland) had constantly shown hostility to this popular devotion. In 1559 the 'emperor' (the layman who financed a cycle of ceremonies and distribution of bread and meat to the poor) was forbidden to speak from the pulpit or other sacramental places in the church. Subsequently the *foliões*, costumed men who assisted, were forbidden to dance in churches or to sing profane songs, or to have dinners at the expense of the confraternity. In 1565 the clergy were instructed to absent themselves from the festival, and in 1697 the bishop of Angra, António Vieira Leitão, prohibited women to establish *impérios*. This conflict between the popular character of the festivals and the desire of the clergy to prevent the infiltration of profane elements continued during the eighteenth century, at a time when the devotion was actually increasing.

Indeed the conflict between popular religion and the desire of the ecclesiastical hierarchy to see a better understanding of the Christian message was at the heart of the disruptions within the church in the eighteenth century. Catholic propaganda all across Europe was often directed against superstitions as though to parry the criticism of unbelievers that religion itself was little more than rituals of magical intent. Bishop Cenáculo Vilas Boas, son of a locksmith, founded an 'Ecclesiastical Academy' in Beja in 1793 which had the declared aim to care for 'the purity of religion, making scrutiny of its observance, and dealing with the questions and doubts of all the parishes'. A study of the incidence of the themes of sermons might reveal how widespread was this concern with divesting contemporary religious observance of all that was extraneous. Certainly in the last decades of the century the coercions available to the clergy, especially the Inquisition, weakened. It went along with this that there should be an emphasis on individual commitment to orthodoxy. Conformity to doctrine was strengthened by customs like that noted by Carrière in winter evenings at Lisbon, when bourgeois and common people stood at their doorways to recite the rosary, in a type of plain-chant. This provided not only an opportunity for sociability during the colder weather, when people would normally stay indoors, but, more importantly, enforced a public observance of religious rituals.

In suggesting this conflict between a popular religion, heavily imbued with social practices of the past, and the effort on the part of the hierarchy to introduce a more qualitatively pure Christianity, we must not forget the inroads made among the clergy by unorthodox religion. This was sometimes a result of theological disputes, like the *Jacobeia* movement, or the attractions of Molinist ideas. Probably a more significant danger than such concerns of the intelligentsia in the Portuguese situation was that the clergy, especially isolated country priests, would accept a quasi-shaman role in popular religion, on the frontiers of ritual and magic. The Inquisition recorded such cases as the porter of a Franciscan convent in Lisbon who persisted in the belief that a condemned *beata* (holy woman) was saintly, or Father Ignacio da Silva, arrested in 1714 for making a pact with the devil, as was another priest in 1724. While the trial of the Italian Jesuit Malagrida was essentially motivated by politics, the grounds given for his conviction which led to his public garrotting and burning on the Rossio Square was his claim to special visions and magical powers 'and to pretend to have Revelations, visions and voices and other especial favours of God, in order to be taken for and reputed as a Saint'.

Popular religion centred on women's concerns. Women in Portugal, save among the peasantry, perhaps enjoyed less social freedom than was the case in France, northern Italy or even central Europe during the eighteenth century. One obvious purpose of the nunneries like Odivelas was to contain unmarried girls of the upper classes with little genuine interest in the religious life, and they gave rise to some notable scandals. Much more typical, however, was the relative comfort of convent life, neither scandalous nor austere, and best summed up by the numerous Portuguese desserts and cakes with names like 'Nuns' Delight'.

The convents provided a setting for the development of local and national reputations of piety. An example in Beja was 'Granny' (*Avó*) Isabel, frequently seized with ecstatic visions during which she ran through the cloisters, often meeting with falls and accidents, after which exaltations she fervently begged for the pardon of the other sisters. Her Franciscan chronicler quoted her as saying that she was quite mad, and did not know what she was doing. He concluded, significantly: 'As these favours were continued, it was known by their repetition how much God cherished his servant.' However, if such nuns were permitted to attain local eminence and semi-cult status (at the death of Granny Isabel large numbers of peasants came to the convent doors to beg for relics of her), this was inside a clerical context. Women outside of conventual surveillance who claimed special religious experience were more likely to be denounced to the Inquisition than accepted as legitimate. The trial of twenty-year-old Andreza Esteves by the Inquisition was brought about by her claim that 'in her body' spoke souls from the 'other world', and that through her mouth spoke Christ, the Virgin and various saints. She even had the idea that she exercised sacerdotal authority, and that she could hear confession, give absolution and administer communion. Of course it is not meant to suggest that extreme religious deviation on the part of the professed was accepted. For example, a nun of Lisbon's Santa Clara nunnery was accused in 1724 of writing to the devil in blood. However, women within convents had greater freedom of religious expression than the *beatas*, wise-women, and so on who were sought out by the familiars of the Inquisition and the clergy. Certainly the *processos* of the Inquisition show more laywomen than nuns among Old Christians.

The archives of the Inquisition provide a massive source of information about the social history of Old Regime Portugal: its four centres were Lisbon, Coimbra, Evora and Goa in Portuguese India. If it was very active during the first half of the eighteenth century, its role in punishing popular superstition, heresies, apostasy and sexual deviation was severely curtailed under Pombal. While New Christian families descended from converted Jews and charged with relapse into the Judaic practices of their ancestors made up the bulk of the cases brought before the tribunals of the Holy Office, some twenty per cent and more were Old Christians accused of sorcery and moral sins, judging from Coimbra in the first decades of the century. The last public auto-da-fé was held in 1766 and the distinction between 'Old' and 'New' Christians was officially abolished in 1773. Students of Judaic practices have shown most assiduity in examining the records hitherto, but much remains to be learned of the organization of the repressive machinery and of the social origins of heresy. The Inquisition probably provides the best source for the study of popular religion often at variance with the intention of the Counter-Reformation. Certainly popular religion studied through such accusations is distorted by the criminal perspective. Other sources, like the *autos sacramentais*, moralizing religious plays for public edification often performed in the seventeenth and eighteenth centuries and based on the lives of the saints, should be consulted, as well as the considerable ethnographical literature collected since the later nineteenth century, although this usually lacks any historical perspective.

By the end of the eighteenth century Portugal's ecclesiastical organization had changed only slightly since the post-Tridentine period, but its religious life had altered in content. The major innovations were forced into effect by the much-feared Pombal between 1750 and 1777: the expulsion of the Jesuits, the transformation of the Inquisition into a royal tribunal, the limits placed on clerical privileges and the prohibition of social discrimination against the New Christians by the Old. Yet even so dread a figure as the great minister cannot alone provide sufficient explanation for the changes taking place in the relations of the Portuguese with their religion. Behind an apparent facade of conformity it is possible to discern at least three groups of Portuguese Catholics at the end of the eighteenth century. First and most numerous among the laity were the adherents of traditional popular religion, second a small number of clergy and laymen in tune with the utilitarian outlook of the century, and third the nostalgic partisans of Counter-Reformation rigorism exemplified by the Holy Office.

5 The Italian churches

MARIO ROSA

For historical and ideological reasons deriving from the risorgimento, the unification of the peninsula and the special relationship between church and state existing until recently, the attention of scholars has focused above all on the 'political' aspects of Italian church history, on the contribution of such movements as Jansenism and Jurisdictionalism to the debate on reform during the eighteenth century, and finally on the political, institutional and social–economic outlines developed in the reform struggle against ecclesiastical structures.

As a result, the 'internal' history of the church, from its institutions to its religious life, has been generally neglected, although now interest and research have begun to move in new directions because of the different awareness of religious problems following upon the Second World War and the deeply felt concern of Italian historians for new historiographical ideas, particularly those suggested by French socio-religious historical methodology. In the light of this historiographical *nuovo corso* not only could previous studies be reutilized, but research could be undertaken on ecclesiastical institutions; such as that leading to the *Atlante storico italiano dell'età moderna* (particularly for the Lombardy of Maria Theresa and Joseph II); or to analyses of religious sociology of the Le Bras school embodied in the work of Candeloro Giorgini on the Tuscan Maremma in the eighteenth century, or Giuseppe Orlandi on the Modena countryside after the French Revolution; or to samples of the socio-religious history of the Mezzogiorno in the eighteenth century by Gabriele De Rosa and his collaborators. These are all contributions in different areas although it is not yet possible to provide a general outline of the church's role. Nevertheless the way has been opened, we hope, for significant progress. This analysis, we must say, is not free of difficulties and does not allow broad generalizations, for there are two fundamental problems involved in forming an interpretation of the history of the Italian church not only during the eighteenth century but throughout the modern period. On the ecclesiastical-religious level there was not a single Italian church as there was in France or Spain, for it existed in each of the Italian states with internal variables, distinct organizational structures and a particular relationship to political power, etc., even though there existed as a unifying factor the link to Rome and the Catholic religious civilization which emerged between the Counter-Reformation and the Enlightenment. There was an institution not found elsewhere in Catholic Europe, the papacy, which is essential to understanding the church of eighteenth-century Italy. In other words, when considering the church in this period, we must remember that besides certain common typical features (the organization of the episcopacy, the formation of the secular clergy, the crisis of the religious orders, rural missionary activity and the development of specific devotions) there were often considerable differences among ecclesiastical-religious phenomena within the diverse territorial and political framework of the peninsula. Let us turn now to concrete examples by first considering the Italian episcopacy in order to understand the development of its structure between the first and second halves of the eighteenth century (between 1740–1, the beginning of the pontificate of Benedict XIV, and 1780–1, the eve of the great revolutionary crisis in Europe). Some trends may be discerned in the peculiar features of the three areas here examined: the Kingdom of Naples, the Papal States and the rest of the Italian states.

In the Kingdom of Naples (131 dioceses), the aristocratic component of the hierarchy remained stable while feudalism was declining as a political, economic and social force; nevertheless, the maintenance of this component (thirty per cent) was guaranteed by an increase in the number of bishops drawn from the religious orders (sixteen to twenty-four per cent), most of whom were generally the younger sons of feudal or noble families of the kingdom. They were chosen from the best and most learned orders (Benedictines and Theatines) and received their appointments from the king within the royal patronage applied to the twenty-four dioceses of the Neapolitan church. In the Papal States (sixty-five dioceses) the number of bishops from the religious orders declined (from seventeen to thirteen per cent), and the aristocratic component of the episcopacy dropped significantly from forty per cent to between thirty and twenty-eight per cent (although the famous 'suburban' dioceses as well as some of the major ones were ruled by noble bishops belonging to the College of Cardinals). Above all there took place a clear process of 'provincialization' of the episcopacy, for the number of bishops originally from Rome and the Papal States rose from sixty-one to seventy-four per cent; they were largely chosen from among the veterans of the papal curia and the local pontifical administrative bodies and generally appear as a very limited group of ecclesiastical officials in the service of the Roman congregations. In the other states (117 to 120 dioceses), the number of bishops from the religious orders (mendicants and regular congregations) remained relatively stable in the first and second halves of the century, approximately twenty-seven per cent. Moreover, aristocratic participation was substantial due to the presence of sons of noble or feudal families.

In Piedmont, in fact, the government showed an increasing preference for the appointment of noblemen to the most important dioceses of the state or those in border regions, or those situated in Sardinia and enjoying the highest prestige. Similarly, the aristocratic Venetian senate sent patrician prelates to the mainland or to the 'de Mar' dioceses, while in Sicily nobles from the landed, feudal nobility headed the island's most important dioceses. In spite of the importance of noble participation in the hierarchy, it should be stressed that there never developed in Italy a completely aristocratic episcopacy such as that in France on the eve of the Revolution of 1789. As in the case of the episcopacies, parishes too do not present a homogeneous character, though they share the same institutional and structural features in spite of the distinction between rural and town parishes. The study of Italian parishes is just beginning. While the parishes of the continental south were sometimes (twenty-nine per cent) *ricettizie* or 'receiving', in some provinces the average was as high as sixty-nine per cent. They were similar, if I am not mistaken, to the Spanish *iglesias propias* where the 'cure of souls' was assigned collectively to the capitular clergy who appointed curates requiring only episcopal confirmation. In north-central Italy we do not find a similar parish structure but rather one based on free episcopal appointment of the parish clergy and appointment either public or private, that is by the community, for example, or by families or individuals enjoying feudal patronage. The reason for the difference between north and south arose from the distinct historical development of the regions in question. The phenomenon of patronage was most highly developed, as far as we know, in the Republic of Venice (at Verona, for example, in the urban and *extra muros* parishes, patronage appointments of the parish clergy reached the range of sixty to seventy per cent) and in Tuscany (where thirty-seven per cent of the parishes fell under episcopal appointment, thirty-two per cent under public, and thirty-one per cent under private) until the reforms of Leopold II abolished all forms of patronage. In an institutional setting marked by an extremely weak episcopal jurisdiction even in medium-size dioceses, by the presence of insufficient ecclesiastical and lay forces and by an inadequate parish life weakened by external causes, two factors like two threads of clashing colours disturbed the ecclesiastical and religious existence of eighteenth-century Italian dioceses: first, the problem of the adequate preparation of the clergy and second, the problem of an expanding ecclesiastical population, at least during the first half of the century. Inadequate seminaries operating on limited resources raised serious obstacles to the formation of a well-qualified clergy throughout the century in spite of the efforts of many bishops to improve clerical education – the picture of the 'good priest' remains an eighteenth-century myth typical of the Enlightenment. The situation finds a spectacular corollary in the plethora of clergy who often could not be used for the cure of souls, who survived on a personal *patrimonio sacro* and who often searched for benefices, religious services and endowments provided by either the piety of the faithful or the interest of private families. Between the end of the seventeenth century and the early eighteenth century the ecclesiastical population of Italy, both secular and regular, reached its height. From the time of Montesquieu's visit to Italy (1728–9) foreign travellers characterized the peninsula as a 'monks' paradise'.

Unfortunately, we do not have precise statistical information on the growth of the ecclesiastical population during the first half of the eighteenth century, but it is available thanks to the documentary efforts of the reformers in the last three decades of the century. We easily can follow a decline in numbers which in some cases verged on collapse. In the Kingdom of Naples the decline was gradual because of a five per cent loss among the secular clergy between 1773–4 and 1780–1 (48 174 to 46 216 individuals), but there followed a more serious reduction to 36 128 by 1801. In Lombardy, the decline of the clergy was even more marked as a result of the restrictive measures imposed by Emperor Joseph II, as the number of those who received holy orders fell by fifty-three per cent between 1782 and 1792, and the number of priests fell by eleven per cent. Reforming governments of the second half of the century cast their sharpest arrows at the regular clergy, although hostility towards the orders developed even in states relatively untouched by reform such as Venice. As for the regular clergy, their numbers reached a peak in the first half of the eighteenth century after the Holy See abolished limitations in effect since 1650 on the number of religious professions (1694). The Jesuits expanded significantly in central-northern Italy as did the various branches of the Franciscan order. The Capuchins, for example, had 4000 more members in 1765 than the 10 821 the order contained in 1650. In Lombardy in 1774 the Minor Observants, Reformed Franciscans and Capuchins had seventy convents of the region's total of 291, and their houses contained 2272 religious of a total of 5536 (forty-one per cent). On the other hand, in the episcopal towns of the south, the number of male convents went from 575 to 664 between 1700 and 1750, while the number of convents for women rose from 240 to 287, a more modest rate of increase. The heaviest losses, without taking into account the problem of the suppression of the Jesuits in European states, occurred in those areas, Lombardy and Tuscany, where the work of the government reformers took its most brutal form; similar losses, however, took place in the territory of the Venetian republic and eventually in the Kingdom of Naples during the 'French' decade following the Revolution which saw a draconian reduction in the number of regular clergy. Without further consideration of figures and percentages we will just underline that in Lombardy alone the number of monasteries and convents fell from 291 in 1767 to 200 in 1790, the number of religious had fallen by forty-eight per cent in 1792, and by seventy-four per cent in 1799. In Tuscany, the number of houses went from 345 to 215 between 1765 and 1789, while, at the same time, the number of clergy in the orders of men declined from 5848 to 3182, a loss of forty-three per cent. The orders of women suffered equally in the Italian states under Habsburg rule.

Throughout Italy the suppression of convents – even of the so-called 'micro-convents' (*conventini*) of twelve members or less in Modena and Venice – did not have a strong effect on the decrease of the clergy. These suppressions did affect, however, the structure of ecclesiastical property, putting into circulation numerous patrimonies from which the state and the secular clergy often profited (as in Tuscany where ecclesiastical patrimonies for the secular clergy were created from the proceeds of such sales). The nobility and the bourgeoisie also took advantage of this situation. Thanks to the careful attention given to socio-economic history, we have some information derived from the remarkable research carried on in this area during the last twenty years, although we do not yet have a full picture of the extension, value and internal structure of church property in eighteenth-century Italy. If it can be said of the Kingdom of Naples that the clergy owned two-thirds of its property, periodic samples taken from the cadastral registers of Charles III show a much lower degree of clerical landownership, although it was higher than in central and northern Italy. The church, moreover, was deeply involved, especially in the south, in the provision of financial credit to both small peasant proprietors through confraternities and to medium and large landowners, lay, feudal and bourgeois groups through monasteries, convents, cathedrals and collegiate chapters until at least 1770. In Lombardy, the extent of ecclesiastical property by the mid eighteenth century was certainly higher than the eighteen per cent in the hands of the church at the time of the cadastral register taken by Charles V in the first half of the sixteenth century. In 1749 ecclesiastical properties accounted for an estimated twenty-three per cent of the value of the property of the region. Using the 1783 cadastral rolls for the Roman *campagna* and those of 1789 for Bologna we can see two distinct zones in the Papal States: in the underdeveloped *campagna*, feudal forms of ownership prevailed over land largely devoted to cereal cultivation and grazing. There ecclesiastics owned forty-one per cent of the land, the nobility fifty-two per cent, the bourgeoisie a very low five per cent. In the second zone, that is around Bologna, church property accounted for twenty per cent of the total, that of the nobility fifty-three per cent, and the property of the bourgeoisie twenty-three per cent. In other words, in the southern part of the Papal States, old and new ecclesiastical property still continued to dominate in the eighteenth century in contrast to the north where the church had suffered losses during the communal period and had not recovered during the Counter-Reformation. This was a situation which prevailed in general terms throughout central and northern Italy. It goes without saying that church property was essentially feudal in form, especially in the south, and that the bourgeoisie regarded it as an obstacle to economic progress. This led to the convergence of governmental, noble and bourgeois attacks on landownership by the church which produced a crisis in ecclesiastical property towards the close of the century. The Italian churches seemed to be caught in the grips of a general crisis during the second half of the

eighteenth century, as they suffered not only from their own internal contra-
dictions but also from the attack directed against them in some states by
reformers demanding a new political and civil order in accord with the
philosophy of the Enlightenment. This was a crisis which clearly undermined
traditional ethical-religious values at many levels. The great polemical disputes of eighteenth-century Italian Catholicism between probabilists and
their opponents, between laxists and rigorists in the first half of the century,
between Jansenists and 'Jesuits', traditionalists and partisans of a Catholic
Enlightenment especially in the second half of the century, are elements which
instead of producing immediate and positive effects contributed to rising
dissension within the church. The famous suggestions of Muratori that during
the 1740s had seemed suitable for moderate and progressive reform within the
church in the direction of a Catholic Enlightenment, were rejected at the end of
Benedict XIV's pontificate to become a subordinate factor in the ideological
amalgam that formed the background for the changes introduced into the
church by Leopold and Joseph II. The pressure of events between 1770 and
1780 and the spread of the Enlightenment placed the Roman curia after
Benedict XIV's concordat policies on the defensive, and hindered the
development of a coherent politico-religious policy in a time of increasing
difficulties for the church. Undoubtedly, considerable efforts were made on the
local diocesan level, but motives differed from place to place, such as the
emphasis on improving the quality of the parish clergy that, for example, in
Lombardy and Tuscany reflected the 'statist' concerns of Jansenist ideas and
Habsburg political objectives embodied in the reform of the bishop of Pistoia
and Prato, Scipione de' Ricci, too famous an episode to be recalled here. The
numerical reduction of the regular clergy, and in some cases its disappearance,
led to the restructuring of religious life in many areas, although in a negative
way, for it meant the removal of all centrifugal forces with respect to parish
organization. Confraternities and oratories disappeared in Lombardy and
Tuscany and their role declined in the south. A similar decline of the Tuscan
'hermitages' occurred as well as the rejection in central-northern Italy and the
Kingdom of Naples of the famous *bigotes* and *beates* who were often members of
the Third Orders attached to the regular clergy. There also disappeared in
Naples the so-called *clerici selvatici*, a numerous group of ecclesiastics only in
the most general sense, but who enjoyed the privileges of the clergy because
they exercised minor responsibilities in country churches and on ecclesiastical
landed properties. No effort was made to adjust parish boundaries in a rational
way, and parishes failed to adapt to the new conditions created by the rapid
demographic growth of the eighteenth century or by the changing demands of
the faithful. In general, the Italian parish lacked that deep community sense
characteristic of its French counterpart in the eighteenth century, and as a
result it increasingly found itself incapable of becoming the real centre of
religious life at the diocesan level and of contributing to the easing of tensions

within a church engaged in a dramatic search for its identity. One institution, which had already proven useful during the crisis years of the seventeenth century and had begun to play a larger role during the eighteenth from the 1720s onward, especially during the pontificate of Benedict XIV (1740–58) with its great emphasis on pastoral work, grew stronger in this period: the mission and popular preaching in the major cities and in the remote countryside. This is a particularly important chapter in the history of the eighteenth-century religious life in Italy, in spite of the periodic nature of missionary activity. The significance of the eighteenth-century missions lay in their impact on popular religious practice through the diffusion of particular devotions and especially through the appearance of new ways of understanding and participating in religious services. They contributed to establishing a new relationship between the clergy and the faithful and to giving the church at the parish level a new social function.

The missions were active not only in the countryside, where the church had lost a large measure of its hold over the populace during a long period of economic stagnation (1630–1720), but also in the towns, so important to Italian society and now open to a vigorous missionary activity. In those urban centres a massive increase of poverty was caused by the disappearance or decline in small country villages of traditional forms of charity and assistance, and there took place a crisis after the famine of 1764–6 in the structure of peasant property which saw the peasantry lose access to the financial credits provided by ecclesiastical institutions (especially of the regular clergy) and the assistance in hard times of the grain supplies furnished by the famous *Monti di Pietà*. This situation was also complicated by a new kind of socio-economic development as the traditional pattern of professional and seasonal mendicity was transformed with the addition of large numbers of hard-pressed peasants in search of aid. It was not accidental that one of the greatest popular preachers of the day, the Capuchin friar, St Leonard of Port Maurice, preached a harsh, penitential, rigorous and evangelistic message in towns and rural districts beset by massive poverty. It is also in this context that the Franciscans promoted the devotions of the Stations of the Cross with great success in spite of opposition within the church from Jansenists and others hostile to the cults of popular religion. In southern towns the most vigorous missionary activity was carried on by the *preti urbani*, the *pii operari* and the Neapolitan Congregation of Apostolic Missions.

But the real religious problem facing the eighteenth-century church lay not in the towns but in the countryside, and there missionary activity was extensive. The Vincentians (Lazarists) and Passionists constantly traversed the Maremma and the Paludian zones of Latium issuing solemn calls to penance. After the 1720s, the Passionists first of all established a network of small convents and hermitages to provide a base for their missionary work in spite of the opposition of the traditional mendicant orders who resented anyone competing for the alms of the faithful. The most successful missionary order, however, was the Redemptorists, founded by St Alphonsus Liguori (1732) whose missionary technique, benevolent, familiar and didactic, had enormous appeal. The Redemptorists worked with considerable success from the 1730s on, and their role was especially important from the middle of the century among the rural masses of southern Italy and Sicily. The number of holy days diminished partly as a result of the efforts of Muratori, while the decline of the religious orders gradually diminished the extent of Lenten and Advent preaching. And reforming governments and bishops suppressed penitential and nocturnal processions – for as the bishop of Sovana declared in a letter of 1776, God must be honoured 'with good sense and discernment', that is, the most extravagant expressions of popular piety had to be brought under control. The missionaries served an important function in this respect, since they substituted new devotions for the extravagances of popular religion, giving the cult a collective meaning. The Passionists, for example, encouraged the public adoration of the Eucharist, especially in the evenings, to allow peasants returning from the fields to participate. Jansenists and others, however, objected to this new devotion on the grounds that it diminished the importance of the Eucharist from its principal setting in the mass. There is no doubt, in fact, that the devotion altered substantially the particular relationship of the faithful to the Eucharist, for at the beginning of the eighteenth century the Eucharist was used in parishes outside the mass only to provide the last rites to the dying and in certain periods of exceptional solemnity such as the devotion of the Forty Hours. If meditations on the centrality of the suffering of Christ and the Virgin, encouraged by the Passionists, were designed to recall renunciation as a lesson of Christian virtue and at the same time served to sublimate social tensions (the popular devotion of the Stations of the Cross can be fitted into this pattern); if there also emerged the development of more gentle 'family' devotions, such as that of the Sacred Heart promoted by the Jesuits, and the Christmas devotions (encouraged by St Alphonsus who wrote the most celebrated popular Italian hymn, 'You descend from the stars' (*Tu scendi dalle stelle*)); it is certainly the cult of the Virgin Mary which spread widely in eighteenth-century Italy, especially in the south. During the first half of the century, confraternities devoted to the Rosary and Our Lady of Mount Carmel attained great popularity, thanks to the indulgences generously attached to them and still deeply felt, while the practice of saying the rosary in public each evening spread as a collective devotion still in evidence today. During the 1740s controversies developed over the so-called 'sanguinary vow' (the promise to shed one's blood in defence of the doctrine of the Immaculate Conception), a practice encouraged by the Jesuits in Sicily but opposed by those committed to 'Devotion under Rule' led by Muratori. But, above all, the activity of St Alphonsus Liguori and his Redemptorists made the most decisive contribution to the evolution of the Marian cult at the level of doctrine and piety. It influenced greatly Marian devotions in the nineteenth and twentieth centuries.

We must ask ourselves, finally, if we wish to attempt a very careful socio-logical approach, what kind of faithful the priests and missionaries met in the course of their ministry and during preaching and evangelization. The present state of research makes it difficult to generalize about the social basis of popular religious beliefs encountered by the missionary clergy. We do have information on the Maremma and the region of Modena and can use the work of Giorgini, Orlandi, De Rosa and his collaborators for the south. In central and northern Italy, the rite of baptism generally took place in the week following birth. The mass was a significant ritual for the population, more as suffrage than sacrifice. Hence, we should say, the still lively persistence throughout the century of devotions on behalf of the souls in purgatory. The use of techniques of control – the Tuscan *polizzino* and the Modena *bollettino* – guaranteed a high level of participation in the obligatory Easter communion. At the beginning of the eighteenth century, the faithful failing to receive communion were often severely censured by the ecclesiastical authorities, although the latter were more tolerant as the century wore on. Marriage followed the typical pattern of Old Regime societies, declining in numbers during March and December, that is in the liturgical seasons of Lent and Advent, and also in July, a time of harvest. As for attitudes towards death, we do not have for Italy studies similar to those carried out for eighteenth-century Provence by Michel Vovelle. It is possible to say, however, that certain baroque funeral rites and devotions on behalf of the souls in purgatory were widespread in eighteenth-century Italy. Even at the close of the century in Tuscany important offerings were made on Sundays or holy days for the celebration of funeral offices on Mondays for the souls of purgatory, because of the widespread pious belief that the flames of purgatory burned more strongly following the day of the Lord. The purpose of these practices was less to appease the judgement of God than to secure the liberation of souls from the sufferings of purgatory. The idea of happiness became increasingly entwined with the collective traditional symbols of religion, altering them but not so abruptly as to provoke discussion.

A different picture emerges from the research carried out by De Rosa in the south, a more tragic and dark picture, so that we can properly speak of two Italies at the religious level just as we have referred to several Italian churches, even though I think this analysis must still be carefully examined. Although De Rosa makes some unjustified generalizations and establishes a too facile contrast between a popular, pagan-Christian religion confined to the folkloric level and a positive, institutional Catholic piety, he notes the characteristic of religion in the south in the area of Cilento, where St Alphonsus's missions were active and where the recourse to magic was frequent and widespread. The population relied on auguries drawn from birds and animals, used magical practices and even committed sacrileges by abusing the sacraments and sacred objects (holy water to protect men and animals, sacramental wine to cure eye diseases, Holy Oil, etc.): on Holy Saturday, those infected with leprosy or simply scabies plunged into the sea to the sound of church bells, believing that their sores would disappear; flagellation rites, used in Tuscany as a simple act of penitence, became in the south a rite which replaced the remission of sins outside the sacrament of penance on the grounds that like baptism the soul was purified by an individual's own blood. Also frequent were individual and collective expressions such as ritual funeral tears and the exaggerated cult of relics (although we find both in central and northern Italy as well), which De Rosa describes as 'magico-sensitive' and in which the clergy itself participated to some extent; some were even counted among the 'magicians' in certain towns: for example, the clergy agreed to carry the Holy Oils in procession like the Eucharist in spite of the efforts of bishops to stop the practice. This protective recourse fed by devotionalism towards the saints and by extra liturgical acts flourished in spite of the hostility of the episcopacy which increasingly called upon the missionary clergy to restrain excesses and introduce practices in conformity to the church's teaching. Failing in these attempts and resisting against the will of the episcopacy, the missionaries were regarded as divine 'protectors' in times of natural catastrophe, as in Calabria after the frightful 1783 earthquake when the populace pleaded with the missionaries for general confession and communion to appease God's wrath.

At this point I should like to suggest a provisional conclusion to this essay on the church in eighteenth-century Italy. At a general level the religious system, clearly in a condition of dislocation during the seventeenth century, sought through the crisis to reform itself, in part by relying on increased state intervention, as Michel de Certeau has pointed out, and in part by placing religion or rather religious practice in line with government aspirations of order as the church sought to find a new balance.

The emphasis was still heavily concentrated on religious practice, on the *sign*, even if during the eighteenth century this meant an effort to organize and rationalize the external expressions of religion, to fit them into the socio-political structure – no longer one of absolutism but of enlightened despotism – and to reach as much of the population as possible by winning the countryside and impoverished groups. The effort made by the church was, however, ambivalent in its purposes and results: in the countryside the missionaries of the eighteenth century recognized in the impoverished rural masses 'the most abandoned of souls' who, according to St Alphonsus's statement, were to become a rampart of faith against the dechristianized elites of the towns and contribute to elaborate the institutional parish structure as a rural model in an urban reality. But Enlightened piety found in the countryside a dark spiritual world, difficult to penetrate, which had to be fought and replaced by the practice of virtue. There developed in eighteenth-century Italy a clear distinction between the bourgeois culture of the towns and the traditional popular culture of the countryside within a reciprocal reorganization and a new coexistence. Parishes and missions begin to play a different but decisive role in the crisis of traditional institutions, from religious orders to confraternities, thus beginning the religious and institutional history of the nineteenth century and a new and difficult relationship between church and laity; but the reconquest of the countryside was to give a strongly rural and traditional emphasis to the new institutional approach and religious proposals which the church was ready to make to Italian society.

6 The German *Reichskirche**

GERHARD BENECKE

The Reformation and Counter-Reformation divided Germany and produced two major civil wars which ended only after extensive involvement by foreign powers. At the same time, the century between 1540 and 1640 produced solutions in federal public law which guaranteed the internal religious uniformity of each of the approximately 300 territorial states, while establishing heterodoxy at the federal or Reich level. After the Peace of Westphalia attempts were made to remove religion from federal politics by forming two blocs of territories in the Reichstag or imperial assembly – the *corpus catholicorum* and the *corpus evangelicorum*. In practice, the right of territories to 'split into parts' at the federal political level was used sparingly, and then only by the Protestants, especially around 1700, an indication that they were the weaker party. In the mid eighteenth century Christian August Beck, tutor in public law to the future Emperor Joseph II, admitted:

> This so-called 'splitting into parts' is indeed granted in the appropriate place in the Westphalian Peace and is recognised as the pinnacle of their freedom by the Protestants, but in practice it leads to very damaging consequences, and in view of the absence of an amicable understanding, the whole matter is left to its own devices, in order that any hint of extolling the virtues of something similar to the 'free vote' as in Poland can be suppressed.

Beck was aware of the threat that religious dissent still posed to peaceful cooperation within federal Germany. In the early eighteenth century, the imperial federal cameral tribunal had temporarily ceased to function and, furthermore, Catholic proselytizing in the Rhineland Palatinate nearly led to civil war. At the same time, the expulsion of Protestants from the archbishopric of Salzburg provided the *corpus evangelicorum* with real grievances. The reason that the Catholics were cautious about retaliating through the

*'Der politische Zustand der altständischen Gesellschaft war insofern ein besserer als der gegenwärtige, als er das Auseinanderbrechen von Staat und Gesellschaft verhinderte.' (The political condition of the traditional society of ranks and orders was in this sense a better one than present day society, in that it prevented state and society from breaking apart): Peter Blickle, *Deutsche Ländliche Rechtsquellen* (Stuttgart, 1977), p. 218.

corpus catholicorum was that they were always the majority in the Old Reich. They were not strong enough to impose drastic solutions on the Protestants in spite of attempts to do so militarily in the 1540s and 1620s, but they kept the Protestants in their constitutional place by buying internal peace which provided the security necessary to keep the French and Turks out of Germany and Austria, especially in the late seventeenth century.

In terms of institutional and territorial power sanctioned by formal religious arrangements after the severe confessional wars, there are three periods to be taken into account. The first period ranges from the 1540s to the 1640s; religious and dynastic conflict went hand in hand and centred above all on the rivalries and activities of the Austrian Habsburgs, Bavarian and Palatinate Wittelsbachs, and Ernestine and Albertine Saxony. The second period, from the 1640s to the 1740s, produced an effective religious truce but dynastic rivalries inclined several German ruling families towards neighbouring European courts such as those of Great Britain and Poland. The third period sees violent dynastic rivalry between the Austrian Habsburgs and the Prussian Hohenzollerns from the 1740s to the later 1860s. It followed the pattern of alternating cooperation, coercion and conflict evident during the first period, but then the objective shifted from a belief in religious uniformity over the entire Reich to one of national unity as each party tried to capture as much territory and influence as possible. During and after the struggle, German-speaking central Europeans came to less satisfactory solutions than had their sixteenth- and seventeenth-century ancestors. This was due to the men of the eighteenth century who had toyed with the idea of rationalized state power and with a mystique of individualism in accord with social and economic changes which made it impossible for politicians to compromise on the basis of feudal ambiguities, overlapping jurisdictions and hallowed traditions.

The major tradition was Catholic and centred on the *Reichskirche*, a unifying concept and not an actual institution of the Old Reich. The *Reichskirche* was a kind of Third World within federal Germany by the eighteenth century. The First World arose from the dynastic conflict among the great powers, including Wurtemberg, Hesse, Mecklenburg, Baden, Guelph, Wettin, Wittelsbach and later the super powers of the Habsburgs and Hohenzollerns. The Second World comprised the vast majority of German territories, Catholic or Protestant, dynastic or republican, which were all building independent governments including state religions, and staffing central and regional federal institutions which provided the mutual services of supervision and security needed in order to compete in a world of larger territories and foreign nations. The Third World was composed of the residue of German episcopal and monastic power and wealth that had provided the backbone of administrative continuity in the centuries since Carolingian, Saxon, Salian and Hohenstaufen times along the Rhine in south and west Germany. This essential, universal and Catholic tradition held the Old Reich together and provided the focus of its ancient loyalties. It was an agglomeration of petty bureaucracies rather like a fragmented latter-day Avignon papacy, Papal States of Italy but on German soil.

The *Reichskirche* was the sum of all the German ecclesiastical high juris-dictions, each striving to become a territorial state in its own right on the basis of episcopal autonomy and a church–state unity, perhaps the best example, outside of papal monarchy, of theocracy in the Catholic world after the Council of Trent. Each elected ecclesiastical territorial ruler was also a *Landesvater* like any secular, dynastic ruler, 'by the Grace of God', controlling his subjects through administrators steeped in the rules and regulations of mercantilism and absolutism. Yet the *Reichskirche* was a construct within the loose tradition of German federal politics. It presented a kind of 'inverse or anti-holism': that is the whole was also *less* than the sum of its parts; not more and not even exactly the sum total. This is crucial to understanding the German past before the rise of modern rationalism in politics after the late eighteenth century. This also applies to other open-ended power agglomerations in the Old Reich, such as the Hanseatic League, the imperial cities, the Swabian League, the imperial circles, federal tax-schedules and law courts, as well as to the cantons of imperial knights. All were untidy, weak and unclassifiable and yet essentially flexible and practical, workable and as strong as the members within wished them to be. The interplay of regional and elective forces meant that solutions could be found on a day-to-day basis for wider religious and ideological responses to political and social change.

No monographic study has yet been made of the *Reichskirche*, and we still do not know adequately why it failed during the course of the eighteenth century. This is due in large measure to the failure of the German historiographical tradition of the nineteenth and twentieth centuries to appreciate the lack in previous times of a powerfully centralized state following a unified national development. The unity of the Reich and of the *Reichskirche* was the traditional and far more politically mature alternative to secular, dynastic nation–state politics which late-eighteenth-century and early-nineteenth-century Germans rejected. Modern German liberal and conservative political traditions go no further back than the French Revolution and the impact of Napoleon's armies on central Europe after 1800. However difficult it may be to chart events, the break in German politics was drastic: the *Aufklärung* was the most serious political mistake any generation of German politicians and intellectuals could possibly have made. Why did it occur? It did so because the last bulwark of the Reich, the Catholic faith, underwent an inner transformation from a sovereign territorial and spiritual entity to a merely spiritual one from about the 1770s. Episcopal ostentation was replaced by more austere practice, thereby unhing-ing the whole German tradition of church and state. What Edmund Burke wrote about France could have been applied to Germany in the 1790s. An appreciation of the medieval and early modern German traditions of politics must break through this barrier, not through the study of the history of ideas, thought and culture, but through understanding loose institutions that failed and disappeared such as the Reich and *Reichskirche*, and the practical moral codes upon which they were built. Nineteenth-century Germans invented archival positivism and legal and academic history as its offshoot, but the more they uncovered detailed events and formal structure, the less they understood of the whole of their national past before 1800.

What was the *Reichskirche* between the Peace of Westphalia and the Napoleonic wars? What was its external organization? What was its inner appeal for worshippers? How did German Catholicism continue to function through the *Reichskirche* in the era of Enlightenment with its emphasis on rationalism, secularism and separation of church and state? What is the best way to account for the transition from *Reichskirche* to *Deutsche Katholische Kirche* from 1800 to 1850? What explains the hostility to the baroque *Reichskirche* evinced by German Catholics such as Döllinger in the nineteenth century? What did the *Reichskirche* of the eighteenth century mean to those who formed its ministry, and who made up its congregations? As there existed Prussian or Bavarian patriotism in early modern times, so there existed Würzburg patriotism, Münsterite loyalty and patriotic state service under ruling bishops as well as obedience to the abbots of Fulda or Corvey. Austria and Prussia did not have a monopoly of territorial state loyalty: the bishop of Würzburg and his fellows also commanded allegiance. In this essay we will present a framework which may in future foster detailed and full-length studies of the *Reichskirche*.

Among the German territorial states prominent in the early-eighteenth-century imperial assembly, there were representatives of secular, ecclesiastical, noble, and burgher-republican systems of government. Numerically, the Catholic, elective, aristocratic bloc was the largest. At the imperial assembly there were sixty-five ruling archbishops, bishops, abbots and priors, forty-five dynastic princes, sixty dynastic lords and sixty imperial cities. But forty-five dynastic princes controlled about eighty per cent of the land and population of the Reich; the sixty-five ecclesiastical rulers, fourteen per cent of the total land area and approximately twelve per cent of the federal population. Ecclesiastical territories had perhaps three and a half million subjects, ruling princes twenty-two and a half million, lords and imperial cities one million each, and the imperial knights half a million. In practice, therefore, the *Reichskirche* was the second largest form of government in the Reich. Although in size it lagged behind the princely territories, it was the only cohesive principle of federalism standing in the way of dynastic forces. The *Reichskirche* exercised too much constitutional power given the reality of its economic and diplomatic influence in the eighteenth century, although its land-holdings and jurisdiction had expanded from a low point in the 1540s. In spite of Calvinist advances from

Switzerland down the Rhine and into the northern Netherlands in the later sixteenth century, the Lutherans entrenched themselves in the north and north-east; they did not expand southwards beyond parts of Swabia and Franconia. Ecclesiastical Catholic Germany shared Swabia, Franconia, Westphalia and the whole Rhineland with the Protestants through the arch-bishoprics, bishoprics and monasteries stretching from the north-west through to the south of Germany: Münster, Paderborn, Corvey, Fulda, Cologne, Trier, Mainz, Würzburg, Bamberg, Augsburg, Constance and the great monastic holdings of eastern Swabia, and ending in dynastic Bavaria, ecclesiastical Passau and Salzburg, and Austria. The Reich was Catholic from the English Channel to the Hungarian Plain, from Habsburg Austria through to the Habsburg southern Netherlands; it was Protestant from north-east to south-west from East Prussia through Brandenburg, Upper and Lower Saxony to Franconia, Swabia and the middle and upper Rhine linked with Protestant Switzerland. At certain points in the west, centre and south, a religious dualism evolved, epitomized by parity between Catholics and Protestants in some imperial cities and symbolized by the alternation of Catholic and Protestant bishops in Osnabrück.

In the secular and dynastic states many ruling princes and lords, the dominant groups in some imperial cities and most imperial knights were Catholic. They often cooperated with members of their own families who in turn were the leading ecclesiastical rulers and canons of the *Reichskirche*. Powerful Catholic dynasties played a part in the ecclesiastical territories after the Council of Trent, as illustrated by the activities of Austrian and Bavarian appointees to bishoprics and abbeys in the Rhineland, Westphalia, Franconia and Swabia. Leading families such as the Schönborns of the imperial knights played a crucial role as did younger members of Catholic dynasties elected rulers of ecclesiastical territories. In each ecclesiastical principality there was also a Catholic nobility and a patrician class of municipal councillors. These groups provided cathedral and monastic canons as well as the regulars who preserved administrative continuity from bishops or abbots elected by the chapters. This was the noble element of the *Reichskirche*, the guardian of its wealth, tradition, privilege and feudal grandeur. It produced the cultural superstructure, the ostentation, pomp and ceremony of baroque Catholicism. To whom did inner illumination appear sacrificed to outward show? Although Jansenist influences travelled from France across the Rhine, the way in which this aesthetic and devotional question was posed by German Catholics in the eighteenth century was different from the preconceptions of nineteenth-century Catholic historiography.

Taste and spirituality are closely linked. To some, the baroque *Reichskirche* was brash and vulgar. It is true that it could be inefficient and corrupt, especially when bribes were used in the election of the ecclesiastical territorial rulers, as occurred in eighteenth-century Paderborn. Moreover, the best positions were reserved to nobles of proper lineage.* But are vulgarity and corruption obstacles to popularity and devotion? In the labyrinth of baroque mysticism there was room for all, especially when hallowed by southern exoticism.

The eighteenth century produced an officially orchestrated campaign against popular excesses in religion. The *Reichskirche* like the Old Reich itself was killed by the meddlesome intellectuals and dynastic pragmatists of the Enlightenment and absolutism. They provided as an alternative the secular practice of citizens' rights and eventually nation-state pretensions, a spurious formalism that soon fragmented into a new kind of bourgeois nationalist individualism copied from a more economically and politically advanced western Europe. The elective principle in politics was connected to ecclesiastical territorialism in Germany, and not with dynasticism. A new split between church and state occurred in the later eighteenth century. Unlike the sixteenth century, there was no new Counter-Reformation to save German territorial Catholicism or the traditional federal and elective-republican-aristocratic system of politics that had kept dynasticism in a kind of order. Instead, public and private modes of thought and codes of action among the German ruling groups and classes were created distinct from each other. Attempts by the *Reichskirche* to forestall and hinder this development met the opposition of the papacy in the 1760s, when the German territorial bishops tried to curtail the powers of papal nuncios in the Reich, and it met the scorn of emperor and papacy when the archbishops of Mainz, Cologne, Trier and Salzburg tried to put their houses in order at the Congress of Ems in 1786. The role played by the over-zealous Erastian Emperor Joseph II left the territorial Catholic traditionalists clutching at straws by forcing them to turn to the aged King Frederick II of Prussia. Machiavellism had indeed come full circle.

An all-embracing, public–private, territorial–spiritual unified church based on ostentation, wealth, privilege and inequality failed to adapt to the ideas of the French Revolution on the one hand, and to the economic practice of the British agrarian, commercial and industrial revolution on the other. Instead it was overrun by an enlightened intelligentsia manipulated by dynastic interests which floundered between the two long before Germany was prepared for its own version of political and economic change. The republican tradition in German politics was in the hands of a German ecclesiastical aristocracy: any native German political revolution should have allied with it, changing it from within, but the opposite happened. With its destruction enshrined in constitutional documents and treaties with revolutionary France and Erastian Austria between 1799 and 1803, the *Reichskirche*, like the Reich itself in 1806, took the

---

*In Catholic dynastic states far more civil service families of non-noble status and origin provided prelates than did local noble families: see M. Spindler (ed.), *Handbuch der Bayerischen Geschichte*, vol. II (Munich, 1969), p. 655. Between 1648 and 1789 the family origins of the Bavarian prelates included the following: 7% nobles, 30% civil servants, 30% burghers and craftsmen, and about 6.5% peasants.

better part of native German federal political practice with it to the grave. If there ever was a clear break in German politics it came not in 1945–9, 1918–19, 1870, or 1848 but around 1800, and German political practice became rootless and unbalanced from that time onwards. The price of abolishing the Old Reich and its *Reichskirche* led to the total neglect of its real and practical achievement up to the eighteenth century.

Hegel exposed this problem in a convoluted but important way as long ago as 1802 when he wished to try his hand at political journalism. He produced an epitaph for the dying tradition of native German federal political practice which was surprisingly appreciative of German Catholic universalism, albeit tolerant of an imposed Protestant lobby, as well as of an increasingly senseless dynastic *Realpolitik*. Hegel wrote in appreciation of some kind of link between a medieval mystique of unity and a modern state of diversity.

> When religion was uniform, and when the still embryonic bourgeoisie had not introduced a great heterogeneity into the whole, princes, dukes and lords could regard one another more easily as a whole and accordingly act as a whole . . . Religion is a still more important fundamental determinant of the relation of individual parts of Germany to the whole; of course it has made the greatest contribution to the rupture of political union and to the legalisation of this rupture. The times in which religion was split were too inapt for the separation of church from state and for maintaining the state despite the division of faith . . . But while religion has completely rent the state asunder, it has yet afforded an inkling in a remarkable way of certain principles on which a state can rest. Since the split in religion has torn men apart in their innermost being, and since none the less a bond was supposed to remain, the bond had to be an external one in relation to external things such as making war: and this bond is the principle of modern states. Precisely because the most important parts of constitutional law were interwoven with the state and then all political rights were made dependent on two, or in strictness three [i.e. Protestantism, Catholicism, and parity between the two] religions. This is apparently contrary to the principle of the independence of state and church, and to the possibility of there being a state despite differences in religion, but in fact the principle is really recognised because there *are* different religions and Germany *is* supposed to be a state.
>
> (*The German Constitution*, 1802)

In 1802, a commissioner of the Grand Duke of Baden was taking charge of the schools in the newly secularized territorial bishopric of Speier on the middle Rhine north of Karlsruhe, a state which had experienced vigorous reform since the 1720s, under its ruling bishop, Cardinal Damian Hugo von Schönborn. The impression given by the commissioner was hardly one of poverty and backwardness usually associated with the conventional view of the territorial states of the *Reichskirche*. He reported:

> The territorial Bishopric [of Speier] is the pearl among the new possessions [of

Baden]. There is prosperity generally everywhere and the whole gives the impression of a state that has been well run for a considerable number of years. The signs of the good government of Cardinal Schönborn and the late Prince Bishop Augustus are still prevalent. The populace really seems to be admirable here, and all classes display a definite outward prosperity. Even the middling and lower class of people [*Volksklasse*] displays better behaviour than is the case in many other places. The populace loves its religion and is truly devoted to its parish priests, who are considered on the whole in town and country to be very worthy and suitable men.

The bishopric of Speier is a good example of the mass of smaller ecclesiastical territories. It had under 30 000 inhabitants and about forty localities with primary schools by the early eighteenth century. Teachers were subject to regular examination, and all school registers were checked by the bishop's own officials. In a survey of the late seventeenth century only one teacher was found to be inadequate and that because of too many side duties. Local authorities tended to overwork and underpay teachers. As a result of the cardinal-bishop's reforms in the 1720s and 1730s, teachers were assigned more reasonable tasks. Parents had to register all children between the ages of six and twelve at school in wintertime from October to March; it cost one kreuzer per child per week plus a fixed quota of heating fuel for the school-room. Children of poor parents were means-tested and became a charge on the parish. Parents had to pay the teacher on pain of a fine to the local government, whether their children came to school or stayed away. It was thus in the interest of teachers to keep full registers, since otherwise they would be losing revenue, which in any case was so low before the 1750s that the ever-paternalistic cardinal-bishop decreed that no school-teacher should handle church service collections or parish charity funds. From 1728 the parish priest was to be present at catechism examinations, and from 1739 rural deans were to examine not only pupils' but also the teacher's deportment, behaviour, reading, writing and devotions every two years. Reports were then filed with the local administration. New teachers were only to be appointed after approval of their baptismal records, testimonials of academic competence and moral character, and a check on their teaching experience.

A real problem was to force parents to send their children to the state schools. In 1731 at the administrative capital and town of Bruchsal the commissioners estimated that there were 600 eligible schoolchildren but that two-thirds were being sent to private schools. Although some ambitious burghers claimed that their children were receiving better tuition including Latin, no doubt most of these 'hole-in-the-corner schools' were workshops. Tailors and cobblers were traditionally favoured, whereby children could work and learn simultaneously, thereby supplementing family income or at least paying for their own keep or equivalent school fees. In the bishop's state schools that was impossible. In 1743 Cardinal-Bishop Schönborn fined seven burghers of Bruchsal ten talers each for refusing to send their children to the state school. It was of little use to fine the poor, but wealthier subjects could be made an example of in this way. Considering that the net fee for school attendance was under one taler per child per year, this was a large fine, and equivalent to the pay of a domestic for well over six months. The cardinal-bishop saved surplus revenue during his reign and left nearly a million talers. In 1757 his successor opened a completely endowed secondary school and also doubled the salaries of all the employees of this exemplary ecclesiastical state.

In mid-eighteenth-century Bruchsal, the ruling bishop of Speier had responded effectively to the need for more state school places by increasing the number of parish schools from one to three. The remaining two schools were funded by the chapter and district nobility on a system of scholarships for students and choristers. Yet even before this expansion, the town's single primary school had been educating about ten per cent of the six to twelve year olds and of these one-third were girls. All three schools had handled about one-third of the school-age population before the expansion. How many other states of the territorial *Reichskirche* ran such extensive educational systems in the eighteenth century?

An examination of the internal administration of the larger ecclesiastical states reveals that they too operated in a reasonable manner. In home affairs great stress was laid on the provision of educational and church facilities at the parish level in town and country. Although this went hand in hand with administrative proliferation, in many respects it was in line with state paternalism and the level of popular devotion at that time. Schools were efficiently administered by a primary school commission in the archbishopric-electorate of Cologne from 1786, and a territorial council of medical control functioned there from 1779. The archbishopric was divided into two parts and in a survey of 1670 all parish boundaries were measured and all dwellings counted. Every church or chapel was reaffirmed as the natural focal point of public life, and each was identified as to its place in the administrative hierarchy of the diocese. This was no mean task since twenty-six of the 471 settlements under the territorial high jurisdiction of the archbishop of Cologne also fell under the jurisdiction of the deans of the neighbouring archbishop of Trier. A century later, the archiepiscopal-electoral administration of Trier undertook a survey of 913 settlements and jurisdictions in its territory and concluded that thirty-two of them were under deans of the bishop of Liège, twelve under the archbishop of Mainz, and no less than eighty-five under the archbishop of Cologne. The complexities of overlapping inter-ecclesiastical administrations within the eighteenth-century *Reichskirche* did not apply only to the clergy and to those clerics enjoying papal exemption from episcopal jurisdiction. At the parish level, these complexities are important to understand given their influence on efficient administration. Each ecclesiastical state wished to keep revenue that otherwise would have been lost to others in the form of fiscal and judicial business, rents, benefices and feudal rights. The early modern *Reichs-kirche* increasingly had to be overgoverned in order to fulfil the tasks of the state. A preliminary view of the *Reichskirche* shows its members burdened with heavy administrative costs and an overstaffed bureaucracy. But the ecclesiastical territorial states produced modern results characterized by the uniformity and supervision of life, devotions, thought and economy of all their subjects. The accent was theocratic and very much church-court centred. That the *Reichskirche* should have been effective may surprise later historians. However, no one in the eighteenth-century *Reichskirche* was spiritually or perhaps even materially neglected, and in the last generations before the advent of industrialization along the Rhine and in Westphalia a territorial church system of government which was sovereign in home affairs reached a high point of development. It will be necessary to examine its social anthropology at the parish level to ascertain what this church-centred environment with its public ritual and family devotional structures meant to those at the base of its social pyramid. What did the term *barocke Volksfrömmigkeit* really mean? What did the 302 inhabitants of the hamlet of Daun, the local administrative centre of a region in the upper division of the archbishopric of Trier really think of their theocratic fatherland with its ecclesiastics, laws and customs?

Since one in eight of all eighteenth-century Germans lived in similar small states it is strange that no overall research has been carried out on a national scale on the problem of the *Reichskirche*. All we can do here is to provide indications of the wider problem, although a synthesis of the available historical literature could be attempted in the near future. Brief descriptions of some of the problems for eighteenth-century Bavaria, parts of Franconia, Swabia and the Palatinates are available in Max Spindler's handbook of Bavarian history, but even this is an exception to the general neglect of the topic.

The Catholic church and the territorial Catholic nobility expanded their landed property in Bavaria. Between 1500 and 1760 in the districts of Dachau and Landsberg church holdings increased from 51 to 56.6 per cent of the whole, while the holdings of the nobility rose from 16 to 31.7 per cent. At the same time near Munich the districts of Moosburg, Starnberg, Weilheim, Cham and Kötzing saw eighty-four farms fall into the hands of the nobility and fourteen into the hands of the church while three moved from noble ownership to the church. To what extent this development applies to the rest of Catholic Germany has yet to be assessed. However, in Bavaria it was the established nobility that saw itself threatened by the growth of church property, especially among the monastic orders. As late as 1704, a decree forbade the further amassing of land by the church in Bavaria, a measure completed by the amortization laws of 1764. By that time, the church owned fifty-six per cent of the land which could not be taxed directly but only through *dons gratuits* worked out with the consent of the papacy. The elector of Bavaria, in contrast, had control of only fifteen per cent of the land, and no less than eight bishops among his fellow territorial rulers also governed some of his Bavarian towns and villages. Freising, Regensburg, Passau, Bamberg, Eichstätt and Constance were all part of the Bavarian sphere of influence and rivalry with Austria. The greatest opportunity for tapping the wealth of the church occurred during the foreign and federal-civil war of 1756–63. An annual ten per cent wealth tax was levied on the clergy for five years with papal approval. It was assessed by episcopal officials much to the disgust of the wealthy regular orders, as only ten per cent of eighty Bavarian monasteries and convents complied voluntarily. In the 1760s taxation was extended by the secular authorities. No monastic order, for example, was allowed to accept gifts even of moveable property worth more than 2000 gulden. However, the Bavarian government stopped short of Jansenist–Gallican church reforms and interference similar to those Joseph II tried to implement after 1768 in the Habsburg lands. By the 1780s the papacy was prepared to ally with the Bavarian government by setting up a nunciature in Munich. The struggle began for control over the independent territorial *Reichskirche* from within the devout, dynastic base of German Catholicism. It was waged against the native, theocratic, elective and aristocratic-republican elements within the church.

After the destruction of the Jesuits in the 1770s, some of the Bavarian Catholic intelligentsia took over some of the defunct order's methods to found an elitist radical order of *Illuminati* operating from the arch-Catholic University of Ingolstadt. Hierarchy, discipline, loyalty and a strict moral code were now directed towards Jansenist, Febronianist and Gallican ends. They concentrated on reason, natural law and a classless, cosmopolitan and republican world order within the concept of a totally emancipated new church. The new currents show to what extent the traditional, privileged, territorial *Reichskirche* was being torn asunder from within by the later eighteenth century.

This was different from the experience of the previous two generations which had seen between 1700 and 1740 the emergence from Italian, French and Austrian influences of a native Bavarian church architecture that was one of the wonders of the world. The imposing world of pilgrimage and devotion moved into the countryside away from larger villages and towns. The great mass of Cistercian Fürstenfeld and the grand facade of Ettal tucked angularly into its high mountain pass became a marvel to pilgrims and the curious alike. Inside, carving, sculpture, mural and fresco painting transported the profane and the devout into the upper reaches of spiritual power towards a mystical union of externalized thought and action. This 'worldly otherworldliness' was the great aesthetic spell that the German *Reichskirche* cast over its own faithful from within itself and it was equally from within itself that the hair-line crack of destruction came in the form of doubt once the alliance of papacy and dynasticism had loosened the ties that held episcopal-monastic German republicanism together as an effective administrative system of theocratic small states attuned to the political tradition of early modern German federalism.

7 The Austrian church

JEAN BÉRENGER

Austria as considered in this essay does not include all the lands under the authority of the Habsburgs of Vienna, but what we have elsewhere termed the 'Austro-Bohemian Complex', or what might be described after 1620 as the Hereditary Lands. Together with the Austria of today, the kingdom of Bohemia, Moravia and Silesia, it was an elongated territory stretching from the Rhine to Poland, and from Prussia to the Adriatic, where Germans and Czechs predominated with a population at the opening of the eighteenth century of around five and a half million. After the great plague of 1713 the population did not stop expanding notwithstanding the loss of the largest part of Silesia in 1745. The time limits for a study of the eighteenth-century church in Austria are best set between 1683 and 1780, from the end of the siege of Vienna to the death of Maria Theresa, for this was a period of triumphant Catholicism reinforced by the 1683 victory over the Turks and which Joseph II tried to end by his radical reforms.

Three special features of the Hereditary Lands should be kept in mind:
(1) We are concerned with areas of *reconquista* with the exception of the Tyrol. The impact of Lutheranism had been very strong in Austria; in 1560 Vienna was in the main a Lutheran city. Since the fifteenth century and the Hussite wars, Bohemia was generally receptive to heterodox currents which led to the development of the Utraquist church, the Unity of the Brethren and the Lutheran churches. These lands were then prime targets for the efforts of the Counter-Reformation, and we are dealing with a combative Catholicism.
(2) The Czech and the Austrian provinces had clearly different political and cultural traditions. In the Alpine provinces the population was of Germanic outlook with the exception of the Italian and Slovak minorities of Upper Austria. The German population was faithful to the dynasty and the ideal of the Holy Roman Empire to the extent that it rose above provincialism. In the lands of the Bohemian Crown two nationalities were contrasted, the minority of Germans and the Czechs, both conscious of belonging to an independent entity and jealous of the privileges enshrined in the right of the state. Let me add that the clergy never tried to germanize the Czechs; on the contrary, the national language was encouraged in the masses said for the peasantry.

(3) The dynasty itself was an essential factor in religious life. It desired a Catholic reconquest, and it provided the means of attaining it to the clergy. Yet the dynasty did not regard itself as an instrument in the hands of the church. Monarchs from Leopold I to Maria Theresa considered it their first duty to ensure the salvation of the souls of their subjects, which meant to say making them good Catholics, but they were unwilling to become the puppets of either the curia or the bishops. Joseph I did not hesitate to make war on the pope at the beginning of the eighteenth century.

The clergy

A first observation which must be made is that there was a scarcity of clerical services to the faithful, an inheritance from the medieval past. All these lands mentioned above were, in the majority, areas of late conversion or of recolonization; for a long time they possessed very large bishoprics which were suffragans of the Rhenish metropolitans. Some more recent diocesan creations, however, had diminished these weaknesses. Moreover the limits of the dioceses did not coincide well with political boundaries.

In Bohemia, the archbishopric of Prague, created in 1073, dominated a kingdom of two and a half million inhabitants. The recent creation of the bishoprics of Litomyšl, Litoměřice and of Hradec Králové began a failed reform which attempted to establish a bishopric in each 'circle', the equivalent of a county. In 1754 Olomouc was raised to a metropolitan see, while Brno became a suffragan bishopric of Olomouc and southern Bohemia gained an episcopal see with the bishopric of České Budějovice. Silesia was responsible only to the bishop of Breslau. Thus at the beginning of the eighteenth century, six bishops and one archbishop served a total population of four million inhabitants.

The situation was worse in Lower Austria which was dependent on the Bavarian bishopric of Passau. The see of Vienna only extended to the capital and its suburbs. It ministered to only 150 000 faithful in 1700, and to 200 000 in 1780. The diocese was spread over seventeen parishes including three enormous *intra muros* parishes. The bishopric of Wiener Neustadt was smaller still. Vienna, the capital of the empire, was raised to the level of a metropolitan see only in 1717 with Wiener Neustadt as a suffragan diocese. A part of Upper Austria owed obedience sometimes to the archbishop of Salzburg, a prince of the Holy Roman Empire, and sometimes to the patriarch of Aquileia, which is to say the Republic of Venice.

In general terms we can say that at the start of the eighteenth century there was one bishop for every 500 000 inhabitants in the twelve dioceses of the Hereditary Lands. Eighteenth-century diocesan creations did not keep pace with strong demographic growth, however: three episcopal seats were added although the population increased by fifty per cent. The situation had worsened in fact to the point when there was one bishop for 800 000 inhabitants, but this is only figurative since the dioceses were uneven in size.

The relatively small size of the episcopacy was balanced by a significant number of prelates in charge of *collegiales* (collegiate churches) and in cathedral chapters. The cathedral of St Stephen of Vienna included eighteen canons, fourteen nominated by the emperor who chose the successful candidates from aristocratic families. Noble sons destined for the church followed a veritable *cursus honorum*: studies at Rome in the *Collegium Germanicum*, a benefice and then a canonry at Passau, Salzburg, Trent, Vienna or Prague. The most fortunate were placed in charge of a small diocese such as Lavant or Gurk where they acquired knowledge of ecclesiastical administration. With a little luck they might be elected by their peers to head a large diocese. According to German custom, the bishop was elected by the canons who chose one of their own so that in reality the episcopacy was in the hands of the aristocracy. The Habsburgs could discreetly put pressure on the canons, but if they wished to elect a family candidate the individual had to be named a canon first, like Archduke Leopold-William at Breslau. This system guaranteed a certain independence of the episcopacy in relation to the dynasty and the state.

A rigorously enforced requirement excluded commoners from cathedral chapters. Any misalliance in the female line of a family mercilessly excluded an aspirant since sixteen quarters of nobility were required to be eligible. The most notable prelates were recruited from the Thun, Auersperg, Firmian, Harrach, Wallenstein, Kollonitz, Schaffgotsch, and Trautson families, all belonging to the *Herrenstand*, to governmental circles and to the richest noble houses. Cardinal Migazzi, archbishop of Vienna from 1757 to 1786, seemed somewhat outclassed although he came from good Tyrolean noble stock: he owed his success to the protection of Maria Theresa, to his reforming ideas and to the premature death of his predecessor. In Austria as in Bohemia bishops, canons and prelates formed a group closely linked to the high aristocracy which thus found a means of extending its influence and increasing its wealth. If we count on average a dozen canons in each cathedral chapter we are in the presence of a group of at least 200 individuals, that is one member of the high secular clergy for every thirty to fifty thousand inhabitants.

In this context one must consider also the abbots and priors of the religious orders who sat in the Estates on the prelatial benches. They were recruited in a more democratic manner; the great Benedictine and Premonstratensian houses were not only confined to nobles. The heads of the great monastic foundations displayed, nonetheless, attitudes typical of feudal seigneurs because of the importance of the landed property they administered; they numbered about fifty.

However, a crucial difficulty for the church lay in the staffing of parishes which were both too large and ill-served. Let us take the example of Vienna. The city proper inside the fortifications, containing 100 000 inhabitants in

1680, possessed only three parishes: St Stephen's Cathedral, St Michael's church, served by thirty Barnabites, and the church served by the Benedictines of the Scottish Convent. Eighteen cathedral canons, some ten secular priests and forty conventuals provided a total of seventy priests, or at the best, one priest for every thousand inhabitants. Each suburb had a parish church. After 1740 the collegiate church of St Peter added some ten secular priests, thus slightly compensating for the growth of population. By this time the capital numbered 175 000 inhabitants.

Much graver was the lack of parish clergy outside Vienna. In Bohemia at the end of the seventeenth century, seventy-five rural parishes lacked priests, despite the *Reformation* edicts which had promoted the reconstruction of 368 parishes since 1637. Despite the efforts of successive governments and Estates, twenty per cent of the parishes lacked priests. The efficiency of a Commission of Enquiry instituted by the Estates was hindered by a lack of cooperation on the part of Catholic seigneurs responsible for these parishes, who did not respond to the Commission in sixty per cent of the cases. The issue was usurped property, tithes and lands, the revenues of which would have permitted the maintenance of a priest and a vicar. A parish could only maintain a priest if it had sufficient resources to assure him a decent existence, much superior to that of the peasant and comparable to that of the gentry. It was not merely a question of comfort for the priest but one of prestige in the eyes of the population. Ill-provided parishes did not keep well-educated priests, and if the incumbent wished to levy surplice fees he soon lost the confidence of the faithful, especially of the newly converted. The clergy was beneficed but its properties and revenues had been usurped. The Catholic aristocrats of Bohemia, even the great convents holding such benefices, were unwilling to restore the property confiscated by their predecessors.

For this reason services of the regular clergy were indispensable. The Jesuits and the Capuchins made up for any loss of zeal or for the absence of secular clergy. Vienna was dominated by the regulars, for if the capital counted only three parishes *intra muros*, it possessed thirty-three churches and forty-seven chapels – in all 200 religious edifices on the present territory of the city – the number of convents having almost doubled between 1683 and 1760. Due to this reinforcement there was one priest for every 500 inhabitants rather than one per 1000. The predominance of the regulars resulted from the shortage of secular priests, but after 1650 the preponderance of the former contributed to a decline in vocations among the seculars since all prebends and endowments had been engrossed by the religious orders.

The success of the Counter-Reformation only accentuated the advantage of the regular clergy. In the face of danger Ferdinand I had done what he could to save the great abbeys, but above all he called upon the Jesuits who achieved a dominant position in the religious life of both Bohemia and Austria. They shaped baroque piety and what has been called Jansenism, which in an

Austrian eighteenth-century context means little more than a current of opposition to the Jesuits. For example, in 1700 the Jesuits possessed in the kingdom of Bohemia eight colleges (Prague in both the Old and New Towns, Kutná Hora, Hradec Králové, Kladsko, Bustnitz and Těšín), eight residences, a school and seminary in Prague Old Town and another seminary at Krumlov. The Habsburgs also favoured the introduction of Italian orders which literally colonized the city of Vienna and gave Austrian piety its special character. Subsequently, the bishops encouraged the multiplication of convents and assisted the contemplative orders as well as those engaged in pastoral work, preaching or teaching.

In the capital, the decisive turning point came in 1683 with the siege by the Turks. On the one hand, the preacher Abraham of Sancta Clara called upon the terror-stricken Viennese to repent, while on the other, the euphoria of victory over the Ottoman army and the need for reconstruction led to a multiplication of churches in the suburbs and religious houses in the city centre. In 1640 Vienna had three nunneries and seven male convents *extra muros*; by 1683 the capital had fifteen convents – eight of men and seven of women in the same area. At mid-century there were thirty religious houses within the ramparts, ten outside. The older orders had come from southern Germany, the newer ones from Italy. Among the latter were the Capuchins, who had thirty convents in Bohemia in 1782, the Carmelites, the Servites, the Piarists and, of course, the Jesuits. Founded at Rome in 1621 the Piarists established themselves at Vienna in 1697 and were concerned with the teaching of youth. They spread in the eighteenth century establishing three provinces: Austria, Bohemia-Moravia and Hungary. A stroke of good fortune, the suppression of the Jesuits, allowed the order to replace them in the majority of their colleges. The religious orders of women made special progress after 1638: the Carmelites, the Ursulines (specializing in the education of girls), the Institute of English Ladies (founded by Mary Ward in the seventeenth century) who also busied themselves with the education of the young, as did the Salesians (Order of the Visitation) who established a house at Vienna on the Rennweg in 1717, and the Daughters of Saint Elizabeth who were concerned with works of charity.

Austrian Catholicism was still most deeply marked by the Jesuits. Invited by Ferdinand I in the middle of the sixteenth century they established themselves at Vienna, Prague and Innsbruck. In the *Collegium Germanicum* in Rome, they trained hundreds of noble canons including all the archbishops of Vienna from 1630 to 1804. Their colleges and schools in Vienna, Graz, Linz, Klagenfurt, Innsbruck and Prague exercised a marked influence on the sons of the nobility. Moreover, they controlled the faculties of philosophy and theology and the Universities of Vienna, Prague, Graz, and Innsbruck. Their impact on the social elite was profound, due also to their activity as confessors and preachers, but they turned their attention to the masses by organizing missions and Marian congregations. In addition they served as almoners to the troops, prisoners, and those infected by disease.

The older orders, less useful in the activities of the Counter-Reformation but profoundly rooted in feudal society, were not neglected. In Austria, it was vital to consolidate the positions challenged in the sixteenth century, but in Bohemia, it was necessary to reconstruct the communities destroyed by the Hussite wars. The Benedictines reestablished six male convents (Břevnov, Rájhrad, Sázava, St Nicholas in Prague Old Town and Emmaüs at New Town, and St John of the Rock) and a convent of women, the abbey of St George of Prague. The Premonstratensians reconstructed their house at Strahov in the suburbs of Prague and six other convents. The Cistercians rebuilt nine convents, the Dominicans reconstituted a province from 1604 and possessed six convents in 1700 (St Egidius at Prague Old Town, St Mary Magdalen in Prague's Little Quarter, at České Budějovice, Plzeň, Litoměřice, and St Ann in Prague Old Town). The Franciscans, less ravaged by the Hussite wars, possessed eighteen convents in the eighteenth century, among them St James and St Agnes at Prague Old Town, St Clare at Cheb and at Litoměřice.

The majority of these foundations did not have a charitable purpose; they were primarily contemplative orders or were oriented towards the reconversion of those who had abandoned Catholicism. We are still in the presence of a combative Catholicism aiming to recapture souls. The majority of these orders received endowments for the saying of masses (quite rare among the Germans but more numerous among the Italians) or for pastoral action like the foundation of the church of St Peter of Vienna. Joachim von Schwander, a banker and government councillor, endowed seven benefices in favour of secular priests charged with pastoral care, the administration of the foundation being conferred on the Confraternity of the Holy Sacrament.

For these reasons, despite the preoccupations of Kollonitz, poor relief in Vienna remained in the hands of individuals. The civil hospital, *Bürgerspital*, founded in 1280, was transferred to the city in 1529 and belonged to the bishopric. In the eighteenth century the authorities began to separate the poor from the sick. In 1693 the Emperor himself established a general hospital (*Allgemeines Krankenhaus*) in a suburb of Vienna in order to care for crippled soldiers: this home for wounded veterans became by 1733 an architectural complex capable of housing 5000 individuals. After 1752 it was joined to the hospital of the renovated Faculty of Medicine, and under Joseph II the 'General Hospital' became a true hospital, and not merely a hospice.

In 1727 archbishop Kollonitz, nephew of cardinal Kollonitz who had persuaded Leopold to create the General Hospital in 1693, founded in turn a workhouse (*Grossarmenhaus*) in a campaign against poverty and vagabondage, while François Billiotte, personal physician to Leopold I, founded a hospital (*Armeleuthaus*) where the poor were cared for free of charge. Finally, the *Lazaret* consecrated to St Roch and to St Sebastian for the care of plague victims was transformed into a military hospital in 1766.

The church believed that by encouraging both urban and rural confraternities it could exercise a profound influence on the faithful. Thus the little town of Hardegg, in Lower Austria, possessed a Confraternity of the Holy Sacrament (*Societatis Corporis Christi*) founded around 1695 and suppressed under Joseph II. Priests from outside the parish were paid to say masses and to celebrate the Epiphany, Corpus Christi and the feast of St Michael. The confraternity had its own budget, fed by the modest subscriptions of its members who are mentioned in the parish death registry. Vienna was a fertile location for confraternities. In 1780 the capital counted 103; they aimed to introduce new devotions and also to watch over the faithful until the definitive triumph of the Counter-Reformation. Particularly exemplary were the Italian congregations such as the Congregation of the Immaculate Conception, founded in 1625 by the Jesuit Lamormaini, confessor of Ferdinand II, and reorganized in 1661. It was composed of pious Italians deemed worthy to belong to its ranks and survive on donations. In 1749, for example, it received from the duke of Positano a legacy of 25 000 florins. In 1775, it became the Congregation of the Virgin of the Snows. Another organization, the Confraternity of the Memory, active between 1690 and 1783, included Italians from every background, bankers, artisans and aristocrats who venerated a small statue of the Immaculate Conception in the church of St Leopold. The confraternity was rich (with 15 000 florins in its coffers in 1783) and paid preachers for each sermon.

The Catholic clergy was perfectly integrated into the feudal system, and this was both a source of strength and weakness. Ecclesiastics constituted the First Estate in each of the respective Hereditary Lands of the Habsburgs and took precedence over even the Order of Peers (*Herrenstand*), that is to say the aristocracy. Prelates were well represented in the diets and because of this participated actively in political life since the clergy furnished a third or a quarter of the administrators chosen by these assemblies. Abbots were *ex officio* members of the financial and permanent commissions of the diets, where they sat in rotation. To the extent that prelates furnished a third of this administrative personnel, the clergy enjoyed a role superior to its wealth and numerical importance even in relation to the aristocracy, which was by far the most powerful order in the Hereditary Lands during the eighteenth century. The financial reforms of Maria Theresa after 1749 tended to reduce the political power of the clergy to the extent that the orders had to agree to pay taxes for a ten-year period and could no longer discuss the amount to be paid annually as they had done before.

The political role of the clergy was based on landed wealth, the great reconstituted estates of Bohemia after 1620 and those of Lower Austria. In 1700, the Bohemian clergy possessed 7775 fiscal, seigneurial tenancies, or 12.3

per cent of the cultivated land subject to the land tax. This represented a tripling of its holdings since 1615 when the church held only 4.2 per cent of the taxable land. Ferdinand II, after the victory at the White Mountain (1620), donated to the church the lands confiscated from noble rebels to the value of three million florins. There were, in addition, gifts from pious donors. However, the Emperor refused to restore all the property which the clergy possessed before the Hussite Revolt. As a result, the church in the eighteenth century was no longer the largest landowner of the kingdom as it had been in 1420. Its place was taken by the aristocracy (*Herrenstand*) which possessed two-thirds of the land. With 554 seigneurial tenancies the archbishop of Prague held modest holdings relative to the 2000 of the Schwarzenberg or of the Lobkowitz. It should be noted that no parish priest in the archdiocese possessed land. The properties of the church were shared among the prelates (cathedral chapters, St Guy, 167 tenancies); the knightly orders (Grand Prior of the Order of Malta, 492 tenancies, Knights of the Cross, 185); the Premonstratensians of Strahov and the Jesuits (345 tenancies for the Prague College in the Old Town).

In Lower Austria, the extent of the holdings of certain abbeys was striking, especially of the Benedictine, Cistercian and Augustinian houses. The property of the bishops was also substantial in the region. Let us take as an example

Table 7.1. Abbatial and episcopal landholdings in Lower Austria

Geographic location and owner	Seigneuries	No. of tenants
Ob dem Wienerwald		
Sankt Pölten	—	621
Melk	—	852
Göttweig	—	1096
Lilienfeld	—	1492
Herzogenburg	—	826
Gaming	—	783
Bishopric of Freising	Waidhofen	690
Bishopric of Passau	—	1021
Bishopric of Regensburg	Pochlarn	361
Bishopric of Salzburg	Traismauer	438
Unter dem Wienerwald		
Klosterneuburg	—	1469
Heiligenkreuz	—	563
Unter dem Mannharsberg		
The Order of Peers predominates	—	NK
Waldviertel		
Zwettle	91 localities	1146

the Cistercian abbey of Göttweig, situated in Lower Austria, which possessed 1096 seigneurial tenancies dispersed within fifty kilometres of the abbatial church. Vineyards were favoured as a form of cultivation. Thanks to a *robot* (unpaid labour) levied on draft animals the abbey retrieved the product of tithes and field rents owed in kind to the lord by the tenants. The wine was placed in the cellars of the abbey; the crop gave an average annual yield of 36 000 litres. At the beginning of the eighteenth century, thanks to adroit commercial policy, the abbey was able to lighten its financial obligations amounting to sixty thousand florins, and to reconstruct the church and other buildings after 1718. At Melk, which had 852 seigneurial tenancies, the land was divided between vineyards and forest. Prelates needed managerial sense, even commercial flair, for Austrian wine had to meet Hungarian competition and was not always easy to sell. Vienna, however, represented an important market for building lumber and firewood.

On the other hand, abbots and prelates as lay seigneurs demanded service from the peasantry through the *robot*. As a kind of second serfdom the *robot* was a heavy burden on the peasantry in the eighteenth century. The edicts of Charles VI setting uniform requirements for the *robot* only worsened matters in Lower Austria, where the requirement was previously fifty-two days a year, whereas in the Czech lands it was three days a week. In Lower Austria, required labour could be replaced by a cash payment, and prelates often preferred money to the actual work.

The clergy was not particularly rich through collecting tithes; these were connected to the right of patronage which often remained in the hands of the descendants of the medieval founders of a 'cure of souls' or a benefice. Abbeys possessed the right of patronage but less extensively than lay seigneurs. In fact, the tithes were largely owned by the aristocracy and levied by their estate managers, and they represented a good part of their revenues. In Austria, the tithe was not a specifically ecclesiastical revenue but a seigneurial one.

In Bohemia, at the start of the eighteenth century, the lower clergy did not possess landed property, and its survival was precarious. Parish priests depended on surplice fees for masses and modest charges for baptisms, marriages and burials. The decision of Joseph II in 1783 to provide all parish priests with an annual revenue of 400 florins (*congrua*) was a measure of justice, first suggested in 1620 but never put into effect. Part of the product of the salt tax was destined for the parish clergy to compensate for the loss of clerical property confiscated in the Hussite period and never restored. The Bohemian State, always financially troubled, was incapable of carrying out this programme and Joseph II assigned the revenues of Jesuit estates, evaluated at 3 750 000 florins in 1773, and those of the religious orders suppressed in 1782, toward payment of the *congrua*.

In the eighteenth century the fate of the clergy rested on the good will, piety and generosity of donors. Countess Maria Saint-Julian, for example, reestablished the parish in 1694 at Hardegg, in Lower Austria, where the priest had lived in penury since 1650 among a community converted under duress in 1654. Now the vassals had to pay annually to the priest 250 florins, twelve measures of wheat and six of wine, as well as twelve cords of wood. In return the priest sang a solemn mass each Sunday in the parish church, and every week said two masses for the family of the counts. To that income could be added the surplice fees (three kreutzer for a baptism, seven for a marriage and six for a burial) as well as the product of the Sunday collection, which is to say some twenty-five florins per year on average during the first half of the eighteenth century. Church property overall produced hardly seven florins a year but by the end of the eighteenth century it represented only sixteen acres which the parishioners tried to expropriate for themselves. The priest, however, had to pay the village teacher part of the surplice fees and a fixed salary of five florins a year. The teacher was essentially responsible for teaching children to read and assisted the priest teaching the catechism. Educational levels clearly below those of Protestant areas very much preoccupied Maria Theresa. In 1774, a commission presided over by Canon Felbiger accepted the principle that school should be obligatory from the age of six; children were to learn reading and writing, although the state remained content to encourage seigneurs and parish authorities to open schools without taking on the expense. The task of inspection fell to secular priests amenable to the reform spirit, like Kindermann in Bohemia.

Until this time the clergy, with the agreement of the Habsburgs, controlled all intellectual activity in order to struggle against latent Protestantism or any other heterodox doctrine. This work was largely in the hands of the Jesuits active in the universities and the fields of censorship and publishing.

Until 1760 and the expulsion of the Jesuits the universities were few – foremost Prague and Vienna, then Innsbruck, Graz – and mediocre. They lacked a clientele of elevated social rank and high intellectual quality. The aristocracy sent their sons on the Grand Tour of Europe and sometimes enrolled them in Italian universities such as Padua and Bologna, while future prelates studied at the *Collegium Germanicum* in Rome. The Austrian universities were confined to the appraisal and certification of foreign academic diplomas (the famous *nostrification*) or to educating youth from modest backgrounds.

In Prague, the Jesuits secured by imperial decree of 10 November 1622 the fusion of their academy, the *Clementinum*, with the formerly renowned Charles IV University. They encountered a redoubtable adversary in the person of Cardinal Harrach, archbishop of Prague, who did not wish to abandon the monopoly of intellectual life to the Jesuits. In 1636, he founded a large seminary, the *Ernestinum*, and entrusted it to the Irish Franciscans who were suspected of Jansenism. In 1653, negotiations reached a compromise. The archbishop was to serve as the university's chancellor; the four faculties dominated by the Jesuits were to elect the rector, while the king-emperor reserved to himself the nomination of a superintendent. And the Charles University and the *Clementinum* were again separated. The latter remained under Jesuit control until the suppression of the order. The five chairs of philosophy and theology were held by Jesuits, but the society carefully saw to it that they were filled by good professors, among whom was B. Balbín, who published thirty-two books during his career, notably an *Apology of the Czech language*. In their way the Jesuits were defenders of Czech language and culture. Another professor of the *Clementinum*, Father Fischer, published a trilingual treatise on agriculture (Latin, Czech, German) in 1674. Neither the Jesuits nor the Catholic church in general wished to cut themselves off from the masses by being ignorant of the Czech language. As a result they were not interested in encouraging the germanization of the country. Thus the *Clementinum* occupied an essential place in Czech Catholic life until the reforms of Maria Theresa. The quality of the teaching carried on in Latin attracted foreign auditors. The students numbered, on average, 500 or 600 each year, mostly destined for the priesthood. As a complement to the *Clementinum*, the archbishop maintained a large seminary where the faculty was favourable to Augustinianism.

The faculty of medicine was of lesser quality. The professors holding its five chairs by royal appointment showed less interest in their teaching than in acting as doctors for the aristocracy. The faculty of law had four chairs prior to 1784, when a chair of public law was created. In 1752, Maria Theresa established a chair to teach history. The Prague law faculty was known as one of the best in central Europe, attended by nobles ambitious for administrative careers.

Joseph I tried to implement reforms, but encountered the opposition of the Society of Jesus; it was only Maria Theresa who succeeded in imposing a more severe control in 1752. A director of studies was named in each faculty of the *Clementinum*. Scholastic methods in instruction were abandoned and new courses created: patristics, church history, liturgy, oriental languages, etc. In addition, the monopoly of the Jesuits was broken, and secular priests were introduced into the examination commissions where the directors themselves were seculars. And in 1760 one of the chairs of dogmatic theology was conferred on a Dominican and the other on an Augustinian. Finally, the curriculum was modernized. A Jesuit, the first director of the philosophy faculty, introduced the teaching of the natural sciences. And in 1763 Seibt began to teach German literature, bringing to Prague the 'bel esprit' of Leipzig. From that time on, the curriculum was constantly modernized. After 1773 the new director of studies, Reitenstrauch, who was close to Jansenist circles in Vienna, caused the *Clementinum* to take another step forward. In 1784, Latin was abandoned as a teaching language in favour of German, a highly significant reform since more than a century would pass before the

Charles IV University gave instruction in Czech. The 1784 reform was the work of Joseph II, not that of the Jesuits. It should not be forgotten that Joseph Dobrovský, often presented as the father of Czech philology, was a former Jesuit. Another religious, Fortunát Durych, hermit of Saint Paul, translated the bible into Czech, and the edition of 1780 enjoyed the official support of Maria Theresa.

The University of Vienna also profited from the solicitude of the empress. First she reformed the faculty of medicine. A course was set up for the midwives and then others on surgery and chemistry. In 1749 she named Van Swieten *praeses facultatis* (president of the faculty) to introduce reform. From that point he began to modify the regulations by putting an end to *nostrification*. He founded a chair of surgery, reinforced the teaching of anatomy and succeeded in founding a school of surgery which in twenty years trained enough instructors to ensure competent teachers in the other medical faculties of the monarchy.

At Vienna the essential problems remained the Jesuit educational monopoly and the obstacles to new ideas. While Cardinal Migazzi, archbishop of Vienna, founded a large seminary, where the professors were favourable to Jansenism, a decree of Maria Theresa of 10 September 1759 removed the Jesuits from the deanery to the profit of the canons of St Stephen's Cathedral.

Secular priests, Dominicans and Augustinians were eligible as at Prague for appointment as professors of theology. At the same time, two new chairs of dogmatic theology were created, one for Augustinianism, the other for Thomism. This created a breach in the traditional monopoly of scholasticism. The posts were given to open-minded Italians, the Neapolitan Gervasio and the Lombard Gazzaniga. The latter, in his manual of theology (*Praelectiones theologicae*) drew his inspiration from St Augustine and St Thomas Aquinas and condemned both the excesses of Molinism and the five propositions of Jansen. These theologians were the defenders of the *sana dottrina* approved at Rome and spread throughout Italy after 1730. Thus Archbishop Trautson, the chancellor of the university, contributed to the reform of the faculty of theology by introducing the study of the ancient biblical languages and patristics. Father Blarer, favourable to Jansenism, was appointed director of the faculty to supervise the implementation of the reforms. He was aided by Dean Ambrose Simon von Stock, a canon of the cathedral and one of the chiefs of the Jansenist 'party'. However, the power of the church in the intellectual realm derived from its control of censorship, or more precisely from clerical influence over secular authorities who used censorship to prevent the circulation of Protestant works. In 1750, the Society of Jesus exercised a *de facto* monopoly over censorship, given to it by Emperor Ferdinand II. In 1550 the Viennese magistrates had lost their rights in this area to a commission presided over by the archbishop. Composed of Jesuits after 1620, the commission's existence was questioned in the middle of the eighteenth century. Civil and ecclesiastical authorities reproached the censors for ignorance, incapacity, prejudice and authoritarianism. In fact, the system worked well in its own terms. The commission, for example, enjoyed the right to search bookshops. A similar right was exercised by parish priests in the case of private individuals so that ordinary folk took care not to possess the bible or other forbidden books. They were content with almanacs and books of piety published and distributed by the Jesuits. The diffusion of heterodox thought was in fact difficult as long as the system functioned well. Any infraction of the law in this respect could lead to corporal punishment until 1733 and to a fine of three florins after that date. In 1752 Maria Theresa modified the composition of the censorship commission at the suggestion of Van Swieten. Three canons of St Stephen and four laymen were named censors, including Van Swieten himself and Martini, a law professor. One section of the commission dealt with ecclesiastical matters (theology) and another with secular publication. 'Belles Lettres', however, did not fall within their jurisdiction. The censors examined imported books but they were liberal on the whole as long as these were not written in German. No longer did theologians judge the merit of books on chemistry and medicine. There took place, therefore, a secularization of intellectual life even at the level of censorship, just as the reform of the universities introduced pluralism into higher education.

A rigorous policy on censorship was due to the presence of a crypto-Protestantism in Upper Austria, in Bohemia, and to a lesser degree in Lower Austria. In spite of the massive emigration of Protestants after the Peace of Westphalia, families and sometimes entire parishes remained deaf to Catholicism: in 1782 some fourteen thousand persons declared themselves to be Protestant in Upper Carinthia. Between 1740 and 1770, a generation of 'enlightened' bishops became conscious of the seriousness of the problem. They recognized the inefficacy of intimidation but also of the Jesuit missions based on spectacular effects, theatrical settings, fear and the evocation of the miraculous. Bishops trained at the *Collegium Germanicum* in the ideas of the *sana dottrina* hoped to use new methods, the pastoral efforts of the bishop, the catechism for example, along with gentleness and rational argument as methods of persuasion. The limited territorial extent of the bishoprics of Gurk, Lavant, Ljubljana, lent themselves to the new methods. Ignorance was seen as a major obstacle to the progress of Catholicism, and this in turn was tied to advances in education. The principal figures of this movement were Count Joseph Maria Thun, Count Leopold Firmian and Count Emanuel Waldstein in Bohemia (bishopric of Litoměřice).

The movement, emphasized today by Austrian historiography, cannot disguise what was the dominant characteristic of the church throughout the eighteenth century, a baroque piety in which emphasis was placed on gesture and ritual in order to impress and convince simple souls as well as to transmit essential truths. Moreover, there was less cleavage with medieval devotions than some historians have maintained. The accent was placed on the cult of the saints and hyperdulia. Jesuits and Capuchins favoured the adoration of the Blessed Sacrament, confraternities, processions, general communions and a eucharistic piety to which the Habsburgs were attached by family tradition. The orders stressed the Trinity in reaction to monotheistic Islam and the uniate heresy which was vigorous in eastern Europe (Poland and Transylvania). In reacting against Protestantism the Habsburgs also showed great devotion to the Virgin Mary and propagated the cult of the Immaculate Conception, to which Ferdinand III consecrated his Hereditary Lands.

Only the prelates touched by the *sana dottrina* or Jansenism condemned the forms of baroque piety. In a celebrated *mandamus*, the archbishop of Vienna, Trautson, emphasized the superior value of preaching for the instruction of the people compared to rites and ceremonials of a theatrical nature (1 January 1752). Count Spaur, bishop of Brixen, reduced the veneration of images. Count Herberstein, bishop of Ljubljana, criticized confraternities. Both were true Jansenists and in this were exceptional. More frequently, prelates were hostile to the preponderance of the Jesuits but once the order was broken they again became conservative, like the archbishop of Vienna, Migazzi, who once filled the Hofburg (Imperial Palace) with Jansenist confessors.

The faithful

The little that is known of popular piety shows how profound the action of the Counter-Reformation had been. Outside the crypto-Protestants and a small elite attracted to Jansenism after 1750 the bulk of the population, in Bohemia as in Austria, had been won over to baroque piety.

There is no study to indicate that Christians abstained from the sacraments. The registers of observance, compiled as everywhere by parish priests, revealed some negligence. The registers contain a margin of error from two to three per cent with respect to births because baptisms were entered after some delay, as, for example, at Hardegg in Lower Austria. This absence of registration is particularly inconvenient for demographers, but the evidence suggests that the Christian people participated in all the momentous rites of passage (baptism, confirmation, marriage and burial) without hesitation. As for Easter communion, it was so closely watched among a formerly Protestant peasantry that it became habitual. Failure to take the sacraments at least once a year was considered grounds for assuming crypto-Protestantism. In reality the nearly universally accepted doctrine of the time was Jesuit insistence on frequent communion. Here again the sovereigns set the example by receiving communion daily. The results achieved by the Society of Jesus in promoting communion were spectacular.

At the Jesuit house in Graz, a former bastion of Lutheranism, 45 000 communions were recorded in 1637, 85 000 in 1683 and 120 000 in 1765.

There was thus a steady progression unshaken by the *Aufklärung*. In Vienna, the church of the *Mariahilf*, served by the Barnabites, destroyed by the Turks and reconstructed by Prince Paul Esterhazy, distributed communion to 97 000 in 1733. This was a suburban church associated with a certain Marian devotion, and the number of communions reveal an undeniable fervour.

Piety also took the form of pilgrimages, in particular the Marian ones which associated a cult typical of the Counter-Reformation to this older and spectacular form of devotion. Mariazell was certainly its devotional culmination. *Magna Mater Austriae*, the black virgin of Mariazell, continued to attract pilgrims from Bohemia, Moravia, and Hungary, as she had done since the middle ages.

The gothic basilica of Mariazell, remodelled in contemporary style by Ferdinand II and decorated by Fischer von Erlach, was the destination of a *via sacra* which left Vienna, passed the abbeys of Heiligenkreuz, Lilienfeld, and the Annaberg, Joachimsberg and Josefsberg. In the eighteenth century from 120 000 to 150 000 pilgrims received communion at the shrine each year; in 1727, there were 188 000, in 1757, 373 000 (a jubilee year it is true), in contrast to 1960 on the eve of Vatican II when 165 000 communions were given. On the north bank of the Danube the basilica of Maria Taferl was located on high ground near Melk; a pietà, brought there in 1642, began to draw crowds. Progress was even more spectacular than at Mariazell. In 1660 there were 36 000 communicants, in 1760, a jubilee year, ten times more. Progress was steady: 71 000 communicants in 1702, 186 000 in 1751 and 250 000 in 1760. The most fervent joined in a single pilgrimage to the Maria Taferl, Mariazell and the Sonntagsberg. Even in the suburbs of the capital, at Enzersdorf on the north bank of the Danube, the eighteenth century saw the development of a Marian pilgrimage attracting 60 000 faithful every year. The image of the Virgin of St Stephen's Cathedral was the object of an aristocratic devotion developed at the initiative of the Empress Claudia-Felicitas who founded a confraternity. In Bohemia, the Marian cult developed after White Mountain, and was supported by the dynasty and the Catholic minority, which favoured at the same time devotions to the image of mother and child and to Our Lady of Sorrows. All social classes and both Czechs and Germans took part in these devotions, which corresponded to a need for consolation after the horrors of war, just as in Austria they met a need for protection against the plague (1679, 1713) or the Turkish invasion. In 1655, Bohemia counted two shrines to the Virgin; in 1672, twenty-six and by the eighteenth century, forty-four. The principal places of pilgrimage were the Virgin and Child shrine at Příbram and the chapel in Prague's Little Quarter which held a statue of Infant Jesus and was dedicated to Mary of Victory, symbol of the triumph at the White Mountain over rebellion and heresy.

Devotion to the Blessed Sacrament was associated with the Marian cult. Traditionally, the House of Austria was attached to devotion to the Eucharist, the sign of the real presence which was so vigorously denied by the Protestants. The sovereign usually participated in the great Corpus Christi procession held each year. Ferdinand III saw to it that the Blessed Sacrament was publicly adored in the city and the army. Numerous baroque poems celebrated the Habsburg cult of the Eucharist. Maria Theresa made her children attend mass daily, an inheritance preserved even by Joseph II. Through the aristocracy eucharistic piety was extended to the peoples of Austria and Bohemia.

Baroque piety rested above all on processions, grandiose in Vienna and the towns and fervent in the countryside. The earliest missionaries had insisted on the role of these festive retinues and the importance of commemorations. Religious feast days and Sunday rest were scrupulously observed. Frequently popular plays of sacred character were presented on these occasions at Jesuit instigation. A precise count of ceremonies and processions is difficult to establish. The *Italian Gazette* mentioned those involving the court, and they numbered sixty between April and November of each year.

The study of the distribution of religious monuments is less complex. We know that Vienna had thirty-three churches and forty-seven chapels. The study of to what saint or Virgin chapel altars were dedicated through the iconography of the reredos is also helpful. In Vienna, for example, Our Lady of Sorrows was gradually replaced by the Virgin and Child during the eighteenth century. Christ on the Cross or associated with Peter and Paul is found less often. The Trinity is an infrequent motif although each town possessed its votive column (*Dreifaltigkeitsäule*) constructed after the plague of 1679 or 1713. The most famous of these is still in Vienna, constructed on the Graben by Burnacini, decorator of the Opera, and a masterpiece of baroque art at once grandiose and tormented.

Among dedications to the saints, variety is considerable: St John Nepomocene occupied second place following representations of the Virgin. St Florian and St Sebastian were to be found next in almost equal numbers, then St George, St Leopold, St Roch, St Charles Borromeo and isolated examples of St Joseph, St Joachim, St Erasmus of Elmo. Among the altar pictures dominating the eighteenth century were the Virgin and Child, Christ Crucified, St Joseph and the Holy Family, then St Anthony and St John Nepomocene, St Theresa of Avila with the Trinity and St Leopold.

There were also many single statues, calvaries and niches which invited prayer or the sign of the cross. All urban and rural space (especially in Bohemia) thus had a sacred character. Popular piety was expressed in these statues. The rapid spread of devotion is best characterized by the cult of St John Nepomocene in the monarchy as a whole. Of fifty-four statues raised in the diocese of Vienna, thirty-one were in honour of this saint; all were created after 1700, most between 1720 and 1740 at the time of the beatification of the celebrated Prague canon. Regarded as a martyr of the confessional, he was thought to exercise thaumaturgic virtues and to shield the faithful against fire and flood. Among the remaining monuments were the Virgin (six), the Trinity (four), and Christ crowned (two).

Baroque piety was inseparable from the cult of the saints, mediators between man and God and rehabilitated by the Council of Trent in the face of Protestantism. Thus developed the cults of St Roch and St Sebastian, thought to protect the population against the plague. The church and the Habsburgs promoted the cult of the Holy Kings, medieval princes who had favoured the extension or introduction of Christianity, which closely linked together Catholicism, the national dynasty and local patriotism. In Lower Austria it was the Margrave Leopold, buried at Klosterneuburg. In Bohemia it was Duke Wenceslas and his grandmother Ludmilla assassinated by pagans in the tenth century and thus martyrs for the faith. The relics of St Ludmilla were to be found at St George's abbey of Prague, those of St Wenceslas at Mladá Boleslav, the presumed site of his martyrdom. To the national saints was added St Adalbert, missionary and first bishop of Prague.

The Habsburgs tried to make St Joseph the patron of the whole monarchy but the Czechs imposed the cult of St John Nepomocene. Canon of Prague, John of Nepomuk was martyred at the end of the fourteenth century. His remains were said to have been thrown into the Vltava from the Charles Bridge of Prague. A member of the Catholic gentry, John of Nepomuk was always honoured by his brothers of the St Guy chapter who enhanced his image in opposition to another national hero, John Huss, the Protestant. The great Catholic families adopted him as did the peasants. He became a national saint whose cult was supported by the Jesuits. Charles VI obtained his beatification in 1723 as the church recognized a popular cult which it halted with difficulty. Martyr of the confessional, and thus a hero of Tridentine doctrines, he soon had a universal vocation which imposed itself on the Austrian and Croatian people. The statue of the canon wearing the rochet and camail and carrying the crucifix spread throughout the towns and countryside of the whole monarchy.

Baroque piety corresponded, moreover, to the deep needs of the rural masses. In a time when calamities abounded (plague, war, death) the supernatural world was a refuge for the peasants and at the same time a way to conciliate obscure forces. The church prayed for good weather and harvests and against hail. The liturgical year accommodated its rhythm to the needs of the seasons. Summer had to be devoted to the heaviest agricultural tasks and was scarcely broken by major feast days until the Assumption (August 15), while the autumn multiplied celebrations when granaries and cellars were full. In Bohemia, the church allowed pagan customs to survive: coloured Easter eggs were blessed, masks were tolerated at Advent, female masks of St Lucy, demon masks (*Krampus*) at Christmas and of course the carnival masks. At Candlemas, tapers were blessed which would be burned during storms to protect houses from lightning. In an even more curious custom, on the *laetare*

Sunday villagers burned a straw effigy of death in a ritual which perhaps went back to the Black Death. At Pentecost, the Bohemian clergy solemnly blessed the flocks. In Prague, the two most important festivals were those of St Wenceslas and of St John Nepomocene. Pilgrimages took place to the tombs of the two national saints in St Guy's Cathedral accompanied by the singing of popular psalms.

However, these rejoicings did not take place without disorder. Pilgrimages were sometimes occasions to carouse. The often led to a variety of profane festivities and disorders, in particular illicit sexual relations.

The serious minded, first economists and 'cameralists' and later *philosophes*, attacked religious festivals because they prevented artisans from working. The Jansenist elite seriously criticized baroque festivals after 1750 and briefly obtained satisfaction from Joseph II, who prohibited processions and pilgrimages just as he had suppressed numerous convents. However, the people remained deeply attached to these devotions of Mediterranean provenance. Although they had been imposed by priests of foreign origin, they were devotions which corresponded to profound needs and constituted a coherent whole.

History should not judge nor take a position on intellectual fashions like the rationalism of the eighteenth or twentieth centuries. The Austrian church found itself confronted by a colossal task around 1650, a religious reconquest in the midst of Protestant lands. The material resources available were slight and were even more reduced by the egoism of the upper classes. The church used efficacious methods with the support of the Jesuits, the Habsburgs and a not numerous but qualified secular clergy. The church marked the elites as profoundly as the peasantries, for the crypto-Protestants and the Jansenist minority remained numerically insignificant. The faithful, impregnated with baroque sensibility, were attached to a religion which emphasized the ritual gestures to excess, but nonetheless was a sincere and a deeply lived experience.

8 The Hungarian church

BÉLA K. KIRÁLY

In 1700 Mátyás Radnay, bishop of Pécs, complained that his diocese was short of 360 parish priests, and that he did not have a single candidate for the priesthood. In the diocese of Nagyvárad, 339 parishes were served by 500 clergy in 1556; by 1711, only three parishes had a priest, and when the bishop first returned to his see his situation was so straitened that he could neither reestablish his cathedral nor even begin a suitable residence for himself. Neither diocese was exceptional. In all Hungary only the diocese of Nyitra had been without a single parish under Ottoman rule during the preceding century and a half. Every other diocese had been occupied partially or completely by the Turks. When they were expelled, Hungary was a depopulated wasteland.

Sixteen years of warfare between the Osmanlis and the Habsburgs (1683–99), and Ferenc II Rákóczi's eight-year war of national liberation (1703–11), devastated Hungary. One a war between two hostile civilizations and faiths, Islam and Christendom, the other a civil war, they were fought with ferocity. After a quarter-century of turmoil, peace was restored in 1711 when the Habsburg dynasty and the Hungarian estates concluded the Treaty of Szatmár. To raise Hungary from the ruins required immense efforts in every sphere, spiritual as well as material. The most important ingredient for moral and spiritual reconstruction ought to have been tolerance, but it was the element most conspicuously absent from Habsburg policies and attitudes. Instead, the dynasty unleashed on an exhausted nation a prolonged campaign of the Counter-Reformation, which like its predecessor of the seventeenth century had failed by the last decade of the eighteenth century.

Among the lands ruled by the Habsburgs, only in Hungary (including Transylvania, a constitutional part of the lands of the Crown of St Stephen) was a substantial part of the population still Protestant by the eighteenth century. In 1550, the legislative diet of Transylvania passed the first of a series of fundamental laws making Lutheranism (and subsequently Calvinism) an established religion (*recepta religio*) equal to Catholicism. The diet of Torda in 1568 extended similar status to Unitarianism and proclaimed tolerance for all religious practices, making Transylvania the most lenient state in an intolerant Europe. This was the situation in 1687 when the Transylvanian estates again acknowledged the wearer of the Crown of St Stephen, Leopold I (1657–1705), as their sovereign. Transylvania was too valuable a base for military operations against the Ottomans to risk alienating, so on 16 October 1690 the king issued a *Diploma leopoldinum* guaranteeing the validity of all Transylvanian laws, including those securing freedom of religion. Freedom of conscience thus continued to exist in Transylvania even under Habsburg rule.

An equally anomalous constitutional situation obtained in royal Hungary, the heartland of the Crown of St Stephen. There in the early seventeenth century, immediately before and during the Thirty Years' War, the Habsburg kings, even while rooting out Protestantism by fire and sword in their hereditary provinces, the Alpine provinces and especially Bohemia and Moravia, promulgated laws on religious freedom passed by Hungarian diets. Matthias II (1608–19) in 1608 had promulgated the diet's ratification of the Peace of Vienna of 1606, which had guaranteed the nobility's religious freedom, the estates' right of habeas corpus, and the autonomy of the state. Ferdinand III (1637–57) had promulgated the diet's ratification in 1647 of the Treaty of Linz, which had extended the freedom of religion to 'subjects'. Succeeding monarchs reaffirmed these laws in their Hungarian coronation oaths, so that in the early seventeenth century Hungary was as tolerant a state as Transylvania.

As soon as the Thirty Years' War was over, however, the Habsburgs, relieved of pressure in the west and with peace on their Ottoman borders, turned their attention to domestic affairs. Their attempts to curtail Hungarian autonomy and freedom of religion soon fomented a *fronde* (1666–70) led by Palatine Ferenc Wesselényi, Count Péter Zrinyi and other dignitaries. When the conspiracy was discovered, its leaders were executed, and on 27 February 1673 the Hungarian constitution was suspended. The Hungarians' response was a general popular uprising led by another aristocrat, Count Imre Thököly. So successful were the insurgents that the dynasty was forced to seek a compromise. Leopold I's summons to the diet of 1681 signified the restoration of Hungary's autonomy, on which the Habsburgs were much readier to yield than on matters of religion. A very watered-down version of the laws of 1608 and 1647 was passed through this diet, restricting the Protestants' freedom to worship to just two localities in every Hungarian county under Habsburg rule. Since each locality was defined by an article of the law, they became known as 'articular places' (*locus articularibus*). The law was reaffirmed in 1687 and became the legal basis for the state's role in religious affairs in Hungary for most of the eighteenth century. War with the Turks resumed in 1682, but no sooner had the tide of battle turned and the Habsburg forces gone on the offensive than Leopold renewed his efforts to introduce absolutist government and further restrict freedom of religion in Hungary. In 1691 he issued the *Explanatio leopoldina*, a decree that purported to elucidate the earlier laws. It subjected all Protestant parishes to the supervision of the local Catholic bishop and forbade Protestant ministers from performing any religious functions outside the articular places. In a country demoralized and ruined by the struggle against the Turks, a normal church routine was out of the question. What was needed was a great missionary drive to re-christianize the nation, to bring about a spiritual renaissance. Under an intolerant monarch it was hardly possible.

The Roman Catholic church

There are no reliable statistics on the repopulation and resurrection of Hungary through most of the eighteenth century. The census of 1786, corrected in 1787, provides the only figures that are reasonably accurate within the limitations of the period. It has been estimated that the whole of Hungary (that is, royal Hungary, Transylvania and the Triune Kingdom of Croatia-Slavonia-Dalmatia, but excluding the military frontier districts along the Ottoman border, which were directly subordinate to Vienna) had a population of 4 100 000 early in the century. According to Joseph II's census, the population had doubled to 8 416 789 in 1787.

During the early decades Hungary gradually rose from its ashes. By the latter half of the century, it was largely repopulated, society had become stabilized and the church was strong and flourishing. The diocese of Eger, which had not had a single parish in 1699, had 353 parishes, 6 auxiliary districts and 125 chaplaincies by 1799. In 1787 there were 7 035 895 souls in the care of 13 263 clergy in royal Hungary and the Triune Kingdom. Each diocese contained an average of 280 000 believers and 167 parishes, that is, 1675 faithful per parish. At the end of the century the ratio of believers to each member of their clergy was 628 for the Roman Catholics, 632 for the Eastern Catholics (Uniates), 1377 for the Lutherans, 975 for the Calvinists, 758 for the Orthodox, and 589 for the Jews – an overall ratio of 700 to 1. By comparison, the overall ratio was 900 to one in Poland, 916 in Bohemia, 1078 in Denmark, 866 in England, 230 in Venice and 27 in Sicily. Hungary and the other states of east central Europe were thus on a par with contemporary standards in western Europe.

The basic structure of the Roman Catholic church in Hungary had been established by St Stephen, ruler of the Hungarians from 997 to 1000 and their first king from 1001 to 1038. He founded the archdioceses of Esztergom and Kalocsa and the dioceses of Veszprém, Pécs, Győr, Vác, Eger, Csanád (with its see in Szeged), Bihar (with its see in Nagyvárad) and Transylvania (with its see in Alba Iulia (Gyulafehérvár)), all of which were still in existence in the eighteenth century. To them had been added the dioceses of Zagreb (Zágráb), founded in 1093, Nyitra, founded in the early twelfth century, and in 1600 Senj-Modruš (Zengg-Modrus). The first monarch to make substantial changes in the system was Maria Theresa (1740–80), who in 1776 created the dioceses of Szepes, Rozsnyó and Besztercebánya out of part of the territory of the huge archdiocese of Esztergom. The following year she carved out the dioceses of Székesfehérvár and Szombathely from the dioceses of Győr, Veszprém and Zagreb. And in 1781 several church territories were consolidated after her death into the diocese of Djakovo (Diakovár).*

Until her reign the Eastern Catholic parishes had come under the jurisdiction of the Roman Catholic episcopacy. She set up a separate, independent episcopacy for them by founding in 1771 the diocese of Mukachevo (Munkács) in Ruthenia (transferred in 1776 to Uzhhorod (Ungvár)), and in 1777 the dioceses of Križevci (Kőrös) in Croatia and Făgăraş (Fogaras) in Transylvania.

The senior member of the hierarchy was the archbishop of Esztergom, who was primate of Hungary after 1279 and usually a cardinal. The primate was a papal legate, who thus communicated directly with Rome rather than through the apostolic nuncio in Vienna. In 1715 the primate was created a prince of the Holy Roman Empire, hence his popular title of prince-primate.

A vigorous and extensive monastic system had come back to life by the middle of the eighteenth century. In royal Hungary and the Triune Kingdom there were 152 monasteries housing 2302 priests, 274 postulants and 658 lay brothers – 3234 religious in all. There were another twenty-five monasteries in Transylvania. Twenty-four of all the foundations were Piarist, twenty-five Jesuit, eighty-four Black Franciscan, eleven Minorite, eleven Capuchin, eight Misericordian, three Servite, three Dominican, and eight belonged to various other orders. Twelve convents housed 274 nuns and 116 lay sisters.

The efficacy of the church depended above all on the spiritual, moral and intellectual standards of the parochial clergy and this was partly a function of their material well-being. In the early part of the eighteenth century, when missionary work was essential, the economic situation of parish priests was wretched. Benefices were in the gift of local landowners, who were theoretically obliged to build and maintain churches, rectories and schools, obligations more honoured in the breach than the observance. As Hungary was gradually rebuilt, it became clear that neither the patrons nor the episcopacy were doing enough to help the parishes out of their destitute and often degrading condition. The state was forced to step in.

As early as 1704 a royal decree ordered lay patrons to provide for the maintenance of the parish clergy. Other regulations sought to increase parish revenues by imposing surplice fees (*stola*) to be paid for baptisms, weddings, funerals and similar services. The bishops were ordered to turn back to the parishes one-sixteenth of the tithe. In 1734 patrons were enjoined to assign each parish between a half and two 'sessions' of land, to be cultivated free by

*For the location of the dioceses, see the map in Bálint Hóman and Gyula Szekfű, *Magyar történet* (Hungarian History) (5 vols., Budapest, 1941), vol. I, between pp. 416 and 417.

the local peasantry. A session (*sessio*) was the area of land, varying according to its fertility, that would yield enough to keep eight serfs and their families and to enable them to meet their obligations to lord, state and church. Glebes of such an area should in principle have provided the priest with sufficient tax-free income to live in modest but respectable circumstances. The diet of 1751 codified these regulations. By then the church hierarchy, with richly reendowed benefices, was living in great wealth, but the general lot of the parish clergy was still far from satisfactory. The average income of a diocesan bishop was 867 776 forint a year; that of the twenty-one cathedral chapters was 530 668 forint each; of the three Eastern Catholic bishops, 24 123 forint each; of the three Eastern Catholic cathedral chapters, 9150 forint each; and of the Orthodox bishops, 80 000 forint each. By contrast, the average annual income of the parochial clergy was 200 forint.

A 1733 enquiry, which had found parish incomes inadequate, held the bishops to blame for not taking proper care of their clergy. To rectify the situation, King Charles III (1711–40; Charles VI as Holy Roman Emperor) issued a decree on 7 March 1733, setting up the *Cassa generalis parochorum* (General Parish Fund) and appropriating 16 000 forint a year for it from state revenues. The bishops and prelates were required to make 'voluntary' contributions to it. Several abbeys were kept vacant and their revenues paid into the fund, as were all the fines for religious offences collected from the 'a-Catholics' (as Protestants were derogatorily termed). In 1769 Maria Theresa decreed that all future appointments to bishoprics and beneficed preferments were conditional on an advance pledge to pay into the fund one-tenth of the income of the benefice. Prelates already installed would pay in only as much as they had already pledged, but pay they must. When Joseph II (1780–90) abolished the monasteries, their wealth was transferred into the fund.

These measures by the Habsburg state appear to have made generous and farsighted provision for the benefit of the most important level of the clergy, the parish priesthood. The General Parish Fund was by no means an altruistic creation; the Habsburg monarchs dipped into it regularly. Only four years after he had set it up, Charles III 'borrowed' 50 000 forint for his war chest from the fund, almost its entire year's income. Once and sometimes twice every year thereafter the Habsburgs would 'borrow' from the fund, never repaying, or even paying interest on, the 'loans', which ranged from 10 000 forint to as much as 80 000. While the aim was undeniably to help the lower clergy, it was inextricably linked with the dynasty's design to tax the church.

The church in the second half of the eighteenth century was a flourishing institution with enormous influence on the way of life of the population, Catholic and non-Catholic alike. It contributed substantially to the intellectual life of the country, to literature, science and art. In contemporary thought, art and taste in general the predominant style was baroque, which was embraced by the church for what was to be the most intensive period of church-building in the nation's history. Churches, schools, clerical residences, libraries rose like aristocratic palaces; even churches originally built in romanesque or gothic styles were rebuilt, restored, enlarged or, some would say, disfigured along baroque lines. The large interior surfaces of baroque buildings afforded domestic and foreign painters and sculptors unrivalled opportunities to apply their arts and they did so in abundance. Baroque, well domesticated, appeared on every hand.

The hierarchy was meanwhile exercising considerable political power. All the diocesan bishops and the abbots of the major monasteries were *ex officio* members of the House of Lords. In the Lower House all titular bishops sat in person and all the cathedral chapters sent deputies, though here all the clergy cast only a single joint vote. The referendary of the Hungarian Royal Court Chancellery was a prelate. The Hungarian Viceregal Council (*Consilium regium locumtenentiale hungaricum*), the executive branch of the Hungarian government, included two prelates: the primate and a diocesan bishop. The primate and four other bishops sat among the justices of the *Judicum septemvirale*, the senior, appelate division of the Supreme Court; the other division, the King's Bench (*Tabula regia*), included two bishops and two nominees of the primate. The archbishop of Esztergom was *ex officio* permanent high sheriff of Esztergom county, and the bishop of Eger that of Heves county. After 1729 parish priests were automatically full members of the county assemblies.

The revival of religious life also affected secular society, aided in part by the establishment of numerous pious and charitable organizations. These included the Congregation of Mary for schoolchildren and educated adults, Holy Rosary societies for the poor, and the Franciscan Tertiaries for the devout. Catechetical congregations of laymen and women gave instruction in religious observance, morality and a Christian way of life. As a popular parallel to the 'apostolic' concept of Hungarian monarchy (see below), the Jesuits propagated the idea that Hungary was the *regnum marianum* (the realm of Mary) under the Virgin's special patronage. The cult of St Stephen was given extra impetus in 1771, when the gilt-encased reliquary supposed to contain the saint's right hand was returned to Hungary from the Dominican monastery in Dubrovnik (Ragusa), whither it had been taken in 1590 for safekeeping from the Turks. August 20 was proclaimed the saint's day and has remained the major national holiday in Hungary to the present.

The *regnum marianum* concept was more than a movement to inspire religious devotion among the masses: it also represented the Hungarian version of baroque political thought. While the idea was bound in the west with the concept of absolute monarchy, in Hungary it became identified with a church-oriented concept of estate parliamentarianism, strengthening the Hungarian estates' hand in the struggle against Habsburg absolutism. The estates saw the *regnum marianum* as resting on five principles: the king is Roman Catholic; he reigns with the advice and consent of the magnates; he resides in his realm, leading its intellectual life and providing incentive for commerce; he protects the privileges of the estates and the integrity of the counties; and he takes an oath to uphold the constitution. The baroque concept was a far cry from its western European counterpart but even in the seventeenth century its partisans had included such intellectual giants as the great orator, former Jesuit and primate of Hungary, Péter Pázmány (1570–1637), and the warrior poet, Count Miklós Zrinyi (1620–64). During the eighteenth century it was espoused unequivocally not only by the nobility but also by the urban middle class, both Catholic and otherwise.

Roman Catholic piety during the baroque period was pervasive. Lent was observed with particular rigour. Prayer books and catechisms were printed and distributed in great number. In 1750 sixty thousand catechisms were distributed in the diocese of Győr alone. Far more frequent parish visitations by diocesan bishops enhanced the quality of religious observance. Sunday schools for young and old were started, and the Jesuits introduced the custom of week-long missions culminating in a procession led usually by a local dignitary carrying a cross over his shoulder. Traditional places of pilgrimage were brought back into use and new ones set up. Huge groups of pilgrims visited sites outside Hungary, the most popular destination being Mariazell in Lower Austria. Calvaries were restored and many new ones erected.

In 1720 and 1733 Charles III decreed punishments for the non-observance of official holy days. With the consent of Pope Benedict XIV, Maria Theresa substantially reduced the number of holy days but made the observance of those left stricter. Joseph II further reduced the number of official holy days and tried unsuccessfully to do away with pilgrimages. These royal rescripts mirror the fact that in a half-century religious life had fully revived in Hungary.

The Protestant, Orthodox and Uniate churches

Hungary was very much a multi-denominational country: 48 per cent of the people were Roman Catholic, 17 per cent Orthodox, 15.3 per cent Calvinist, 10.3 per cent Eastern Catholic, 7.7 per cent Lutheran, 1.4 per cent Jewish and 0.3 per cent Unitarian. Though the Roman Catholics predominated in the country's religious and political life, both the Protestants and the Serbian Orthodox were considerable forces. Almost all the Calvinists and most of the other Protestants in Hungary were Hungarians, and they included a large number of the nobility and in Transylvania even some aristocrats. The Habsburgs' efforts at Counter-Reformation diminished very little the influence of the nobility in the county assemblies and the national diet, the cornerstones of Hungarian autonomy. In fact, the court had to enlist the support of the Protestant nobility to secure passage through the Hungarian diet of laws on taxation and recruitment, and in 1723 of the Pragmatic Sanction, by which

Charles III sought to secure the succession to all his domains for his eldest daughter, Maria Theresa. This need blunted somewhat the zeal of the Habsburg anti-Protestant drive.

Yet one of the most characteristic features of Habsburg religious policy in Hungary was the renewed effort at Counter-Reformation rooted in the restrictive laws of 1681 and 1687 and the *Explanatio leopoldina*. In 1731 these restrictions on the Protestants were increased and consolidated by the *Carolina resolutio* of Charles III. This ordinance issued on 21 March extended further the Roman Catholic clergy's broad control over the Protestant churches, placed Protestant marriage suits under the jurisdiction of the Catholic ecclesiastical courts, decreed conversion from Catholicism to Protestantism to be a crime punishable by the lay courts, declared mixed marriages valid only if performed by Catholic priests, compelled Protestants to observe Catholic holy days, and ordered that all official oaths, apart from those taken by witnesses in courts of law, had to be sworn in the decretal form, which invoked the Virgin Mary and Catholic saints and was thus unacceptable to Protestants. This last provision was intended to exclude Protestants from public office.

Maria Theresa reaffirmed the *Carolina resolutio* on 24 December 1742, and a whole series of anti-Protestant decrees followed. The archbishop of Esztergom was commissioned in 1763 to draft a project on the propagation of the Catholic faith in Hungary. The document he prepared became the mainstay of Maria Theresa's anti-Protestant acts. It included a ban on 'heretical' (i.e., Protestant) publications, a ban on those educated abroad from entering holy orders, a requirement that Protestants attend Catholic services before going to their own, the deportation of Protestant ministers who challenged Catholic doctrine, the enforcement of earlier decrees restricting Protestant worship to the articular places, enforcement of the use of the decretal oath, and a declaration that all the Protestants' remaining rights were to be considered valid only *ad huc* (*sic*). It contained a long list of Protestant disabilities, all of them invidious, some of them affronting. These abstruse restrictions on freedom of conscience were being introduced in Hungary precisely as the ideas of the Enlightenment were burgeoning in the west.

If any comfort was to be drawn from the archbishop's drab compilation, it was from his need to reiterate many bans that had already been in existence for two generations. If enforcement was still a problem in 1763, then many restrictions on the Protestants must have been imposed very spottily. Yet in many places 'illegal' houses of worship, even if they were no more than wattle and daub huts, were razed. So onerous were the administrative obstacles hampering such routine matters as the appointment of ministers and the repair of church fabric that extraordinary conviction was needed for Protestantism to survive. And survive it did.

Most of the Orthodox in Hungary in the eighteenth century were Serbs, Rumanians and Ruthenes. Ever since the successful Union of Brest-Litovsk in the Polish-Lithuanian Commonwealth in 1596, the idea had been entertained of persuading the Orthodox Rumanians of Transylvania and the Ruthenes of northern Hungary (Slovakia) to unite with the Catholic church. The idea was given definitive form by two Jesuits, Gábor Hevesi and Márton Szentiványi, who formulated a plan for union on the basis of the principles enunciated in 1439 during the ecumenical Council of Ferrara-Florence. These principles held that the pope was supreme head of the church, that only unleavened bread could be used for the host, that purgatory existed, and that the Holy Ghost proceeded not only from the Father but also from the Son. With acceptance of these principles went the pledge that all the Orthodox rites could be retained after union.

The first to accept union in Hungary were the Ruthenes in 1689. A *Diploma leopoldinum* issued in 1692 emancipated Uniate priests, their families, residences and places of worship from servile burdens and placed the Ruthene Uniate parishes under the jurisdiction of the Catholic bishop of Eger.

Soon thereafter the Transylvanian Orthodox followed suit under the guidance of another Jesuit, Pál László Bárányi. Union was first accepted by Metropolitan Teophilus at a synod in Alba Iulia in 1697 and was reaffirmed by his successor, Metropolitan Athanasie Anghel, at a synod there the following year. A *Diploma leopoldinum* issued on 23 February 1699 extended to the Rumanian Uniate priesthood the same rights as the Ruthenes. The union was given final form at a third synod in Alba Iulia in 1700, when 58 Rumanian prelates and 1563 priests acceded to it. A royal decree of 19 March 1701 placed the Rumanian Uniate parishes under the jurisdiction of the archbishop of Esztergom. Leopold I invested Athanasie on 25 June, though it was not till 1721 that he received papal investment. His see was transferred in 1738 to Blaj (Balázsfalva), which became a focal point for the religious, cultural and national development and aspirations of Rumanians both inside and outside Hungary.

The most politically significant group of Orthodox in Hungary was the Serbs. A host of 200 000 Serbs migrated into Hungary in 1690 under the spiritual and political leadership of Arsenije III Černojević, the metropolitan of Pécs and patriarch of their church. They had risen in rebellion against their Ottoman overlords and fought alongside the Habsburg armies as they drove deep into the Balkans during the war of the Holy League. When a vigorous Turkish counter-offensive drove the Habsburg troops back over the Danube, their Serbian allies followed them rather than face Ottoman retribution. A *Diploma leopoldinum* had guaranteed the Serbian immigrants religious freedom and autonomy within the newly liberated Hungarian state. By 1695 eleven Serbian Orthodox dioceses had been organized in Hungary. The Serbian Military Frontier District was set up in 1702 with the manpower provided by the immigrants. The Serbian patriarch, the spiritual leader of the Serbs in Hungary and their national leader until 1771, so zealously guarded the unity and cohesion of his people that he was able to forestall any move toward union with the Catholics, even if he had to resort to coercion or force on a few occasions. The only Uniate diocese that could be formed was that of Križevci in Croatia. It was so tiny – it consisted of only four parishes – that the patriarch apparently did not consider it worth the effort to extinguish.

The church and education

The principles and structure of Roman Catholic education in Hungary had been laid down by an ecclesiastical council in 1560, which had made it mandatory to provide in every parish an elementary education that would teach pupils singing, prayer and an understanding of the catechism. The earliest efforts at educational reform were undertaken by the Jesuits, who opened their first secondary school in 1586. In 1602 they had 400 students. By the middle of the seventeenth century they were operating twenty-three secondary schools in rump Hungary and four in Transylvania; a hundred years later the total had risen to thirty-six. At the same time there were twenty-three secondary schools run by Piarists, four by Black Franciscans, four by Minorites, two by Paulites, and one each by Benedictines, Dominicans and Premonstratensians – in all, thirty-six Catholic secondary schools. In 1772 there were 4145 elementary schools with 4437 teachers in the 8742 villages of royal Hungary; in the thirty-seven cities another 401 elementary teachers were at work. An increasing proportion of these were lay teachers.

Catholic colleges, known as academies, were opened in five towns, three of them by Jesuits. The university founded by the Jesuits in Nagyszombat in 1635 and transferred to Buda in 1780 had 134 theology and philosophy students in 1715. A law faculty was added to it in 1767 and a medical faculty two years later when the state took over its supervision and invited Protestant students to register. During the academic year 1792–3 the university had 281 students, 131 of them reading philosophy, 110 law and 40 medicine. Between 1771 and 1793 it conferred 132 doctorates of law, 186 of medicine and 146 of philosophy; 228 masters' degrees in pharmacy, 315 in obstetrics, 892 in surgery and 5 in optics; and 341 midwives' certificates.

Many priests studied abroad, mostly in the Hungarian colleges at the universities of Rome and Bologna, in the Pázmáneum at the university of Vienna, or at the university of Graz. In 1790 eleven of the nineteen Catholic diocesan bishops had been through the German-Hungarian college of the university of Rome and most of them were opposed to Josephinism, not least the primate, József Cardinal Batthyány. Parallel to the Roman Catholic system was an extensive and efficient Protestant school system.

At the beginning of the eighteenth century when there was an acute need for priests for Hungary's religious revival, there were only three seminaries in the country. As a result priests were ordained after only one year's training, so it is little wonder that their educational level was low. In 1733 a royal decree ordered every diocesan bishop to set up a seminary for his see. Teaching in the seminaries was undertaken either by Jesuits or Piarists; only the bishop of Eger staffed his seminary with seculars. By the middle of the century all the seminaries required four years of study, with courses in canon law, theology, scriptural exegesis, ethics, oratory, and inter-faith polemics. This last was considered essential to combat Protestantism.

Maria Theresa initiated a limited modernization of the whole educational system. Under the influence of the Enlightenment, secularization was central to her reforms, though a great many churchmen remained educators. When the Society of Jesus was disbanded in 1773, most of the Jesuits' wealth in Hungary was put into a fund set up to support educational reform. Two members of an Education Commission appointed in 1776, the reformers József Ürményi and József Terstyánszky, drafted the queen's reform edict. The *Ratio educationis* of 1777 imposed a uniform structure on all education in Hungary. Every village had to have an elementary school. All secondary schools, colleges and the university were brought under the supervision of the Education Commission. The seminaries remained under the bishops' control but their curricula had to be approved by the commission and only university graduates were permitted to teach in them. The country was divided into eight school districts, each headed by a lay superintendent, who supervised the elementary schools. In each school district, a secondary school and several middle-level schools had to be established wherever they did not already exist, and at least one teachers' college. Elementary schools were to give classes in the native language of their pupils. The secondary schools consisted of three junior, grammar grades and two senior, humanities grades, which were to give students a general education in Latin, history, natural sciences, mathematics and geography, a departure from the scholastic tradition of the Jesuits. On the college level, 'lyceums' taught two-year courses in philosophy and 'academies' two-year courses in law.

The reform diet of 1790–1 granted the Protestants freedom to offer the full range of education and a Protestant college system then came into being. Both Protestant secondary schools and colleges offered a higher standard of education than that in the rest of Hungary's places of learning.

The apostolic kingdom, the 'placetum regium' and Josephinism

The Habsburg dynasty had tried since the middle of the seventeenth century to consolidate its historically, ethnically and linguistically diverse realms, provinces and territories into a centralized, modern, mercantilist, unidenominational state in the contemporary spirit of absolute monarchy. The greatest obstacle to this was Hungary, because of its well-developed system of government through the estates in the diet and its multidenominationalism. Not only did the Habsburgs' efforts cause continual strife with the Hungarians but they also severely strained relations with the Holy See, because dynastic absolutism tended to increase the monarchy's control over the church at the expense of papal authority. The crux of contention with Rome was the doctrine of the 'apostolic' kingdom of Hungary.

According to this doctrine, the title of apostolic king bestowed on St Stephen by Pope Sylvester II carried with it both symbolic and real privileges. The symbolic privilege was the right to be preceded on ceremonial occasions by an 'apostolic' cross; his real privilege was to be a papal legate with the right to organize the church in Hungary, to confer benefices and preferments on the clergy, and to appoint bishops at will. These rights, it was claimed, devolved upon the heirs of St Stephen. The Habsburgs, as his successors, now sought to exercise these extensive powers over the church in Hungary as an ecclesiastical equivalent of the absolute political powers they asserted and repeatedly enforced.

The authenticity of the Habsburg claim was hotly contested. In Rome in 1644 the Jesuit Menyhért Inhoffer published his *Annales ecclesiastici regni Hungariae*, which alleged that the original papal bull had been found and that it bore out the doctrine completely. It was also sanctioned equally unhesitatingly in the *Tripartitum*, the fundamental definition of the constitutional structure of the Hungarian kingdom and the privileges of its estates, first published in Vienna in 1517 by the jurist and statesman, István Verbőczi (or Werbőczy; d. 1541). Though never officially promulgated, the codex was republished several times in Latin and Hungarian and acquired the force of law. It asserted that the apostolic sovereign was the supreme patron of the Roman Catholic church in Hungary and enjoyed all the rights of St Stephen. It was Ferdinand III who began to put heavy pressure on the Holy See to acknowledge his apostolic title and privileges. He was supported by most of the Hungarian bishops, who benefited by the custom that in Hungary they bore the title, wore the vestments, acquired the benefice and exercised the rights of their preferment immediately after their presentation by the king without having to wait for papal investiture. The Holy See contended that the apostolic title and the papal legate's privileges had been conferred on St Stephen alone and that, even had they been inheritable by his successors, they would have lapsed through long disuse. The papal curia strongly objected to the Hungarian prelates assuming office before investiture by the pontiff.

Leopold I carried on the efforts begun by Ferdinand III. When they continued to bear no fruit, he unilaterally issued a decree on 29 April 1701 establishing in practice the absolute power of the crown over the affairs of the church in Hungary. This decree became the cornerstone of Habsburg ecclesiastical policy for the rest of the century. Leopold's pious claim was that his decree was simply a benevolent fillip to the revitalization of church life in the newly liberated lands of Hungary. At the same time he assumed the titles of apostolic king and 'Refounder of the Hungarian Catholic Church'. His decree also announced that he would brook no outside interference in the reconstruction of the church in Hungary, neither by Rome nor the Hungarian diet. It stipulated that ecclesiastical benefices in the reconquered territory would be restored to their patrons only if the Turks had seized them by force, not if they had been voluntarily abandoned. The right of patronage had to be proved with the original deed by which it was established and reinvestiture was encumbered with a heavy tax. In the dioceses along the new Turkish border, one-tenth of the tithe was to be paid to the state. Another royal decree two years later, also issued without reference to the Holy See, ordered the estates of deceased prelates to be divided into three equal parts. One part was to be made over to the state treasury (*Kamara*), one part was to be applied to the needs of the church, and only the remaining third was to be disposed of according to the terms of the deceased's will.

All the prerogatives ascribed to apostolic kingship were exercised by the three immediate predecessors of Maria Theresa, but she determined to obtain papal consent to her enjoyment of them and to the apostolic title. Her overtures finally achieved the success denied for a century: on 19 August 1758 at his very first consistory Pope Clement XIII issued an apostolic brief conferring the coveted title on Maria Theresa and her successors. His patent recalled the Hungarians' gallantry in defending Christendom against the infidel and the deeds of János Hunyadi (1387–1456), voivode of Transylvania and regent of Hungary (1446–52), who won lasting fame as commander of the Christian forces that successfully defended Belgrade (Nándorfehérvár) against the Ottoman onslaught of 1456. The brief cited the bull of Pope Sylvester II (999–1003), who made St Stephen king in recognition of the merit he earned in propagating Christianity. He permitted him and his successors to have the cross carried before them on ceremonial occasions as a token of their apostolic work. From that time forth the monarchs of the Hungarians have been addressed on occasion as apostolic kings, but whether by right or custom is not known.

Apostolicity was closely linked with the *placetum regium* (king's pleasure), the right of a sovereign to ban the publication and circulation of papal writs not consonant with state policies. The concept was common to all of Europe but the Hungarian kings' handling of it had its own peculiarities. Its first known application in Hungary was in 1404, when King Sigismund (1387–1437), coregnant with Queen Mary of Anjou (1387–95), subjected all papal documents to his *placetum regium* – on the paradoxical grounds that it was his apostolic right to do so – in order to curb excessive papal taxation of the church and temper papal legates' unrestricted interference in church affairs in Hungary. The principles on which he acted were given more formal shape in laws framed by Kings Vladislav I (1440–4) and Matthias Corvinus (1458–90). Their enactments were republished in 1776 and 1796 as a reminder of their continuing validity. Maria Theresa herself noted in 1746 that the *placetum regium* was not a dead letter and had recourse to it in 1768 to ban continued circulation of the papal bull *In Coena Domini*, which asserted the Holy See's supremacy over civil power. Even the apostolic brief suppressing the Society of Jesus in 1773 was not allowed to be published in its entirety; omitted were its provisions for the disposition of the Jesuits' property, which was dispersed differently from what Pope Clement XIV had ordained.

Joseph II did not bother with apostolic rights. He based his dealings with the church on his belief in the divine and absolute right of kings to answer only to the Deity for their actions. While Josephinism was in full bloom, he thus issued more than 6000 decrees affecting every aspect of religious life even to the form of the liturgy of high mass. Josephinism has been too thoroughly examined to require extensive exposition here. Suffice it to say that Joseph II did not have himself crowned king of Hungary so that he would not have to swear the coronation oath and be bound by the Hungarian constitution. Instead he ruled all his lands as an enlightened despot and introduced in Hungary measures little different from those he took elsewhere. In religious matters his policy was both a success and a failure. His regulation of church–state relations in the spirit of the Enlightenment was a success that lasted until April 1850, when Francis Joseph issued a rescript abolishing the *placetum regium* as a step toward the signature of a new concordat on 4 August 1855. The concordat so extended the authority of the pope that it turned the clock back to the middle ages in all the Habsburg lands; but for two generations the principles of Josephinism had triumphed. However, in matters of detail, Joseph II's policies were such a failure that he himself repealed most of the reforms on his deathbed. He was a victim of the misconceptions that bedevil many a splendid rationalist who mistakenly believes that reason alone rules men and society. They fail to grasp the power of the irrational. Passion, tradition, custom, superstition are forces that can be disregarded at peril even in the most sophisticated modern society. Reforms, even the most benevolent, must take into account the irrational side of man. Joseph II ignored historical tradition and deep-rooted custom and tried to leap to a stage of society that eighteenth-century men simply could not accept. He failed because he was too far ahead of his time.

The transitory elements of Josephinism included the virtual separation of the church in his domains from Rome and the transformation of the church organization to all intents and purposes into a government department. As early as 26 May 1781 the *placetum regium* was imposed on all correspondence of the Holy See with Hungarian bishops, heads of religious orders, the foreign-resident abbots, and generals of orders with houses in the Habsburg land. Joseph II's most notable effort to reduce papal power was his order to destroy all copies of the bulls *Unigenitus* of 1713, anathematizing Jansenist propositions, and *In Coena Domini*, which his mother had already banned. Pope Pius

VI's visit to Vienna in March 1782, the first time a pope had crossed the Alps in three centuries, was to no avail. On the contrary, Joseph thereafter abolished the contemplative orders in his territories, closing down 134 religious houses. All told, 1484 male and 190 female Carthusians, Camaldolites, Clarists, Capuchins and anchorites were expelled. A decree of 10 October 1782 put all church revenues under state control and allocated a substantial part to the creation of new parishes. A survey ordered by the decree established the need for 950 new parishes and 559 new chaplaincies. The minimum revenue (*congrua*) for each parish was increased to 300 forint a year, in addition to which each was to have a parsonage, an orchard and the use of enough of the common land to pasture two to three milch cows and one to two horses. To meet expenses, the income of the General Parish Fund was increased by keeping vacant the archdiocese of Kalocsa and the dioceses of Nyitra and Győr and paying their revenues into it. Clergy for the new parishes were found from members of the dissolved monastic orders.

Once the state assumed responsibility for creating parishes and assigning clergy to them, it also acquired the liability for training the clergy. The diocesan seminaries were therefore closed down and state seminaries opened in Eger (soon transferred to Pest), Zagreb and Pozsony. One of the declared goals of state education of the clergy was 'the conquest of the hydra of superstition and ultramontanism'.

While the general principles of Josephinism were progressive, Joseph himself became so immersed in the details of putting it into effect that Frederick the Great dubbed him 'mon frère le sacristain'. And indeed some of Joseph's regulations were picayune – banning candles on altars, ordering the removal of ex-votos, and prohibiting the sale of metal votive gifts to saints. In some cases, putting his orders into effect was tantamount to vandalism.

The crowning achievement of the Enlightenment was the Edict of Toleration proclaimed on 29 October 1781. Joseph anticipated developments in Europe by this declaration of the principle of the freedom of conscience. In the preamble of the edict it was stated: 'All pressure that does violence to the conscience of man does great harm . . .; true tolerance emanating from Christian charity does the greatest good.' This one decree annulled both the *Explanatio leopoldina* and the *Carolina resolutio*. No longer required to take the decretal oath, Protestants were free to enter public office and Joseph appointed many to key positions. The concept, however, was still that of toleration. Many restrictive regulations remained in force and complete freedom of conscience was not yet the rule, but more than a century of Habsburg Counter-Reformation efforts came abruptly to an end.

It was left to the remarkable Hungarian diet of 1790–1 to reenact the provisions of the laws of 1608 and 1647 and so extend legal protection to true freedom of conscience. Indeed estate parliamentarianism, which fought tenaciously against Habsburg absolutism and enjoyed the support of a peculiar alliance between the Hungarian version of baroque thought and the nascent forces of the Enlightenment, finally carried the day. Hungary with Transylvania entered the era of the French Revolution at the end of the century with a system of parliamentary government by the estates in diet and real religious freedom both in the ascendant.

9 The Polish church

JERZY KŁOCZOWSKI

Before 1772, Poland joined to Lithuania with 730 000 square kilometres and approximately twelve million inhabitants represented one of the largest states in Europe. This period, however, was a time of a severe, many-sided crisis which resulted in the partition of the territory of the Polish-Lithuanian state between 1772 and 1779 by three neighbouring dynamic and developing states, Russia, Prussia and Austria. To engage in the long and difficult discussion of the causes of Poland's fall lies beyond the scope of this essay, but it is important to stress that the history of this great state cannot be viewed exclusively through the prism of this catastrophe. It must be linked to changes that took place gradually within Poland after a series of disastrous epidemics, invasions and wars during the early eighteenth century. Within the framework of the comparative study of Catholic societies in eighteenth-century Europe, this essay attempts to define the nature of Polish society and within it the place of the church. The discussion will be limited to the period before the first partition of 1772–3, since during the last quarter of the century important changes occurred which affected religion in Poland, but which are not relevant here.

In comparison with western Europe during the eighteenth century, Poland was more heavily agricultural and less urbanized. The urban population comprised only a small proportion of the total, most of which lived in hundreds of small villages and worked the land. Moreover, in many towns Jews were a majority of the population. 500 000 of a Jewish population of 750 000 lived in urban centres where they formed an isolated society enjoying limited legal rights and emphasizing religious and cultural separateness. Even the boldest eighteenth-century reformers drew back from demanding full equality for Jews, for the Christian and Jewish urban populations were two different and diametrically opposed groups. The most notable characteristic of eighteenth-century Polish society was the existence of a large nobility forming ten per cent of the population of the entire state and nearly twenty-five per cent of the ethnic Polish population. The nobility, of course, consisted of very diversified groups and included an aristocracy, owners of large estates, and masses of gentry who survived by working the land. The nobility, closely attached to the ideals of noble freedom and democracy, traditionally identified itself with the Polish state which it regarded as superior to any other. The nobility was in theory completely Polish due to the mass 'polonization' of the Lithuanian and Russian nobles that had taken place as early as the sixteenth and seventeenth centuries. The peasantry, the largest and least privileged part of society, was forced to fulfil burdensome obligations to their landlords. The nationality problem was especially complex in the case of the peasantry, for in addition to those speaking Polish, several million of them spoke either Russian or Lithuanian.

Significant socio-economic changes took place in eighteenth-century Poland. Difficult economic conditions during the first half of the century gradually gave way to an improving situation during the second half, as state income increased by thirty to forty per cent and a demographic expansion of similar proportions took place. Partition seriously affected the country which had emerged from stagnation and was developing economically. The resulting weakness of the political and military structure of Poland after the initial partitions was reflected in the level of military expenditures in the critical period 1788–90, when Poland spent 30 million zloties, and its strong absolutist neighbours Russia, Austria and Prussia spent 250 million, 180 million, and 70 million respectively.

In view of the weakness of the state, the existence of a relatively strong religious structure was of great significance for Poland, although the denominational make-up of the state was extremely complex. The Catholic church, representing a large majority of the population, had two separate organizations for communicants of either the Latin or Greek rites (Uniates). The strength of the Catholic church was enlarged at the beginning of the seventeenth century by the addition of the Protestant churches of the bishoprics of the Polish Rus, Przemyśl, Lwów and Łuck, which accepted union with Rome, but on condition that they continue to enjoy substantial autonomy. The Latin rite of the Catholic church covered the entire state and included approximately fifty per cent of the population. It identified itself with the Polish population or, in ethnic Lithuania, with the Lithuanian people. Hence, the Latin-rite church enjoyed a clear numerical superiority only in territories where Poles or Lithuanians were a majority of the population. It owed its strong position to several factors: its material resources, efficient organization, and its centuries-old tradition of cooperation with the state, i.e. the presence of bishops in the senate. The Catholic church employing the Greek rite was mainly of a Russian-speaking peasantry. It was poorer than the Latin church, and its lower clergy, who were allowed to marry, were less educated than their Latin counterpart. The political importance and prestige, moreover, of the Uniate bishops was modest, since they were not members of the senate. Before 1772 there were four and a half million Uniate Catholics and five to six million Latin Catholics. By contrast, the Uniates had a larger number of parishes which had developed relatively freely by comparison with the more limited parochial development of the Latin church.

In the early 1770s, there were approximately 4500 parishes using the Latin rite and 9300 the Greek. The network of Uniate parishes was especially dense in the southern part of the territories covered by the Eastern Church, in the area later known as the Ukraine. This parish distribution had great significance for the religious and political history of the region.

Other religious groups were less important. Within the framework of the Catholic church, it is necessary to mention the separate Lwów bishopric of the Ormians with its more than twenty parishes and several thousand worshippers. There were, in addition, more than 500 000 Protestants living mostly in the north-eastern borderlands. Several especially large Lutheran communities lived in the towns of Pomerania and in Gdansk and sixty Calvinist churches dotted the country as well. If one considers the presence of the Jews, a small number of Moslems and of Protestant sects in addition to the above, one can see a complex religious and national mosaic. Although the atmosphere of tolerance characteristic of sixteenth-century Poland changed for the worse during the second half of the seventeenth century and early eighteenth, according to most sources religious freedom in Poland was more securely established than in most other states.

The Latin-rite church functioned within this social and denominational context; it was the only church that we can realistically compare with the Catholic churches of eighteenth-century Europe. The metropolitan province of Gniezno included ten dioceses, mostly founded during the middle ages. From the fifteenth century, the archbishop of Gniezno held the title of primate of Poland and was the most important person in the kingdom after the monarch. It was a mark of his distinction that he served as regent during periods of interregnum. The archbishopric of Lwów, with six dioceses, covered the Russian lands and had a strongly developed system of Uniate parishes as well as 731 parishes of the Latin rite, although the size of the latter varied from 358 square kilometers to 100 to 200 in the ecclesiastical province's western regions. The diocese of Warmia was subject to Rome. The imbalanced structure of the Polish church in the size of dioceses and number of parishes is illustrated by table 9.1.

The network of parishes was denser in some areas than in others; indeed, in some cases it was virtually non-existent. Information on average parish size shows a substantial difference between the eastern dioceses where the Greek rite predominated and the western dioceses where parish sizes were relatively uniform. Parishes in the west were quite large, covering often a dozen or more villages, thus imposing a burden on villagers living several kilometres from the parish church.

The dynamic growth of the religious orders performing various social functions was a basic characteristic of the post-Tridentine church in Poland.

Table 9.1. Metropolitan sees and dioceses in 1772

Diocese	Area in square kms	Parish	
		Number	Average area
Ecclesiastical province of Gniezno			
Chełmno	6 700	175	38
Cracow	53 000	980	54
Gniezno	39 000	951	49
Livonia	40 800	22	1854
Płock	23 500	304	77
Poznań	28 900	500	58
Smoleńsk	15 900	3	5300
Wilno	231 000	403	573
Włocławek	18 300	242	76
Żmudź	24 800	98	253
TOTAL	481 900	3527	137
Ecclesiastical province of Lwów			
Chełm	18 800	84	224
Kamieniec	19 700	65	303
Kiev	65 900	30	2197
Lwów	30 500	150	203
Łuck	109 000	221	493
Przemyśl	18 100	181	100
TOTAL	262 000	731	358
Dioceses subject to the Apostolic See			
Warmia	4 200	76	55
Wrocław*	37 300	651	57
TOTAL	41 500	727	57

*Wrocław, which included all of Silesia, was part of the ecclesiastical province of Gniezno until the eighteenth century, although even in the fourteenth century Silesia lay outside of the borders of the Polish state. From the eighteenth century the diocese was subject directly to Rome. The tradition of the old ties was, however, very strong and the Polish side often stressed this fact during the eighteenth century.

Growth in the number of foundations and personnel continued until the tragic date of the first partition in 1772–3, a period which corresponds also to the suppression of the largest and most popular order in Poland at the time, the Jesuits. It is interesting to note that during the seventeenth and eighteenth centuries, the number of new parishes increased only moderately and that the rise was almost exclusively concentrated in the east. New monasteries were founded at a much greater rate between 1600 and 1772 by the great magnates and wealthy landowners who emerged comparatively unscathed from the country's general economic crisis. The process can be seen in table 9.2.

A break-down of table 9.2 by religious order shows that the greatest growth took place among regulars devoted to the active life in comparison with nunneries devoted exclusively to contemplation and the strictly monastic

Table 9.2 Growth of Latin-rite monasteries, 1600–1772/3

Year	Number of orders	Number of provinces of regular clergy	Number of religious houses	Number of members
1600	15	15	227	3 600
1650	20	24	470	7 500
1700	27	34	674	10 000
1772–3	27	46	884	14 500

orders (table 9.3). The mendicants maintained a clear superiority over the other regular clergy, especially during the second half of the century. During the seventeenth and eighteenth centuries, there emerged a strong group of clerics regular dominated by the Jesuits and Piarists. Of the orders, the Observant Franciscans, known in Polish as *Bernardyni*, the Dominicans and the Jesuits were the most significant in numbers and social importance. Over the eighteenth century the number of religious houses increased substantially as did the number of religious in the larger foundations. During the period 1700–1772/3 the greatest increase took place among the Jesuits, Calced Carmelites, Piarists and Franciscans of Strict Observance.

Table 9.3. The number of religious houses in orders of the Latin rite, 1550–1772/3

	1550	1700	1750	1772–3
Monastic orders	26	37	38	38
Canons regular	53	86	103	111
Mendicant orders	122	450	528	559
Clerics regular	ND	101	152	176
Nuns	31	111	ND	152

The network of religious houses covered the entire country; they were found especially in the western dioceses, Lwów and Przemyśl, where there was a religious foundation for every 350–700 square kilometres and one religious for every 15–30 square kilometres. The number of monasteries and convents was sparser in the eastern dioceses but taking into account the numerical relationship of parishes to religious houses, it is clear that the orders here too played an important role.

Tables 9.4 and 9.5 reflect a significant development for the history of the eighteenth-century church. The number of secular clergy of the Latin rite stood at approximately 10 000 in 1772–3, the number of regular clergy, 14 500, of whom 9185 were priests. Thus there were nearly as many priests from the religious orders as secular clergy, a fact which reveals the importance of the

Table 9.4. Number of religious in the largest orders of the Latin rite (more than 400 members) in the eighteenth century

	1700	1772–3
Observant Franciscans		
(*Bernardyni*)	1800	2359
Dominicans	1800	2093
Jesuits	1400	2330
Conventual Franciscans	900	1250
Reformed Franciscans of the		
Strict Observance	740	1341
Cistercians	450	456
Calced Carmelites	400	966
Discalced Carmelites	300	446
Piarists	ND	499

orders to the life of the church. Moreover, in ethnic Polish regions there was a balance between seculars and regulars with a slight advantage to the former, but in the eastern territories monks and friars were far more numerous. This is a striking fact since the number of parish priests in the east was much lower than elsewhere. Bishops of the Uniate church constantly complained of the scarcity of clergy in their dioceses. The number of clergy in the Uniate church stood at approximately 10 000, but their cultural and social prestige was low. The Basilian order, however, was an exception and formed a well-defined elite within the Uniate church. The episcopacy and the leadership of the Uniate church were dominated by Başilians, much to the irritation of the secular clergy who often protested against their role. The Basilians, established during the seventeenth century on the Jesuit model, grew rapidly in the first quarter of the eighteenth century. By 1772–3 they numbered 1225 members distributed in 144 houses. It should be stressed that there were many examples of cooperation between Latin and Uniate churches despite substantial differences. Members of the latter, for example, often participated in the activities of Latin monasteries and convents, and Latin Catholics took advantage of the services provided by the dense network of Uniate churches.

The strong position of the orders accounts for the continuation into the eighteenth century of the traditional conflict between the secular and regular clergy, particularly between bishops and the orders. Bishops frequently complained to the papal nuncio or to Rome about the regulars but at the same time they took advantage of the services monks and friars provided.

Table 9.5. The relationship of the number of orders and religious to parishes*

Diocese	Number of parishes	Number of religious houses	Ratio of religious houses to parishes	Average number of religious per parish
Livonia	22	24	0.9	4.1
Kiev	30	18	1.7	3.4
Wilno	403	228	1.8	4.4
Łuck	221	112	2.0	4.6
Lwów	150	67	2.2	4.0
Kamieniec	65	23	2.8	2.0
Smoleńsk	3	1	3.0	2.0
Chełm	84	27	3.1	3.2
Przemyśl	181	45	4.0	2.1
Żmudź	98	19	5.1	1.3
Poznań	500	79	6.3	2.0
Cracow	980	147	6.6	1.7
Płock	304	44	6.9	1.2
Gniezno	800	105	7.6	1.2
Włocławek	242	27	8.9	1.5
Wrocław	651	71	9.2	ND
Warmia	76	7	10.8	0.8
Chełmno	175	15	11.7	1.1
TOTAL	4985	1059	4.7	2.1

* Includes all religious houses, even those containing one or two members, hence the difference between these figures and those in table 9.2, which do not include very small foundations.

The strength of the church arose from several factors, not all of which have been thoroughly explored and analysed by historians. Economic factors were not of primary importance, for according to a register of landownership taken after the first partition, only nine per cent of the land belonged to the church as opposed to thirteen per cent owned by the crown and seventy-eight per cent by the nobility. These proportions were roughly the same before 1772. Since medieval times, the nobility had opposed the transfer of land into the hands of ecclesiastical institutions. The oldest and largest church holdings, those belonging to the Cracow and Gniezno dioceses, dated from the eleventh to the thirteenth centuries. In the later period of the church's complete triumph over Protestantism, the Polish Estates (Sejm), fearing that the monarchy might be dominated by a landowning church rivalling the economic position of the nobility, passed the Amortization Decree of 1635 which forbade the transfer of real estate to the church. During the seventeenth century local and national estates implemented the provisions of the 1635 legislation, although permission was sometimes granted for the transfer of land to new religious foundations. This was exceptional, however, and did not alter the existing situation.

Many of the new foundations, moreover, were established by the mendicant orders which depended more on alms than on property revenue.

For centuries the numerous Polish nobility (*szlachta*) reserved for itself the most important and lucrative church posts, namely bishoprics and cathedral canonries. It also exercised the right of patronage over a majority of parish appointments. However, the urban population also contributed to the organization of the Latin church. Many prestigious ecclesiastical institutions provided employment in the largest cities, Cracow, Warsaw, Wilno, Lwów, Poznań and Lublin. The churches and ecclesiastical institutions of the towns were in general better endowed than those of the countryside. Urban parishes maintained impressive church buildings, large clerical establishments, lay brotherhoods, hospitals and schools. Many of the houses of the religious orders were found in the towns. Thus during the seventeenth and eighteenth centuries, monasteries were often established in new towns in recognition of their civilizing role. In numerous older towns caught in economic decline the religious orders played a crucial role. Orders owned extensive urban properties which were exempt from municipal taxation and engaged in commercial activity. The expansion and increasing participation of the orders in urban economic life was a social characteristic of declining Polish towns during the second half of the seventeenth century and the first half of the eighteenth, and it coincided with the growth of urban Jewish communities which, though religiously and culturally distinct, were heavily involved in the economy. The economic activity of the church provoked opposition and protests on the part of municipal authorities who often protested along with existing religious institutions against the erection of new churches and monasteries. Frequently, the intervention of national and provincial authorities was necessary to overcome such opposition.

Research on the social origins of the Polish clergy in the seventeenth, eighteenth and early nineteenth centuries reveals that the majority of both the parish and regular clergy came from the towns. It was difficult for the peasantry to enter the ranks of the clergy, much easier for the urban population. Religious considerations, social prestige and the economic condition of the clergy were the principal reasons motivating those entering the church. In an agricultural society lacking a large and well-developed state bureaucracy, the church offered one of the few opportunities for a career. Whether the clergy was recruited from the most able and talented among the urban population or from among the lesser nobility, the second largest source of priests, is impossible to say. It is certain, however, that successive generations of the eighteenth-century clergy dominated the nation's intellectual elite and contributed substantially to Poland's cultural history.

Until 1772–3 the social role of the clergy, especially the regulars, expanded considerably. The Jesuit and Piarist colleges were particularly important in a network of Catholic secondary schools. The number of institutions doubled from 60 in 1700 to approximately 115 in 1772–3. A similar increase occurred among professors and a student body recruited largely from the ranks of the gentry and the towns. Curricula also were expanded and diversified. The Jesuits maintained the largest system of colleges and saw them grow from forty-seven in 1700 to sixty-six in 1772–3, although the Piarists with eleven colleges in 1700 and twenty-seven in 1772–3 competed successfully. Ten colleges came under the control of the university of Cracow, a place of learning traditionally opposed to the Jesuits. In eastern Poland the Basilians established ten colleges on the Jesuit model. It is interesting that they traditionally accepted Latin church students as well as Protestants and Uniates. The faculties of the largest colleges generally exceeded ten members in contrast to the reduced staffs of the smaller institutions. It is difficult to estimate the number of students although some sources suggest it was high. A contemporary observer, Jędrzej Kitowicz, noted: 'Children entering the schools, public, Jesuit and Piarist to be found in every city, are so numerous that some schools have more than 1000 pupils.' On the basis of available data we estimate that the number enrolled in the colleges rose from 10 000 in 1700 to approximately 30–35 000 in 1772–3. This reflected a significant quantitative expansion of education which occurred throughout the kingdom.

Gradual but important curricular changes took place especially during the 1740s and 1750s. A greater emphasis on the teaching of modern languages, particularly Polish, at the expense of the hitherto dominant Latin, and on instruction in history, geography, mathematics and physics occurred as a result of educational reform. In philosophy, criticism was directed against traditional scholasticism and appeals made for the use of seventeenth- and eighteenth-century philosophical writers including the popular Wolff, although teaching of modern philosophy still had to fall within the norms of Christian principles. The objective of reform in the schools was to produce the model man who was both a good citizen and a good Christian. Educational change also stressed the need of basic political reforms in the immediate future for a Poland aware of its weakness relative to the powerful nations surrounding it. Educational revision was not implemented easily because of conflicts within colleges and religious orders over its direction, but it was of great significance for both the state and Polish society. The Theatine order in Warsaw was the first to initiate the modernization of the curricula of its colleges in an effort to attract aristocratic students already familiar with new intellectual trends. As a small order with only two colleges, the Theatines were able to introduce changes more easily and thoroughly than the Jesuits and the Piarists. It is interesting to note that reform was also extensive in the Lutheran colleges of Prussian towns such as Gdansk, where the influence of the German Enlightenment was substantial. Of greater significance, however, was the reform carried out in the Piarist colleges under the direction of the celebrated writer and teacher, Stanislas Konarski. One notable achievement of the Konarski reform was the 1740 establishment in Warsaw of the *Collegium Nobilium*, a model school with a reformed curriculum designed to educate the nation's future political elite, although it had a small enrolment. The Piarists then proceeded to reform their network of provincial colleges through decrees of 1759 approved provisionally by Benedict XIV, in spite of opposition from some in the order. The Jesuits also undertook the reform of their colleges, although the highly centralized organization of the order prevented it from attaining the degree of innovation accomplished by Konarski.

Numerous graduates of the colleges entered the ranks of the diocesan clergy and the religious orders. Only during the first half of the eighteenth century did a system of diocesan seminaries on the model decreed by the Council of Trent become established. Of the thirty-four seminaries existing by 1772, eighteen were administered by the Congregation of the Mission known as the Lazarists (Vincentians), eleven by the Jesuits and the Oratorians, only three by the secular clergy. Bishops for the first time required at least one to two years of attendance in a seminary for all candidates for the priesthood, a measure which also reflected increasing episcopal control over the parish clergy. The recognized need for a more educated clergy led during the second half of the eighteenth century to a further increase in the education required of future priests, especially in theology. And W. Müller has recently pointed out that the Polish bishops of the eighteenth century were more highly educated than their predecessors.

Every large religious order maintained a system of education for its own personnel and allowed its most competent members to go abroad to complete their studies. From the end of the sixteenth century Italy attracted large numbers of Polish priests who formed the elite of the secular and regular clergy upon their return home. Of the 150 Polish bishops nominated by the papacy between 1786 and 1795, seventy-seven or 51.3 per cent had taken higher educational degrees in Italy, especially in Rome. This fell below the level of the seventeenth century, however, as many clergy began to take degrees during the eighteenth century at Cracow, Wilno and Zamosc, and this decline in foreign study applied to the religious orders as well. The tendency to remain in Poland reflected the improvement in the teaching of theology through the so-called general course of study and development of dynamic and highly select religious orders such as the Jesuits and the Piarists. Information on the number of religious performing professional duties in colleges and monasteries in 1772–3 shows that in Cracow, for example, there were 1000 religious involved in teaching at this level versus 100 clergy teaching in the university. Of the former 417 were Jesuits, 181 Dominicans, 154 Piarists, with the remainder scattered among the Basilians, Lazarists (Vincentians), Conventual and Strict Observance Franciscans. Thirty to forty per cent of the priests in the 'educational orders,' Jesuits, Piarists and Lazarists, were engaged in teaching, a proportion which was substantially lower among the other orders. However, many teachers in the orders received a relatively sporadic education which limited the possibilities of serious intellectual work. At the same time, the number of intellectually aware members of the orders grew continuously during the eighteenth century. There is evidence indicating that the changes which took place in education had an impact on the church; the pace and extent of these changes varied from period to period although gaining momentum in the second half of the eighteenth century.

A description of a clerically dominated educational system is incomplete without some reference to the convents of nuns where girls received training in elementary subjects. Poland did not have, however, congregations similar to the Ursulines who specialized in education. The one attempt to establish such a congregation, that of the *Prezenteki* in Cracow, led to the establishment of only one convent exclusively concerned with female education. Although it still exists and is the oldest girls' school in Poland, its foundation did not lead to the creation of similar institutions during the eighteenth century. There also existed a network of parish schools which had been developing since the sixteenth century but which fell into disarray during the eighteenth. The impoverishment of the rural masses and of the lesser gentry in the countryside caused the decline of parish schools. The tendency of the higher gentry and the aristocracy to send their offspring to be educated by the schools of the orders or by private tutors limited the recruitment of the parish schools to the peasantry and the lower gentry. The orders competed quite successfully with the parish schools for students, but the decline of parish schools during the eighteenth century was not as extensive as some scholars have maintained. Stanislas Litwak has noted that in the large diocese of Cracow, thirty-six per cent of the parishes maintained schools and this percentage may have been close to the national average. It appears that many thousand pupils, most of them boys, received elementary education in the parish schools.

Other factors contributed to the intellectual formation of the secular and regular clergy. Recent scholarly studies of libraries, publishing houses and literature provide better grounds for understanding the evolution of culture over the course of the eighteenth century. Many parishes had libraries usually with small collections while some monasteries had larger holdings of over 1000 volumes, and there were a few religious houses with collections exceeding 10 000 books. The Jesuit and Dominican houses in the cities had the largest libraries which were constantly being expanded by the acquisition of both Polish and foreign published works. It was not accidental that Bishop Jędrzej Załuski in 1761 bequeathed the largest library in the kingdom, 200 000 volumes, to the Jesuits. Moreover, the decline of the publishing industry in many towns during the seventeenth century led certain orders to establish their own publishing houses which nearly monopolized the trade in the eighteenth century.

From the period of the Counter-Reformation the Catholic clergy took its pastoral responsibilities more seriously and became extensively engaged in a variety of social activities. The Polish church followed this pattern. The religious orders, for example, were not only engaged in education but also in significant pastoral work. During the eighteenth century the social and spiritual activities of the Polish church became extensive and highly organized and exercised as well a profound impact on the social and civil cultures of both the peasantry and the gentry. Within the context of the parish, compulsory religious practices of all kinds became common. The records of eighteenth-century ecclesiastical visitors who examined the condition of parish religious life reveal that the level of observance was high. There also developed an extensive programme of popular missions conducted by the religious orders, especially the Jesuits and the Lazarists (Vincentians), although other orders also participated. Missions generally lasted for several weeks and were held in a central parish drawing congregations from parishes in the vicinity. According to a recent study, in one limited period of the mid eighteenth century, 169 of the 753 parishes of the Cracow diocese held missions. This means that over a generation virtually the whole diocese was covered by missionary activity. The Lazarists, one of the prominent missionary orders, maintained twenty-one missions in 1772–3, and each contained a group of missionaries who organized approximately a hundred missions over the course of a year. Between 1654 and 1740 the groups of the Warsaw congregation organized 169 missions; between 1744 and 1799, 336. The Cracow missionaries organized 495 missions between 1682 and 1768, those in Wilno conducted 240 between 1686 and 1763. The Jesuits who maintained statistics on the results of their missions have provided us with valuable data, as table 9.6 indicates.

The dioceses in which the Jesuit mission in table 9.6 operated included a dense network of Uniate parishes, and there is evidence that members of the latter attended the Jesuit missions. Missions could last for several weeks or for shorter periods during major holy days. The missionaries themselves preached frequently and heard confessions. In the latter, they were sometimes helped by the parish clergy. On a national scale, 800–1000 missions were conducted annually by the Jesuits alone and hundreds of thousands of confessions heard.

In addition to missionary activity, the clergy of the religious orders often devoted themselves to preaching; the Jesuits, for example, preached 200–500 sermons a year. Priests and friars also served as chaplains to prominent families and often assisted the parish clergy, especially during Easter and other important feast days of the year. The churches maintained by the orders often became the centres of cults attracting pilgrims from long distances. The most famous within Poland and among the celebrated pilgrimage centres of Europe was the Pauline monastery (Jasna Góra) Częstochowa. We know of other important pilgrimage centres, many of which have survived until the present like the celebrated Kalwaria Zebrzydowska, south of Cracow. The

Table 9.6 Jesuit missions in the diocese of Przemyśl (by college)

College	1767			1768			1769		
	Masses	Confessions	General confessions	Masses	Confessions	General confessions	Masses	Confessions	General confessions
Jarosław (St John)	6	1 540	90	10	1 807	36	8	1 250	12
Jarosław	14	6 056	56	11	4 680	50	18	8 195	25
Przemyśl	19	2 949	958	15	2 500	840	19	633	400
Sambor	3	600	ND	6	2 120	ND	45	23 870	ND
TOTAL	42	11 145	1 104	42	11 107	926	90	33 948	437

pilgrimage centres, even the smaller ones, required the services of large numbers of clergy for confessions. The hearing of confessions provides an example of the extraordinary extent of the church's social impact in eighteenth-century Poland. The Jesuits alone in 1770 heard approximately 100 000 confessions in the four collegiate churches cited above and approximately 2 000 000 in the eighty churches under their direction.

The activity of the clergy of the Uniate church also became more intense and varied during the eighteenth century. An impoverished peasantry linked to the land through serfdom made the parish church and clergy extremely important to the life of peasant communities. The pilgrimages, for example, organized by these parishes gave the peasantry their only real opportunity to escape from a harsh daily routine and see some of the outside world. Early-nineteenth-century descriptions of peasant pilgrimages often noted the excitement they generated among local populations.

In the towns, the residents were linked in various ways to ecclesiastical institutions so numerous in urban centres, although tension often developed between the civil and ecclesiastical authorities. The towns, moreover, formed the principal recruiting base for the clergy, especially in the Latin church. It is noteworthy that the Catholic population of the towns developed a collective hostility against a growing and economically influential Jewish population. Indeed, with the eighteenth-century decline of the towns, new and stronger antagonisms of a largely economic character developed between these two groups. The eighteenth-century church often elaborated on the dangers of an expanding Jewish population and encouraged conversion efforts. On the whole these were not very successful, although there are some examples of mass baptisms such as those promoted by the charismatic preacher Jakob Frank in 1759.

The traditional culture of the Polish gentry was heavily influenced by the church. In spite of the increasing social dominance of the gentry, their religious consciousness became stronger during the eighteenth century. The church and its clergy came into intimate contact with the gentry and influenced its members through the ceremonial rites of the church, baptism, funerals, etc.

We should not overestimate or idealize, however, the place of the church in the culture of eighteenth-century Poland. The church's most obvious contribution lay in the field of education where the intense activity of the century represented the continuation of a long national tradition. An assessment of the results of this effort is difficult to make and still provokes discussion. Future research must differentiate between short- and long-term effects, the latter clearly evident in nineteenth- and twentieth-century Poland. We must note the differences among distinct social and national groups as well as regional characteristics of the eighteenth-century Polish Commonwealth, which embraced those areas which are part of contemporary Poland or are now included in the present republics of the Ukraine, Belorussia, Latvia and Lithuania. Little research has been done in this area to allow for an analysis of socio-religious patterns during the last 200 years. Within this context, the place of the church in eighteenth-century Poland is necessary for understanding the *longue durée*, without forgetting the achievements of earlier generations from the sixteenth century onward.

It is also important to remember that the role of the Polish church was conditioned by other factors affecting successive generations. Post-Tridentine Catholicism in eighteenth-century Poland existed in a special socio-cultural setting shaped by the victorious gentry and its culture, often called the 'Sarmacka', a variation of European, baroque culture, and one of the factors which made Polish Catholicism distinct. There took place the 'polonization' of Catholicism which came to be identified with 'Polishness' (*polskość*) and contributed to a long series of wars directed against non-Catholics, Protestants, members of the Orthodox church and the followers of Islam. The cultural decline of the Polish elite during the second half of the seventeenth century was accompanied by a similar deterioration in the church in spite of its concentration on pastoral and educational activity. Even the Jesuits so prominently involved in education between the sixteenth and eighteenth centuries allowed the quality of their schools to slip drastically during the second half of the seventeenth century. There developed during the eighteenth century, however, especially during the 1730s and 1740s, a strong reforming movement within the elite and the church, a movement which is of great significance for understanding this key period of the history of Poland, the time of the Polish Enlightenment. Liberal Polish historiography of the late nineteenth century saw this Enlightenment as anticlerical and even antireligious. But this interpretation must be revised. Future research must clearly show that the history of eighteenth-century Poland should be placed in the context of what is today called the Catholic Enlightenment, for the Polish intellectual elites focused their attention on religious and ecclesiastical problems. Although this critique led to Deism for some, its basic purpose was to question the external features characteristic of baroque religion and the organizational weaknesses of the church. In my view the critique did not question the place of the church itself which remained a powerful force within Polish society. Advocates of the reform of the Polish church did so in a spirit similar to the suggestions for change made elsewhere in Catholic Europe, but adjusted to the situation and needs of the church in Poland.

There is no doubt that national and clerical elites involved in the Polish Enlightenment would not have developed as they did without the reforms that had taken place during the first half of the eighteenth century. In spite of the criticism directed against the church on a problem like that of the monastic orders, the reformers of the second half of the eighteenth century continued the work of earlier generations. Supporters of the Polish Enlightenment influenced the peasant masses far more than the social elites, and it was precisely among the former that there took final shape during the eighteenth century a religious culture formed by the pastoral activities of the Polish church which would endure with few changes until the revolutionary upheavals of the twentieth century.

10 Popular religion in the eighteenth century

MARC VENARD

When an historical problem becomes fashionable, the historian must be especially cautious. In the flood of publications, conferences and debates appearing in recent years on popular religion, we have seen an extraordinary contribution of new materials and suggestions for research. But the subject sometimes risks being submerged in confusion. This essay intends to help clarify the issue by indicating promising directions for future enquiry.

The subject of popular religion imposes two preliminary contraints. The first is a problem of definition: what is meant by popular religion? The second is deciding on a clearly determined historical period, in this case, the eighteenth century, in a question which in many ways seems to defy time and delights in the idea of tradition or even 'the immemorial'. Regardless of the ambiguities, I shall take a position on these basic points.

Popular religion: a problem of definition

The present collection of essays places the problem of popular religion in the context of Catholic Europe. Even accepting this judicious limitation, it is possible to consider the notion of popular religion in two very different senses, emphasizing either its social significance or its cultural content.

From the social point of view, the emphasis placed on the term 'popular' implies that the religion being studied is only part of a broader spectrum, a part, but in contrast to what? In the structure of the Catholic church one thinks of the distinction between clerics and laymen. Does not the word 'lay' come from the Greek word signifying people? Popular religion is seen as the religion of the laity in contrast to that of the clergy. This approach is common and often recommended by historians, particularly medievalists. But it seems inadequate in spite of its apparent simplicity, especially for the eighteenth century. Is it so easy to draw a clear frontier between clergy and laity? What of the tonsured clerics who remained *in the world*, lay brothers and the members of the Third Orders? Moreover, everyone realizes that even in a village the difference between priest and parishioner is equal to or greater than that between lord and peasant. In ecclesiastical language there are expressions revealing social distinctions among the people of God such as *vulgus, rudes*, etc. Rather than rely on ecclesiastical categories, it may seem appropriate to use broader social classifications to elucidate the idea of popular religion, but even these terms are no clearer than those such as 'common people', 'povo', 'peuple', 'lud' and others regularly employed during the eighteenth century. Historians must define the nature and distinctions inherent in concepts such as occupational status, economic means, level of education, social recognition and similar criteria, although all who have used them know the pitfalls. In brief, popular religion concerns the lower classes of society, those who without being necessarily the most deprived do not touch the levers of power, whether economic, political or cultural. If I were pressed to select a criterion, I would choose the cultural, given the object of our enquiry. I would draw within society a double line, between those who did or did not know Latin and between those who did or did not know how to read. We are no longer dealing with the popular above the first. But below the second, we are at the heart of the matter. Yet are the limits so distinct?

Clearly there is no definite criterion of distinction. But we should not speak of religion, whether qualified as popular or not, without saying *whose* religion, doubtless an obvious truth. I fear that the current vogue of popular religion, more generally the history of *mentalités*, may have caused us to forget the well-established distinctions of social history. Would it not be wise to begin to discern as best we can who the popular classes were, and then to study the concrete forms of their beliefs and religious behaviour, if we wish to avoid the anachronistic and the arbitrary in the definition of popular religion?

There is another approach to the study of popular religion, the cultural. The adjective 'popular' is used not only to identify the religious fact (the religion of the popular classes) but also to enter it from within to study what is in effect another religion different from the official, that is the religion institutionalized by canonists, defined by theologians, taught and watched over by the parish clergy. Here we must take account of the inheritance passed on to us. This 'official' notion of popular religion arose from the clergy listening to the laity with whom they dealt, whose beliefs they heard expressed and whose attachment to objectionable rites they saw affirmed. Popular religion existed, and the official church encountered it, if not as a fully articulated system at least as a mass of forms of religiosity which was not the 'true' Christianity which the church wished to establish in the face of popular resistance. The official church called these forms of religious expression superstitions, or often abuses or indecencies, and always in a reproving tone.

Leaving aside the militancy with which the official church regarded popular religion, this attitude of reproof was transmitted from the end of the eighteenth century onward and especially in the nineteenth to folklorists. But now the intent had changed. It was no longer a case of defending orthodoxy, that treasure of revealed truth, against the survivals of pagan thought embodied in popular religion and which could not be uprooted, but of gathering and protecting the treasures of a collective soul transmitted through the ages against the threat of the new rationalist and scientific orthodoxy. In collecting rites, legends, etc. of this treasure, folklorists were guided by certain signposts, oral transmission, cosmic correlations, etc. that they believed characteristic of popular religion. Today, we are still influenced by this approach to the point of not criticizing it. It appears obvious, for example, that the *curé comtois* who exorcized the caterpillars and the field mice ravaging crops in the mid eighteenth century was participating more in popular religion than when he led a rogation procession. In both cases he was merely following his liturgy, but the distinction between these two acts, already sketched in the minds of 'enlightened' parish priests before the end of the eighteenth century, became definitely established in the nineteenth.

We cannot use the category of popular religion, therefore, to characterize such and such a gesture or belief without ascertaining who used it and for what purpose. In my view the most urgent task for researchers is to ascribe to its author every statement on popular religion, to analyse the cultural distance which it implies and the testimony which its echo provides about the content of official religion. For such researches, the word superstition which for centuries is to be found in the ecclesiastical vocabulary might serve as a useful guideline, particularly since we already possess an effective guide in the person of the *curé* Jean-Baptiste Thiers, author at the end of the seventeenth century of a famous *Traité des superstitions* which enumerates both myriad examples and the ecclesiastical texts condemning them.

As a practical consequence of the double meaning in the expression popular religion, the historian wishing to examine its content must carry on his research in two directions:

(1) He must study and measure, as far as possible, the adherence of the popular classes to 'official' religion: their degree of conformity to what they are commanded to observe. And he must ask the questions: to what extent was there an interiorization of a religious culture and language imposed from without? What resistance was offered to contrasting *sollicitations*? This we may call a sociological approach to the problem.

(2) At least as a hypothesis, we can affirm the existence among Catholics of autonomous forms of religion, either accepted or tolerated by the authorities. These forms were complementary to the expression of official religion or existed hidden in the secrecy of individual consciences or in collective rituals. This may be described as the ethnological approach to the question.

These two approaches are not mutually exclusive, it is worth repeating. They pass each other on many cross-roads on which we are most likely to encounter popular religion in its most authentic form. Just as the official church never ceased recognizing and authorizing cults of popular inspiration, so the popular milieu made its own telling choices among the religious 'styles' offered to it. Sometimes we even encounter folklore generated by official themes and practices.

Popular religion: perspectives proper to the eighteenth century

As for the ethnological direction of this enquiry, the eighteenth century, as we have seen, offers particularly favourable possibilities for research. Zealous pastors, suspicious of any deviance, turned their attention to relatively stable societies whose habitat and basic structures had hardly changed since the twelfth century, as did the apostles of the *Lumières*, often ecclesiastics as well as doctors and magistrates, who began to observe their compatriots as though they were the natives of some distant land. On the other hand, the spread of written culture was favourable to direct testimonies coming from the people themselves. In a period of relative prosperity not far distant from the present, the eighteenth century has bequeathed a considerable collection of objects of religious symbolism, ritual vessels and iconographical material. A brief visit to any French ethnographical museum reveals how many of the displays, particularly of religious subjects, point us to the eighteenth century and the first half of the nineteenth.

The sociological approach to popular religion in the eighteenth century is affected by two viewpoints found in contemporary historiography. One directs our attention to the development and culmination of the Catholic reform movement carried on since the sixteenth century, because it is in the eighteenth century that the essential institutions of post-Tridentine Catholicism, especially the seminaries, the catechisms, the domestic missions, etc., fully yield their fruits. It is also the time when the churches, restored to their major task, are decorated in a style corresponding to new values and to baroque sensibility. In short, according to a chronology which certainly differs from one country to another, the eighteenth century is for numerous authors part of the 'ascendant phase' of a Catholicism which increasingly surrounds and educates the masses: what Jean Delumeau has described by the term 'christianization'. This has not prevented observations on the weaknesses and failure of the system, or comment on the slowing-down or even petrification of the reform movement. The studies in this collection on the eighteenth-century church reveal that this perspective predominates in the religious historiography of the majority of European Catholic countries when it turns its attention away from politico-theological quarrels and the intellectual evolution of the highest levels of society in order to examine popular religion.

The other perspective is especially French. It is marked by the revolutionary upheavals which, at the century's end, led to the explosion of the whole institutional and cultural framework on which French Catholicism rested. This explosion permits insights into the process of changing levels of belief to be observed in the religious map of France in the eighteenth and nineteenth centuries. Now it is the problem of 'dechristianization' in the twofold meaning of the term: first, an active and dramatic dechristianization brought about at the height of the revolutionary crisis, and, second, a *de facto* dechristianization revealed by empty churches and an indifferent or even hostile population already existing in certain regions from the time of the Concordat. This form of dechristianization became more deeply entrenched in contemporary France despite all efforts to reverse it. Awareness of this phenomenon has led to the questions which have preoccupied historians from Gabriel Le Bras and André Siegfried to Louis Pérouas and Michel Vovelle: what explains the sharply contrasting religious geography of France? How did regions once completely 'practising' change to zones of both fervour and of indifference? Was the level of practice really uniform and of similar degree from one end of the century to the other? What was the influence of temporal and specific facts on the attitude of populations, like the greater or lesser virulence of the dechristianizers of the year II, the zeal and the insistence of the missionaries of the Catholic Reform or the Jansenist position of bishops or clergy in specific dioceses?

Beyond these specific situations providing a poor explanation of the contrasts in practice and belief which emerged subsequently, it is clear that the lines of breakage and the uneven contours of religious vitality were present under the apparent uniformity of 'la France très chrétienne' and that disestablishment served to reveal them to the light of day. Thus, if the eighteenth century appears in some ways not to possess the key to this problem of historical religious sociology, it remains an excellent period for an attempt to chart the main outlines, if not the deeply buried sources, of the subterranean relief of faith, thanks to the abundance and quality of the documentation available. This is a peculiarly French perspective imposed by the abruptness of revolutionary events. However, why should this approach not be applicable to other countries where the contrasts of popular religious practice in the contemporary world are no less striking: when and how did a fervent Navarra and an indifferent Catalonia emerge? Why the red Emilia and the clerical Veneto?

I have noted on various occasions that documents exist for the historian wishing to study popular religion in the eighteenth century. The moment has come to make an inventory of these sources and to examine their potential for research.

Inexhaustible sources

Speaking of the documentary sources of any study on popular religion is artificial. As several recent books have demonstrated strikingly, the historian 'invents' his sources in relation to the problem which he is attempting to illuminate. The overview which follows has the intention, therefore, of recalling those materials which have already shown their potential rather than to make an inventory of all the available resources.

Whatever the interest of certain studies putting into question other types of evidence, written documents (printed or manuscript) are not about to lose their preponderance. In this domain let us recall the importance – for today there is sometimes a tendency to leave them on one side – of texts teaching the official statements of the church. How can one claim to study popular religion without knowing what the religious authorities expected from the faithful for whom they were responsible? The level of religious observance cannot be measured except in relation to required forms of practice. Provincial and synodal statutes should be studied carefully without forgetting, however, that they are repetitive texts in which it is not easy to know what can be applied to a special and contemporary situation. For example, is it certain that the increasingly numerous warnings to be found in eighteenth-century statutes against the suffocating of young children in the beds of their parents correspond to a renewal of actual outbreaks of such incidents? Episcopal letters, with precise dates, are without doubt nearer to the reality. Nor should frequently printed and widely distributed pastoral handbooks like *Il buon Vescovo* of Giuseppe Crispino, analysed by Gabriele De Rosa, be neglected. It would be valuable to discover whether these are derived from important common sources, notably the *Acta* of St Charles Borromeo. The same can be said of the manuals used by missionaries. As for the manuals for confessors interest has been stimulated by the works of Noonan, but we are far from exhausting their riches both on the psychological and the anthropological levels.

Of more popular character there are the catechisms. It would be desirable to extend over the eighteenth century and to the Catholic world the inventories and analyses of Jean-Claude Dhôtel and Elisabeth Germain. To these should be added devotional works which hitherto have attracted little attention. Since the eighteenth century there has been a common idea that this was not an era of great spirituality. However, the popular echoes of the major authors and schools of spirituality deserve study. For example, at a time when the idea of placing in the hands of the faithful a translation of the missal was ardently debated, it would be useful to collect all the prayers 'à réciter pendant la Sainte Messe'.

Since Gabriel Le Bras, the attention of historians has been drawn to documents verifying the religious activity of the people, especially the records of clerical visitations and pastoral enquiries. The value of visitations in the study of popular religion no longer needs to be demonstrated. Whether the work of the bishop, archdeacons or deans, this documentation records closely the realities of parish life. Its periodic character, moreover, permits a study over time. Such documents, however, must be used with at least minimal critical precautions, the first of these being the necessity of establishing the attitude of the visitor. A *procès-verbal* only reveals the condition of a parish and its members from the standpoint of the visitor. Moreover, within the continuing series of post-Tridentine visitations those of the eighteenth century are clearly distinctive. They were more methodical; the visitors used printed questionnaires, sometimes astonishingly detailed, testifying to increasing interest in the parishes. How many parishioners were there? How assiduous at services were they and how pious? What was the level of morality (i.e. what were the 'predominant vices')? What were the community customs, and finally what social services were available such as schools, hospitals and charitable works? Repeated from parish to parish, often imitated from diocese to diocese, these questionnaires provide information which can be used in a statistical way, like that to be found in the major enquiries carried out at the end of the eighteenth century in several French dioceses (Rheims, Bordeaux, Rodez, etc.). In contrast to the French visitations of the seventeenth century, those of the eighteenth give a general impression of routine sometimes bordering on negligence; visitors passed less often and in greater haste, sometimes contenting themselves with correcting written documents prepared by the *curés*. Does this indicate a slackening of diligence which appeared less necessary than in the early period of the Catholic Reform, or does it reflect greater confidence in the local clergy now better prepared and more easily kept in line? It would be necessary to compare from country to country the evolving typology of pastoral visits. What we know, for example, of the visits of Bishop Angelo Anzani in the diocese of Campagna indicates that in southern Italy in the mid eighteenth century they preserved all their reforming vigour.

From the minutes of the pastoral visits we naturally turn to the reports of *ad limina* visitations which are in some ways the synthesis of the former. The Italians and Belgians provide an example of their systematic use. This documentation has its own special character, but a survey of the recently published reports of the Lithuanian dioceses reveal an ample harvest of information on pilgrimages, confraternities and other aspects of popular religion.

Trials employed by the ecclesiastical authorities to control and repress are also useful. A rationalist and tolerant eighteenth century does not offer in the same way as in earlier times heresy and sorcery trials, which are an unrivalled mine of information on beliefs and behaviour through the interrogations of the accused and even more by the cross-examination of the witnesses. However, less dramatic cases can be just as instructive, like the trials by the *Officialité* (ecclesiastical tribunal) against priests accused of 'mauvaise vie', which permit us to see the real relationship between the clergy and the faithful. Also in the *Officialité* archives we find the cases of 'separation in body' used by Alain Lottin to reveal much about the daily life of families. It would be helpful to see extended to the eighteenth century the methods of systematic and serial statistical analysis being carried out by Bartolomé Bennassar on the archives of the Spanish Inquisition, a major source for the history of attitudes and morals at the level of an entire country.

Not all clerical investigations were repressive. Enquiries of canonization, especially when started soon after the death of the candidate for sainthood, reveal the reactions of witnesses in the face of the supernatural, and the same can be said, obviously, of the investigation of miracles. Here again, however, the terminology and assumptions used by the enquirer when interrogating the witnesses must be kept in mind.

Besides these secondhand testimonies, the archives of the eighteenth century do not lack direct expressions of religious experience both collective and individual. Among the first are the archives of the commune and the collections of the parish fabric: their value differs from one region to another, according to whether the control of religious affairs was in the hands of the municipality (as in Provence, for example) or of a *conseil de fabrique* (as in Normandy). In any event these contain the records of discussions and the lists of accounts, material on the texture of the daily concerns of local religious life, such as repairs on the church, purchases of liturgical objects, sermons, processions and festive celebrations, etc., of the same kind as in the registers of confraternities: well-kept registers, with the statutes laid out on the first pages followed by the list of members, the records of elections of officers, deliberations and accounts. Such registers are not unusual in the eighteenth century, but even when they are missing, some information of this kind may be gleaned from other and more fragmentary archives.

For testimony on individual religious attitudes there are private account books (*livres de raison*) and correspondence, but such documentation is rare among the common people. By contrast, in notarial registers there are echoes of a wide variety of people of all classes and both sexes expressing in wills their frame of mind through the ritual acts by which they bid farewell to earthly life. Let us not be deceived: the pious formulae of the wills are expressed in the notary's language, but that does not diminish the significance of seeing them change over the century in accord with the development of collective attitudes. As for funeral rites, prayers and legacies of pious intent laid down by the testator, they can be fitted into a subtle dialectic between personal preoccupations and social conventions. Since Michel Vovelle has shown with such startling success what can be drawn from this material research, analysis goes forward vigorously, although it is not certain that it will be everywhere as informative as in Provence.

Learning from ethnographers, historians of popular religion are discovering how to use unwritten 'documents', no longer merely as adjuncts to the spoken and written word, but as a corpus which can be collected and analysed statistically. Such information is perhaps most significant in societies composed largely of illiterates. Not, however, that material objects are in themselves more 'popular' than the 'written', since they draw inspiration and obey rules often laid down by the educated. However, the forms of meaning chosen, and the ways in which these are used, generally place this type of evidence at the heart of the concerns of the faithful. Consider eighteenth-century episcopal disapproval of pictures judged 'indecent' which was followed by the iconoclastic campaigns of the French Revolution in order to measure popular attachment to devotional objects.

At first, historical interest focused on sacred vessels and the ornamentation of churches. Study may concentrate on one type of object, perhaps a shelf or frame enclosing decorated panels rising above the high and secondary altars (reredos). It is a difficult task to catalogue and date them, to try to classify them according to the workshops where they were produced, to find the original work orders, although this has been done well for Brittany and Roussillon.

However, to go beyond this risks failure because of the complexity of the social considerations that come into play. It may be preferable to follow research along the lines followed by G. and M. Vovelle on the altars of purgatory in Provence, an approach which could be equally informative applied to the receptacles for carrying the host (pyx) or other eucharistic vessels as well as to altars dedicated to the Rosary. Equally promising are the iconographic inventories systematically established for a particular saint such as St Fiacre or St Roch. These enable us to establish the regional incidence of specific devotions.

The ornamentation of a church often reminds us of the confraternities which held their services there. The confraternities left other tangible relics of their activities, which better express popular creativity than formal works of art commissioned from an urban artist: banners, staffs and lanterns for processions and various insignia. Similarly the environs of pilgrimage sanctuaries can yield evidence of the manufacture of devotional images. A precise catalogue could establish the main centres of production and the means of distribution and could also lead to fruitful iconographic and symbolic (*sémiographique*) research. In contrast to the mass production of the graphic arts we also should consider the individualized ex-voto placed on the walls of the sanctuary by those benefiting from miraculous interventions. The research already in progress will not only save from destruction an endangered form of historical information; it will enable us to see, in the very diversity of objects and scenes represented in the case of a painted ex-voto, the main lines of collective piety.

At the suggestion of Alphonse Dupront there is growing interest in how the space of sacred places was organized in addition to the objects found within them. The location of pilgrimage sanctuaries, the distribution of chapels over a given territory, the itineraries followed by processions are all subjects which can be traced back through the centuries. But as Marie-Hélène Froeschlé has demonstrated recently, churches at the time of the Catholic Reform were remodelled according to a specific hierarchy of rituals and functions. It is only necessary to enter a church today to find there the Catholic arrangement of objects and space first fully realized in the eighteenth century. There is the high altar with tabernacle and reredos isolated by a balustrade, the side altars of which that of the Virgin has a commanding situation, the pulpit and the confessionals, the lectern and the tribune: the nineteenth century added little more than plaster statues.

Two centuries later we can only bear in mind the ethnographic methods of oral enquiry and direct observation. However, in certain relatively isolated regions the rituals practised today (festivals, processions, conjuration rites) can be cited usefully. The information drawn from old documentation just as the testimony of local people may throw light on their truly understood popular meaning.

The sources I have discussed above have been known for many years. Current research is characterized by an attempt to assemble complete collections of documents, or at least to draw them together systematically so that the information gathered can be quantified and placed in an analysis of the character of linguistic usage evolving over time, thus enabling us to make comparisons which are valid from one area to another. The most sophisticated computerized and statistical techniques for analysing information are increasingly being used. Indeed, the moment may have come to recall the virtues of intuition without which even the most complicated and exhaustive techniques may risk historiographical sterility.

Some avenues of research

In a field of research which has changed substantially over the last several decades it is important that recently posed problems do not cause more traditional questions to be forgotten. In the area that I have labelled the sociological perspective, one must enquire into the means used by eighteenth-century Catholicism to popularize the official 'models' of religion.

What pastoral methods were used? And by whom? It is vain to think that the study of popular religion can be separated from that of the clergy, especially their social and geographical origins. The type of education they received conditioned in large measure their influence on the population. In the eighteenth century one must be especially sensitive to the effect on pastoral techniques of Jansenism. Has there not been a tendency purely and simply to confuse this with rigorism? In what areas and how deeply did it penetrate? What relationship can be established between Jansenist pastoral techniques and those which might be better labelled Catholic *Aufklärung*?

In the centuries-old effort to instruct the people in religion, the eighteenth century made few innovations. One cannot overlook, however, the function and content of catechetical teaching. The same can be said of the conditions and themes of preaching. Attention should be focused on the missions, particularly since the major missionaries, Grignion de Montfort and Bridaine in

France, Leonard of Port-Maurice and Alphonsus Liguori in Italy, among others, show that the missions had not lost their creative dynamism nor their popular impact. There were as well less celebrated missionary groups supported by a network of foundations. The sermons, the psalmodies, the spectacular ceremonies characterizing the missions, have too often been examined superficially. They represent in fact an exceptionally coherent religion as it was then expounded. How did this affect the public? Let us at least note the desire, more marked in the eighteenth than the seventeenth century, to teach ordinary people in their everyday language with the risk – the example may be drawn from the far-off diocese of Samogitia in Lithuania – of turning away the educated classes.

Moreover, the use of popular language was a concession which led to discussion. Catholic acculturation increasingly looked to campaigns encouraging literacy. Progressively, the church extended its control over educational institutions. From simple episcopal checks on the morality and orthodoxy of teachers, there developed a positive movement to create schools, and especially those of girls separated from those of boys. This campaign was supported by the notables who saw in the establishment of a school a praiseworthy act of charity, and one rendered still more effective by the creation of specialized congregations of male and female teaching orders. Regional studies well advanced in Poland and France may soon lead to a map of eighteenth-century elementary education. One would not be able, however, to deduce from it a map of literacy: the studies made on this subject, usually from signatures on *actes de catholicité* or notarial documents, show surprising distortions. Moreover, there is some indication from them that education with an essentially catechetical aim may have limited itself to teaching children how to read.

The study of the means used to popularize official Catholicism should have as a complement the study of opposing influences. Eighteenth-century Europe saw elaborated amongst its social and intellectual elites new paradigms of behaviour which we can loosely describe by the expression 'enlightened'. By what channels, with what rhythm, at what social level, did these ideas penetrate the popular classes of town and country? Works like those of Maurice Agulhon, which analyse the transformation from penitential confraternities to masonic lodges in the context of *méridional* sociability, provide a course to follow, as does the 1789 vocabulary used in the French *Cahiers de doléances* which permit us to measure the progress of new cultural attitudes.

However, the fundamental statement which must be made for the Catholic countries of eighteenth-century Europe is one of massive popular conformity. This is true to an extent that some historians in the past believed that the question did not merit examination. Gabriel Le Bras himself, at the end of a study of Châlons which presented a picture lacking in sharp contrasts, observed: 'the general impression . . . is of a routine observance and, save the exceptional souls, one without depth'. He doubted that during the century there had taken place any perceptible evolution in this humdrum attitude. His conclusions were similar for Rouen and Auxerre.

Must we then give up the idea of a quantifiable evolution of religious practices in the eighteenth century? But the laments frequently and insistently expressed by the clergy about the progress of irreligion cannot be considered as mere rhetoric. One must not lose sight of the fact that the statistical documentation provided by the pastoral visits gives generally poor information on the towns by contrast with rural parishes better supervised by their *curés*. Yet even in the countryside abstentions from Easter duty had reached substantial proportions before the upheavals of the Revolution. Gérard Cholvy followed this development from 1697 to 1772 around Montpellier: from an initial quasi-uniformity of practice until by 1772 the average of those who did not observe Easter had reached 11.4 per cent.

There can be no doubt, then, that the observance of Easter declined in eighteenth-century France. Was this so in other countries? Contemporaries also had the impression of a similar and parallel decline in morals, especially sexual morals. It is true that demographic studies reveal a very clear rise in illegitimate births: at Lille from 4.5 per cent of total births in 1740 to 12.5 per cent in 1785, and at the later date the proportion reached twenty-two per cent at Bordeaux and twenty-five per cent at Toulouse. Several factors, however, enter into play here, especially that of rootless urban populations. Can one consider sexual continence as a good test of the quality of popular religion? The same question is equally valid in regard to contraception. From the mid eighteenth century and particularly towards 1790 the demographic consequences of the spread among the petite bourgeoisie of the 'deadly secrets', as birth control methods were euphemized, became evident. Did couples who henceforth 'deceived nature' do so with a sense of violating a Christian moral law which it is not entirely certain had been taught them?

By contrast with these approximate or contestable yardsticks of religious conformity the information drawn from wills is characterized by a remarkable finesse. Not only can we follow through the century the impoverishment of ritual formulae and pious legacies (an evolution which can be quantified by using requests for the saying of masses), but the social range of testators enables us to discern changes in testamentary styles. Thus in Provence it has been shown how moral leadership passed from the *parlementaire* aristocracy of Aix to the wealthiest groups of the commercial middle classes of Marseille. Michel Vovelle has been criticized for not having explained *why* the attitudes of the Provençaux changed in the face of death, but it seems to me that demonstrating *how*, with a degree of precision and rigour, is at present the most important task facing the historian of popular religion.

At the level of descriptive analysis we need to know how the population received official devotions. From the records of pastoral visits it appears that many of the confraternities that had proliferated during the seventeenth century as a result of the Catholic Reform (confraternities of the Blessed Sacrament, the Rosary and others) had disintegrated by the following century or had become lifeless institutions, while elsewhere the fervour of religious creativity was not yet exhausted. The lists of confraternity members deserve close study, especially in anything concerning their sexual and social composition. Wills also provide a means of examining the vitality and the range of the confraternities through examination of bequests and legacies. However, eighteenth-century piety was the vehicle for new devotions, the most notable being that of the Sacred Heart. What regions, what milieux were touched by this devotion which, by the end of the century, had succeeded in establishing itself firmly in popular Catholicism? Is it not also in the eighteenth century that the exercise of the Stations of the Cross, created in the fifteenth century by the Franciscan Observance, made a definitive break-through in several Catholic countries? To follow development of these devotions would be especially interesting in that we may discover behind them the influence of religious orders against whom secular ecclesiastical authorities did not hide their suspicion and even hostility.

In the wide range of questions posed by the adherence of the popular classes to the models of official Catholicism two topics have especially attracted researchers: the sexual dimorphism of the laity's practice, and regional contrasts in religious vitality.

As for the first, it appears that the eighteenth century is a key period between a nineteenth century where practice and devotion is especially the concern of women and a seventeenth century where men dominate religion as they do society and culture at large. Close investigation of the confraternities, works of piety and charity, and the reception of the sacraments could support this initial hypothesis based on research in wills and which seems to show chronological evolution taking place at different rates according to the social level. One senses that feminization and the clerical influence on religious life go together, but this is no more than a hypothesis.

Since the celebrated thesis of Louis Pérouas on the diocese of La Rochelle, socio-religious history has paid great attention to regional contrasts: zones of fervour and apathy have been outlined gradually and have revealed long-established patterns. These zones come to light through the use of a multiplicity of indices which generally point to the same conclusions. Indices like the number of foundations, the success of confraternities, the number of priestly vocations and the ornamentation of churches are the most important. Each of these indicators may be criticized, as in the case of sacerdotal vocations, as almost anachronistic. When they reveal similar positive or negative characteristics they cannot be dismissed as fortuitous. If we observe in a region of fervent piety the continued existence of islands of Protestantism, as in the *Bocage* of Poitou or in the Vivarais, this points to the idea, irritating in its lack of clear definition and still less explicable, of religious temperament. Much remains to be done to throw light on the ecological, sociological and cultural components of the problem of religious temperament, and even the political history of those parts of Europe which remained redoubts of popular religion in a Europe undergoing secularization. One suspects that in future such analyses will lead us well beyond the workings of official Catholicism.

Clearly, popular religion cannot be reduced to a simple imitation of models established elsewhere. It is part of a creative milieu with its own inspiration, but still more with its distinctive accents and rhythms of historical existence, which official Catholicism was obliged either to accept or struggle against, depending on the situation.

In large measure popular religious culture is the domain of the unspoken, of the lived, immediate experience. Too often to understand it we must rely on the hostile enunciations about those ideas by the ecclesiastical authorities. But at the same time their hostility, or at least incomprehension, the suspicion and disdain for a particular religious act, is precisely what leads us to describe it as popular.

A whole section of popular religious life took place in areas of complicity which the clergy controlled imperfectly, beginning with the residents, especially the rural community where cohesion was strongest. Directly or through supervision of the fabric, inhabitants of a parish over the centuries managed their cultural patrimony and insisted on the carrying out of certain popular rites: these are the 'good customs' which the *curés*, like it or not, were obliged to respect if they wished to be accepted by their parishioners. Bells had to be rung for particular reasons, festivals had to be celebrated and processions accompanied. Every community thus lived in close contact with *its* saints, sometimes honoured with a vow. In the same way the community kept contact with its dead with a familiarity which surprised and shocked visiting prelates (will these peasants never stop eating and drinking in the cemeteries, even dancing and letting their cattle graze there!). Constantly reiterated ordinances against these practices had no effect. François Lebrun has shown how deeply popular sentiment objected to the transfer of cemeteries brought about by the urban hygienic policies of the *Lumières* at the end of the eighteenth century.

A similar sensitivity can be observed in many confraternities, and not only in those of particular trades, the religious significance of which was blurred by the eighteenth century, although one should not accept without scrutiny the pictures of them presented to us. Lay sensibility is found in devotional confraternities which remained true to their original statutes. Let us consider the Norman *Charités* or the Penitents of the Mediterranean world, especially, whose vitality and even fervour were accompanied by a strong institutional autonomy. Each had its chapel, services, ornaments, against which bishops and *curés* scolded but in vain. Moreover, was it not precisely this autonomous character of the Penitents which ensured their secular success in parishes where clerical confraternities, despite official encouragements, were quickly exhausted?

A study of popular religion must then obviously follow the continuing efforts of the Catholic-Reform clergy to spread its control over these institutions of secular origin (to which one can add youth societies, and the 'bees' (*ouvroirs*) where people met together to work and amuse each other with conversation in the hours between supper and bedtime). This attempt at control met the resistance of a population wishing to preserve its cultural and social heritage. In areas where the clash was strongest we may see the deep motivations of anticlericalism and disaffection with codified religious practice.

Even after the work of several generations of folklorists and ethnographers much remains to be done before a corpus of popular rites and beliefs can be established. Pastoral visits, especially those at the end of the seventeenth and the beginning of the eighteenth centuries, are rich with observations on the cults of saints and festivals, processions, pilgrimages, and so forth. The information is scattered, certainly, but as it is well dated it furnishes a chronological yardstick to which 'immemorial' facts found during research can be related.

The aim of research, at least for someone who looks beyond exoticism, must be to bring to light deep and basic aspects of the popular mind and to discover their sources. The exemplary investigations carried on by Alphonse Dupront on pilgrimages show almost a type of commerce being carried on with the divine which ignores in favour of the immediate both ecclesiastical institutions and its doctrinal precepts: what matters is *place*, marked with cosmic signs of summit, grotto, tree or fountain which are more essential to the site than the sanctuary built there, and the *image* in which is concentrated and manifested the supernatural virtue which the pilgrims seek to absorb. What counts, however, in the pilgrimages and the festival, is *time* which is focused on the change of the seasons more than on the unfolding of the liturgical year. The cycle of the first of May–Pentecost and of St John constitute the key points. In this context of an immediate relationship with the sacred, the miraculous entered into the normal course of things, from the 'resurrection' of still-born children with the intention of baptism, implored and obtained from the Virgin in a variety of 'Sanctuaires à répit' spread throughout Catholic Europe, or of cures obtained from some 'good' saint, or of conjuration rites to ward off storms and protect crops.

Nothing shows better how rooted these popular religious structures were than does their resistance to episcopal control – an image adjudged obscene and then buried is soon afterwards dug up again and put back into its place – but also to revolutionary dechristianization. There are numerous accounts of peasants who defended their parish bells, who obstinately refused to work on Sundays and feast days, or of experiences on the site of a sanctuary, episodes so numerous that they go beyond anecdote and would be worth collecting systematically.

Is it necessary to advance so far in the interpretation of popular 'superstitions' as to see in them a sort of counter-religion which had been suppressed but remained alive among the masses? The apostles of the Counter-Reformation and before them the humanists and the Protestant reformers spoke of pagan survivals, and Jean Delumeau, today, does not hesitate again to use this language. At the turning point of the sixteenth and seventeenth centuries inquisitions and demonologers denounced a more or less explicit recourse to Satan under cover of questionable rites. If we believe those investigators, there were many pseudo-christians, mainly women, and territories under scant control by the official administration and culture of the church. These people were adepts of Satan, celebrating in grandiose sabbaths the inverted rites of the Catholic religion. One may still encounter historians who share views which flatter an ever contemporary taste for sooty hypotheses. However, if one wishes to stay on solid ground it is necessary to avoid the idea that popular religion was organized in a system. What I have said of its immediacy places this possibility at a distance.

Rather than trying to analyse popular religion as though it had an object or specific content made up of coherent beliefs and rites, attention should, it seems to me, be turned to the carrying out of certain processes which typify the popular practice of religion.

A first development derives from a slippage of time frames between popular and formal religion. While official religion constantly renews its terminology and its acts, popular religion is the locus of long-term usage in practice. Many popular attitudes described as superstitious are only archaisms in relation to the fashions of the day, showing persistent fidelity to what was previously recommended, as in the example of reading the Gospel over the head of a child. This continuity can be observed in popular publications, spread thanks to pedlars in the eighteenth century, which made available the lives of saints and pious legends which three centuries earlier had delighted an aristocratic audience.

A second development is tied to phenomena of physical possession and fits. The eighteenth century has many examples which it is important to draw together beyond the barriers of doctrinal differences. Between the prophetism of the traumatized Protestants of Dauphiné and the Vivarais, the convulsions of the Jansenists of Saint-Médard and the panic-stricken reactions of the Marseilles plague victims, one might find comparable aspects of religious marginality. Under less extreme guise one should direct attention to the manifestations of devout exaltation which were produced around the tomb of a saint like St John Francis Regis, obliging the bishops, overwhelmed, to regulate the observance and to ask for its recognition from Rome.

A third form of development, doubtless both the most important and widespread, is what we might call that of doubling. The same religious rite, practised by the church with the enthusiastic cooperation of the faithful, holds two meanings. One is spiritual, justified by the theologians, while the other is conjuratory, bathed in a sort of animist magic. These are like the two faces of the Catholic principle *ex opere operato* which makes any attempt to separate them vain. One could give a multitude of examples. It is sufficient to see how the sacrament of marriage is at the same time lived as a ritual of fertility, or Catholic funerals as a kind of non-aggression treaty between the dead and the living. One could see also in ex-votos both a statement of gratitude for a grace received and an object securing sacral power, in particular, the wax limbs hanging in the sanctuaries. As for the Eucharist, too closely supervised by the clergy to permit such distortions, one should observe the role played by the consecrated bread which became the real act of communion. From such coexistences of meaning which are also contaminations is not the most significant success in the Catholicism of the eighteenth century that of children's first communion? Conceived and propagated by missionaries as a touching ceremony destined to draw adults, the 'solemn communion' was adopted by the masses who saw in it a rite of passage, that of the initiation of adolescents instructed by the catechism, which was henceforth established as a custom. Strangely this rite of passage was lacking in European society until this time.

In sum, leaving aside an opposition (which seems to me mythical) between an official religion and a popular religion which would be its more or less subterranean obverse, the most promising avenue of research is the exploration of the zones of contact – zones best revealed by the modes of cultural structuration proper to the popular classes.

To conclude this summary and overview which is open to debate on many points and is too much affected without a doubt by a French perspective, I would plead simply for a resolutely dialectical conception of popular religion. To start from an enquiry of the sociological type on the religion lived by the popular classes – and let us understand by that not only external practice but the 'témoignages d'interiorité' – does not dispense with the need for research of an ethnological nature into what meaning should be ascribed to that lived experience. It is essential to understand the relationships of adhesion–resistance or acculturation–folklorization in the eighteenth century. The century of the culmination of the post-Tridentine reform, the century of the triumph of the *Lumières*, the final century of the old agrarian societies in which germinated the revolutions of the modern world, these offer a privileged field of observation to the historian. There is still an abundance of crops to be harvested and not a few terrains lie fallow.

Select bibliography

GENERAL

Conference on New Approaches in Social Anthropology (Jesus College, Cambridge, England, 1963). *Anthropological approaches to the study of religion*, edited by Michael Banton (1966)

Deffontaines, P., *Géographie et religions* (1948)

Delumeau, J., *Le Catholicisme entre Luther et Voltaire* (1971)

Germain, Elisabeth, *Langages de la foi à travers l'histoire: mentalités et catéchèse, approche d'une étude de mentalités* (1972)

De Sandre, Paolo, *Sociologia della religiosità: introduzione al metodo e alle techniche della ricerca* (1967)

ATLASES, DICTIONARIES AND BIBLIOGRAPHIES

Baudrillart, A., *Dictionnaire d'histoire et de géographie ecclésiastiques* (1912–)

Berkowitz, M., and Johnson, J. E., *Social scientific studies of religion: a bibliography* (1967)

Martin, Jochen, *Atlas zur Kirchengeschichte: die christlichen Kirchen in Geschichte und Gegenwart* (1970)

Oxford dictionary of the Christian Church, 2nd edn edited by F. L. Cross and E. A. Livingstone (1974)

Revue d'histoire ecclésiastique (bibliographical issue), LXIX, 3–4 (Oct.–Dec. 1974)

Verkené, Emile van der, *Bibliographie der Inquisition* (1963)

AUSTRIA

Coreth, A., *Pietas Austriaca: Ursprung und Entwicklung barocker Frömmigkeit in Osterreich* (1959)

Freschot, Casimir, *Mémoires de la Cour de Vienne* (1705)

Hantsch, Hugo, *Die Geschichte Osterreichs*, 5th edn (2 vols., 1969)

Hersche, Peter, *Der Spätjansenismus in Osterreich* (1977)

Kann, R. A., *A study in Austrian intellectual history from late Baroque to Romanticism* (1960)

Kelle, Johann Nepomuk von, *Die Jesuiten-Gymnasien in Osterreich* (1876)

Klingenstein, Grete, *Staatsverwaltung und kirchliche Autorität im 18. Jahrhundert: das Problem der Zensur in der theresianischen Reform* (1970)

Lehners, Jean-Paul, 'La paroisse de Hardegg, 1650–1750', unpublished thesis, University of Strasbourg (1971)

Rinck, Eucharius Gottlieb, *Leopolds des Grossen, Röm. Käysers wunderwürdiges Leben und Thaten* (1709)

Seibt, Ferdinand, *Bohemia sacra: das Christentum in Böhmen 973–1973* (1974)

Tapié, V.-L., *Monarchie et peuples du Danube* (1969)

Thiriet, Jean-Michel, 'La mort d'après la clause testamentaire welsche dans la Vienne baroque 1580–1750', unpublished thesis, University of Haute-Bretagne (1976)

Tomek, Ernst, *Kirchengeschichte Osterreichs* (3 vols., 1937–59)

Valjavec, Fritz, *Der Josephinismus, Zur geistigen Entwicklung Osterreichs im achtzehnten und neunzehnten Jahrhundert* (1945)

Winter, Eduard, *Der Josefinismus: die Geschichte des österreichischen Reformkatholizismus, 1740–1848* (1962)

Wodka, J., *Kirche in Osterreich: Wegweiser durch ihre Geschichte* (1959)

FRANCE

Agulhon, Maurice, *Pénitents et francs-maçons de l'ancienne Provence* (1968)

Appolis, E., *Entre jansenistes et zelanti: le 'tiers parti' catholique au XVIIIe siècle* (1961)

Cholvy, G., *Géographie religieuse de l'Hérault contemporain* (1968)
   Le diocèse de Montpellier (1976)

Dainville, F. de, *Cartes anciennes de l'église de France: historique, répertoire, guide d'usage* (1956)

Fracard, M. L. *La Fin de l'ancien régime à Niort: essai de sociologie religieuse* (1956)

Gadille, J., Julia, D. and Venard, M., 'Pour un répertoire des visites pastorales', *Annales, Economies, Sociétés, Civilisations*, xxv (1970), 561–6

Gagnol, P., *La Dîme ecclésiastique en France au XVIIIe siècle* (1910)

Le Bras, Gabriel, *Etudes de sociologie religieuse* (1955)

Lesne, E., *Histoire de la propriété ecclésiastique en France* (1910–43)

McManners, John, *French ecclesiastical society under the Old Regime: a study of Angers* (1960)

Pérouas, L., *Le Diocèse de La Rochelle de 1648 à 1724: sociologie et pastorale* (1964)

Playoust-Chaussis, A., *La Vie religieuse dans le diocèse de Boulogne au XVIIIe siècle, 1725–1790* (1976)

Plongeron, B., *Conscience religieuse en Révolution: regards sur l'historiographie religieuse de la Révolution française* (1969)
   La Vie quotidienne du clergé français au XVIIIe siècle (1974)

Ravitch, N., 'Robe and sword in the recruitment of French bishops', *Catholic Historical Review* (1965), 494–508

Tackett, T., *Priest and parish . . . a social and political study of the curés in a diocese of Dauphiné, 1750–1791* (1977)

Trenard, L., 'Le Catholicisme au XVIIIe siècle d'après les travaux récents', *Information Historique* (1964), 53–65

Vovelle, M., *Piété baroque et déchristianisation en Provence au XVIIIe siècle* (1973)
Religion et révolution: la déchristianisation de l'an II (1976)

GERMANY

Benecke, G., *Society and politics in Germany, 1500-1700* (1974)
'Teutsche Libertät: a comment on German politics two hundred years ago', discussion paper, University of British Columbia (1976)

Blanning, T. C. W., *Reform and revolution in Mainz, 1743–1803* (1974)

Dru, A., *The church in nineteenth-century Germany* (1963)

Feine, H. E., *Kirchliche Rechtsgeschichte*, 4th edn (1964)
Die Besetzung der Reichsbistürner, 1648–1803 (1921)

Geschichtlicher atlas der Rheinprovinz, im auftrage des Provinzialverbandes hrsg. von der Gesellschaft für rheinische geschichtskunde (6 vols., 1894–1914), Vol. II, *Die karte von 1789: einteilung und entwickelung der territorien von 1600 bis 1794*, von dr. Wilhelm Fabricus (1898, reprinted 1965)

Grassl, H., 'Maria Anna Josefa à Lindmayr und die Entwicklung der spanischen Mystik in Altbayern', *Der Zwiebelturm*, 10 (1952)

Heussi, K. and Mulert, H., *Atlas zur Kirchengeschichte* (1919)

Rechenmacher, L., 'Der Episkopalismus des 18. Jahrhunderts (Febronianismus)', unpublished thesis, Würzburg University (1908)

Roegele, O. B., 'Ein Schulreformator des 18. Jahrhunderts', *Historisches Jahrbuch*, 74 (1955)

Rowan, S. W. and Vann, J. A., *The Old Reich. Essays on German political institutions, 1495–1806* (1975)

Sagarra, E., *A social history of Germany, 1648–1914* (1977)

Schlesinger, W. and Uhlhorn, F., *Die deutschen Territorien* (1974)

Schrams, K., *Die religiöse Volks – und Jugendbewegung in der Diözese Regensburg vom 15. bis zum 18. Jahrhundert* (1929)

Spindler, M., 'Der Ruf des Barocken Bayern', *Historisches Jahrbuch*, 74 (1955)
(ed.). *Handbuch der Bayerischen Geschichte* (4 vols., 1967–75), vol. II.

Tüchle, H., 'Die bulle Unigenitus und die süddeutschen Prämonstratenser', *Historisches Jahrbuch*, 74 (1955)

Veit, Andreas Ludwig, *Kirche und Volksfrömmigkeit im Zeitalter des Barock* (1956)

HUNGARY

Acsády, Ignác, *Magyarország népessége a Pragmatica Sanctio korában 1720–21* (The population of Hungary at the time of the Pragmatic Sanction, 1720–21) (1896)

Ajtay, József, *A magyarság fejlődése az utolsó kétszáz év alatt* (The development of the Hungarians during the last two hundred years) (1905)

Bernard, Paul P., *Jesuits and Jacobins: enlightenment and enlightened despotism in Austria* (1971)

Biro, Sándor, *et al.*, *A magyar református egyház története* (The history of the Hungarian Reformed Church) (1949)

Domanovszky, Sándor, *Magyar művelődéstörténet* (Hungarian cultural history) (5 vols., n.d.)

Fraknói, Vilmos, *A magyar királyi kegyúri jog szent Istvántól Mária Teréziáig: Történeti tanulmány* (Hungarian Royal Advowson from St Stephen to Maria Theresa: a historical survey) (1895)

Grünwald, Béla, *A régi Magyarország, 1711–1825* (Old Hungary, 1711–1825) (1888)

Illésy, János, *Az 1754–55. évi országos nemesi összeírás* (The 1754–55 national census of the nobility) (1902)

Irányi, József, *Az 1790–1–iki 26–ik Vallásügyi törvény keletkezésének története* (A history of the origins of Statute Law No. 26 of 1790–91 on religion) (1857)

Kann, Robert A., *A history of the Habsburg Empire, 1526–1918* (1974)
    A study in Austrian intellectual history: from late Baroque to Romanticism (1960)

Karácsonyi, János, *Magyarország egyháztörténete főbb vonásaiban 970–től 1900–ig* (The main features of the ecclesiastical history of Hungary from 970 to 1900) (1915)

Király, Béla K., *Hungary in the late eighteenth century: the decline of enlightened despotism* (1969)
    'The Sublime Porte, Vienna, Transylvania and the dissemination of the Protestant Reformation in Royal Hungary', *Tolerance and movements of religious dissent in Eastern Europe*, ed. Béla K. Király (1975), pp. 199–222

Kovácsics, József, *Magyarország történeti demográfiája: Magyarország népessége a honfoglalástol, 1949–ig* (Hungary's historical demography: the population of Hungary from settlement to 1949) (1963)

Lányi, Károly, *Magyarföld Egyháztörténetei Ausztria-Házi korszak* (Ecclesiastical history of the Hungarian lands during the time of the House of Austria) (3 vols., 1844)

Lassu, István, *Az ausztriai birodalomnak statisztikai, geográphiai és históriai leírása* (A statistical, geographical and historical description of the Austrian Empire) (1829)

Mályusz, Elemér, *Iratok a türelmi rendelet történetéhez* (Papers on the history of the Edict of Toleration) (1940)
    A türelmi rendelet II. József és a magyar protestantizmus (The Edict of Toleration, Joseph II and Hungarian Protestantism) (2 vols., 1939)

Marczali, Henrik, *Magyarország története III. Károlytól a bécsi kongresszusig 1711–1815* (History of Hungary from Charles III to the Congress of Vienna, 1711–1815), *A magyar nemzet története* (The history of the Hungarian nation), ed. Sándor Szilágyi (1898), vol. VIII
    Ungarische Verfassungsgeschichte (1910)

Meszlényi, Antal, *A Jozefinizmus kora Magyarországon 1780–1846* (The era of Josephinism in Hungary, 1780–1846) (1934)

Révész, Imre, *Esquisse de l'histoire de la politique religieuse hongroise entre 1705 et 1860* (1960)

Magyarországi protestantizmus történelme (History of Protestantism in Hungary) (1925)

Révész, Imre and Kováts, J. Stephen, *Hungarian Protestantism: Its Past, Present and Future* (1927)

Schwartner, Martin Von, *Statistik des Königreichs Ungarn*, 2nd edn (2 vols., 1809)

Thirring, Gustáv, *Magyarország népessége II. József korában* (The population of Hungary in the time of Joseph II) (1938)

Valjavec, Fritz, *Der Josephinismus: Zur geistigen Entwicklung Österreichs in achtzehnten and neunzehnten Jahrhundert* (1945)

Vázsonyi, Vilmos, *A királyi placetum a magyar alkotmányban* (The King's Pleasure in the Hungarian constitution) (1893)

ITALY

Alessandro, A. d', 'I proprietari delle tenute dell'Agro Romano nel 1783', *Rivista di storia dell'agricoltura*, IX (1969), 363–81

Giammusso, S., 'Le missioni dei Redentoristi in Sicilia dalle origini al 1800', *Spicilegium Historicum Congregationis Sanctissimi Redemptoris*, X (1962), 51–176

Giorgini, C., *La Maremma toscana nel Settecento: aspetti sociali e religiosi* (1968)

Gregorio, O., 'Sant 'Alfonso de Liguori e l'evangelizzazione del Cilento nel Settecento', *La società religiosa nell'età moderna: Atti del convegno di studi storia sociale e religiosa, Capaccio-Paestum, 18–21 maggio 1972* (1973), 845–57

Matteucci, B., *Scipione de' Ricci: saggio storico-teologico sul giansenismo italiano* (1941)

L. A. Muratori e la cultura contemporanea: atti del convegno internazionale di studi muratoriani, Modena, 1972 (1975) esp. vol. I

Orlandi, G., *Le campagne modenesi fra Rivoluzione e Restaurazione (1790–1815)* (1967)

'Missioni parrocchiali e drammatica popolare', *La drammatica popolare nella Valle Padana: atti del IV convegno di studi sul folklore padano, Modena, 23–26 maggio 1974* (1976), 305–33

Passerin, E., 'Il fallimento dell'offensiva riformista di Scipione de' Ricci secondo nuovi documenti (1781–1788)', *Rivista di Storia della chiesa in Italia*, IX (1955), 99–131

'La riforma "giansenista" della chiesa e la lotta anticuriale in Italia nella seconda metà del Settecento', *Rivista storica italiana*, LXXXI (1959), 209–34

'Studi e problemi politico-religiosi dell' Italia del 700', *Quaderni di cultura e storia sociale*, II (1953), 22–8

Passerin, E. and Traniello, F., 'Ricerche sul tardo giansenismo italiano', *Rivista di storia e letteratura religiosa*, III (1967), 279–313

Placanica, A., 'Cassa sacra e beni della chiesa nel '700', *Cahiers internationaux d'histoire économique et sociale* (1972)

'Chiesa e società Settecento meridionale: vecchio e nuovo clero nel quadro della legislazione riformatrice', *Ricerche di storia sociale e religiosa*, N.s. 7–8 (1975) 121–87

'Note sull'alienazione dei beni ecclesiastici in Calabria nel tardo Settecento', *Studi storici*, VI (1965), 435–82

Il patrimonio ecclesiastico calabrese nell'età moderna (1972)

Prandi, A., 'Spiritualità e sensibilità' in V. Branca (ed.), *Sensibilità e razionalità nel Settecento* (1967), pp. 65–94

Rosa, G. De, 'Pertinenze ecclesiastiche e santità nella storia sociale e religiosa della Basilicata dal XVII al XIX secolo', *Ricerche di storia sociale e religiosa*, N.s. 7–8 (1975), 7–65

'Problemi religiosi della società meridionale nel '700 attraverso le visite pastorali di Angelo Anzani', *Rivista di sociologia*, VI, 15 (1968), 1–48

Vescovi, popolo e magia nel Sud: ricerche di storia socio-religiosa dal XVII al XIX secolo (1971)

Rosa, M., *Religione e società nel Mezzogiorno tra Cinque e Seicento* (1976)

'Sviluppo e crisi della proprietà ecclesiastica: Terra di Bari e Terra d'Otranto nel Settecento' in P. Villani (ed.), *Economia e classi sociali in Puglia nell'età moderna* (1976)

Sebastiani, L., *La tassazione degli ecclesiastici nella Lombardia teresiana. Con una memoria di Pompeo Neri*, Biblioteca della Nuova rivista storica 31 (1969)

Stella, P., 'Devozioni e religiosità popolare in Italia (sec. XVI–XX). Interpretazioni recenti', *Rivista Liturgica*, LXIII (1976), 155–73

Vecchi, A., *Correnti religiose nel Sei-Settecento veneto* (1962)

Venturi, F., *Settecento riformatore* (1969–76)

Zangheri, R., *La proprietà terriera e le origini del Risorgimento nel Bolognese, 1789–1804* (1961)

Zoffoli, E., *S. Paolo della Croce: storia critica* (1975)

POLAND

Bednarski, Stanisław, *Upadek i odrodzenie szkół jezuickich w Polsce* (1933)

Bieńkowski, Ludomir, Kłoczowski, Jerzy and Sułowski, Zygmunt (eds.), *Zakony męskie w Polsce w 1772 roku. Ordines regulares virorum in Polonia anno 1772* (1972)

Kitowicz, Jędrzej, *Opis obyczajów za panowania Augusta III* (1951)

Kłoczowski, Jerzy, 'Zakony w diecezji przemyskiej obrzadku lacinskiego' (The monasteries of Latin Rite in the Przemyśl Diocese) in *Nasza Przeszlosc* (Our past), forthcoming

(ed.), *Kósciól w Polsce* (1968–)

Kumor, Boresław and Obertyński, Zdzisław (eds.), *Historia Kosciola w Polsce* (1974–)

Lesnodorski, B. (ed.), *Polska w epoce Oswiecenia. Panstwo-Spoleczens two-Kultura* (1971)

Müller, Wiesław (ed.), *Relacje o stanie diecezji krakowskiej 1615–1765* (1978)

Rabikauskas, Paulus (ed.), *Relationes status dioecesium in magno ducatu Lituaniae* (1971–)

Sawicki, Jakub (ed.), *Conciliae Poloniae* (1945–63)
Tazbir, J., and Rostworowski, E., *History of Poland* (1968)
Weinryb, Bernard Dov, *The Jews of Poland: a social and economic history* (1973)

PORTUGAL

Almeida, Fortunato de, *História da Igreja em Portugal*, new edn (4 vols., 1967–71)
Borges de Macedo, J., *A situação económica no tempo de Pombal* (1951)
Ferreira, J. A. Pinto, *Antigo concelho de Freixo de Numão, memórias paroquiais do séc. XVIII* (1974)
Godinho, V. Magalhães, *A estrutura da antiga sociedade portuguesa* (1971)
Guerra, Luiz de Bivar, *Inventário dos Processos da Inquisição de Coimbra 1541–1820*, Fontes documentais portuguesas, IV (1972)
Marcadé, Jacques, *Une comarque portugaise – Ourique – entre 1750 et 1800* (1971)
'D. Fr. Manuel do Cenáculo Vilas Boas, Provincial des Réguliers du Tiers Ordre Franciscain, 1768–77', *Arquivos do centro cultural português* (1971), 431–58.
Querido, Augusto, 'Eléments pour une sociologie du conformisme catholique au Portugal', *Archives de sociologie des religions*, VII (1959), 144–51
Rêgo, Raul do, *O último regimento da inquisição portuguesa*, introduction and modernization by Raul Rêgo (1971)
Ricard, R., *Etudes sur l'histoire morale et religieuse du Portugal* (1970)
Salomon, H. P., 'The Portuguese Inquisition and its victims in the light of recent polemics', *Journal of the American-Portuguese Cultural Society* (Summer–Fall 1971), 19–28
Saraiva, A. J., *Inquisição e cristãos novos* (1969)
Silbert, Albert, *Le Portugal méditerranéen à la fin de l'ancien régime* (2 vols., 1966)
Silva, A. Pereira da, *A questão do sigilismo em Portugal no século XVIII* (1964)

SPAIN

Aldea Vaquero, Q., *et al.*, *Diccionario de historia eclesiástica de España* (4 vols., 1972–5)
Appolis, Emile, *Les jansenistes espagnols* (1966)
Callahan, William J., 'Two Spains and Two Churches, 1760–1835', *Historical Reflections*, 2 (1975), 157–81
Cuenca Toribio, José Manuel, *D. Pedro de Inguanzo y Rivero (1764–1836): último prelado del antiguo régimen* (1965)
  Sociología de una élite de poder de España e Hispanoamérica contemporánea: la jerarquía eclesiástica (1789–1962) (1976)
Hermann, C., 'Les revenus des évêques espagnols au dix-huitième siècle, 1650–1830', *Mélanges de la Casa de Velázquez* (1974)
Marichal, Juan, 'From Pistoia to Cádiz: A Generation's Itinerary,

1786–1812' in *The Ibero-American Enlightenment*, ed. A. Owen Aldridge (1971)

Martí Gilabert, F., *La Iglesia en España durante la revolución francesca* (1971)

Martín Hernández, Francisco and J. Martín Hernández. *Los seminarios españoles en la época de la Ilustración* (1973)

Martínez Albiach, Alfredo, *Religiosidad hispana y sociedad borbónica* (1969) *Etica socio-religiosa de la España del siglo XVIII* (1970)

Mestre Sanchis, Antonio, *Ilustración y reforma de la Iglesia: pensamiento político-religioso de Don Gregorio Mayans y Siscar (1699–1781)* (1968)

Noel, C. C., 'Opposition to enlightened reform in Spain: Campomanes and the clergy', *Societas*, 1 (1973), 22–43

Olaechea, Rafael, *Las relaciones hispano-romanas en la segunda mitad del siglo XVIII* (1965)

Sáez Marín, J., *Datos sobre la Iglesia española contemporánea, 1768–1868* (1975)

Sarrailh, Jean, *La crise religieuse en Espagne à la fin du XVIIIe siècle* (1951)

Saugnieux, Joel, *Un prélat éclairé: Don Antonio Tavira y Almazán, 1737–1807* (1970)

Le jansenisme espagnol du XVIIIe siècle, ses composantes et ses sources (1976)

Sierra Nava, Luis, *El Cardenal Lorenzana y la Ilustración* (1975)

POPULAR RELIGION

La Società religiosa nell'età moderna. Atti del Convegno studi di Storia sociale e religiosa, Capaccio-Paestum, 18–21 maggio 1972 (1973)

Miscellanea Historiae ecclesiasticae V. Colloque de Varsovie (27–29 octobre 1971) sur la Cartographie et l'histoire socio-religieuse de l'Europe jusqu'à a la fin du XVIIe siècle [sic, for XVIIIe] Bibliothèque de la Revue d'histoire ecclèsiastique, (1974)

Recherche et religions populaires. Colloque international 1973, ed. A. Desilets and G. Laperrière (1976)

La piété populaire de 1610 à nos jours. Actes du 99e congrés national des sociétés savantes, Besançon, 1974 (1976)

Plongeron, B. (ed.), *La religion populaire, approaches historiques* (1976)

Plongeron, B. and R. Pannet (eds.), *Le christianisme populaire. Les dossiers de l'histoire* (1976)

Russo, Carla (ed.), *Società, chiesa e vita religiosa nell'Ancien Regime* (1976)

Bercé, Y-M., *Fête et révolte. Des mentalités populaires du XVIe au XVIIIe siècle* (1976)

Richerche di storia sociale e religiosa, n.s. 10 (July–Dec. 1976)

'La religion populaire', special issue of *Le monde alpin et rhodanien: revue régionale d'ethnologie* (1977)

Index